CIVIL SERVICE ADMINISTRATIVE TESTS

Edited by

HY HAMMER

Chief of
Examining Service Division
New York City
Department of Personnel (Ret.)

ARCO PUBLISHING, INC.
New York

First Edition, First Printing, 1985

Published by Arco Publishing, Inc.
215 Park Avenue South, New York, NY 10003

Copyright © 1985 by Arco Publishing, Inc.

Library of Congress Cataloging-in-Publication Data
Main entry under title:

Civil service administrative tests.

  1. Civil service—Examinations. I. Hammer, Hy.
II. Title. JF1351.C463 1985   350.1′076   85-9046
ISBN 0–668–05768–8 (Paper Edition)

Printed in the United States of America

CONTENTS

WHAT THIS BOOK WILL DO FOR YOU v
SAMPLE ANSWER SHEETS vii

PART ONE
THE FUNCTIONING ADMINISTRATOR

ADMINISTRATIVE JUDGMENT 5
    Answer Key and Explanatory Answers 13
ADMINISTRATIVE-SUBORDINATE RELATIONSHIPS 17
    Answer Key and Explanatory Answers 23
PROBLEMS OF SUPERVISION AND ADMINISTRATION 27
    Answer Key and Explanatory Answers 38
OPERATING EFFICIENCY 45
    Answer Key and Explanatory Answers 61

PART TWO
PERSONNEL

TRAINING 71
    Answer Key and Explanatory Answers 83
EMPLOYEE EVALUATION 89
    Answer Key and Explanatory Answers 95
DELEGATION OF AUTHORITY 99
    Answer Key and Explanatory Answers 103
POSITION CLASSIFICATION AND PERSONNEL ADMINISTRATION 105
    Answer Key and Explanatory Answers 113
COMMUNICATIONS, RECORDS, AND REPORTS 119
    Answer Key and Explanatory Answers 133
MORALE 141
    Answer Key and Explanatory Answers 144
CONFERENCES, MEETINGS, AND INTERVIEWS 147
    Answer Key and Explanatory Answers 152
RECRUITMENT 155
    Answer Key and Explanatory Answers 160

PART THREE
CONTROL AND AUXILIARY FUNCTIONS

FISCAL AND BUDGETARY CONTROL 165
    Answer Key and Explanatory Answers 171
PUBLIC RELATIONS 175
    Answer Key and Explanatory Answers 180
STATISTICS AND CHARTS 183
    Answer Key and Explanatory Answers 188

WHAT THIS BOOK WILL DO FOR YOU

ARCO Publishing, Inc. has followed testing trends and methods ever since the firm was founded in 1937. We specialize in books that prepare people for examinations. Based on this experience, we have prepared the best possible book to help you score high.

To compile this book we carefully analyzed every detail surrounding examinations for administrative positions . . .

- the duties and responsibilities of administrative positions
- official examination announcements
- previous examinations, many not available to the public
- technical literature designed to forecast upcoming examinations

CAN YOU PREPARE YOURSELF FOR YOUR TEST?

You want to do well on your examination. That's why you bought this book. Used correctly, your "self-tutor" will show you what to expect and will give you a speedy brush-up on the subjects tested in your exam. Some of these are subjects not taught in schools at all. Even if your study time is very limited, you should:

- Become as familiar as possible with the type of examination you will have.
- Improve your general examination-taking skill.
- Improve your skill in analyzing and answering questions involving reasoning, judgment, comparison, and evaluation.

- Improve your speed and skill in reading and understanding what you read—an important part of your ability to learn and an important part of most tests.

This book will tell you exactly what to study by presenting in full every type of question you will get on the actual test.

This book will help you find your weaknesses. Once you know what subjects you're weak in you can get right to work and concentrate on those areas. This kind of selective study yields maximum test results.

This book will give you the *feel* of the exam. Almost all our sample and practice questions are taken from official civil service examinations. On the day of the exam you'll see how closely this book follows the format of the real test.

This book will give you confidence *now*, while you are preparing for the test. It will build your self-confidence as you proceed and will prevent the kind of test anxiety that causes low test scores.

This book stresses the multiple-choice type of question because that's the kind you are likely to have on your test. You must not be satisfied with merely knowing the correct answer for each question. You must find out why the other choices are incorrect. This will help you remember a lot you thought you had forgotten.

Over eight hundred carefully selected questions covering most aspects of the administrative process are contained in this book together with answers. Each correct answer is fully explained so that the reader will be able to grasp the reason for the selection of the correct answer and the concept upon which the question was based.

ANSWER SHEET FOR
ADMINISTRATIVE JUDGMENT

1 Ⓐ Ⓑ Ⓒ Ⓓ	12 Ⓐ Ⓑ Ⓒ Ⓓ	23 Ⓐ Ⓑ Ⓒ Ⓓ	34 Ⓐ Ⓑ Ⓒ Ⓓ	45 Ⓐ Ⓑ Ⓒ Ⓓ
2 Ⓐ Ⓑ Ⓒ Ⓓ	13 Ⓐ Ⓑ Ⓒ Ⓓ	24 Ⓐ Ⓑ Ⓒ Ⓓ	35 Ⓐ Ⓑ Ⓒ Ⓓ	46 Ⓐ Ⓑ Ⓒ Ⓓ
3 Ⓐ Ⓑ Ⓒ Ⓓ	14 Ⓐ Ⓑ Ⓒ Ⓓ	25 Ⓐ Ⓑ Ⓒ Ⓓ	36 Ⓐ Ⓑ Ⓒ Ⓓ	47 Ⓐ Ⓑ Ⓒ Ⓓ
4 Ⓐ Ⓑ Ⓒ Ⓓ	15 Ⓐ Ⓑ Ⓒ Ⓓ	26 Ⓐ Ⓑ Ⓒ Ⓓ	37 Ⓐ Ⓑ Ⓒ Ⓓ	48 Ⓐ Ⓑ Ⓒ Ⓓ
5 Ⓐ Ⓑ Ⓒ Ⓓ	16 Ⓐ Ⓑ Ⓒ Ⓓ	27 Ⓐ Ⓑ Ⓒ Ⓓ	38 Ⓐ Ⓑ Ⓒ Ⓓ	49 Ⓐ Ⓑ Ⓒ Ⓓ
6 Ⓐ Ⓑ Ⓒ Ⓓ	17 Ⓐ Ⓑ Ⓒ Ⓓ	28 Ⓐ Ⓑ Ⓒ Ⓓ	39 Ⓐ Ⓑ Ⓒ Ⓓ	50 Ⓐ Ⓑ Ⓒ Ⓓ
7 Ⓐ Ⓑ Ⓒ Ⓓ	18 Ⓐ Ⓑ Ⓒ Ⓓ	29 Ⓐ Ⓑ Ⓒ Ⓓ	40 Ⓐ Ⓑ Ⓒ Ⓓ	51 Ⓐ Ⓑ Ⓒ Ⓓ
8 Ⓐ Ⓑ Ⓒ Ⓓ	19 Ⓐ Ⓑ Ⓒ Ⓓ	30 Ⓐ Ⓑ Ⓒ Ⓓ	41 Ⓐ Ⓑ Ⓒ Ⓓ	52 Ⓐ Ⓑ Ⓒ Ⓓ
9 Ⓐ Ⓑ Ⓒ Ⓓ	20 Ⓐ Ⓑ Ⓒ Ⓓ	31 Ⓐ Ⓑ Ⓒ Ⓓ	42 Ⓐ Ⓑ Ⓒ Ⓓ	53 Ⓐ Ⓑ Ⓒ Ⓓ
10 Ⓐ Ⓑ Ⓒ Ⓓ	21 Ⓐ Ⓑ Ⓒ Ⓓ	32 Ⓐ Ⓑ Ⓒ Ⓓ	43 Ⓐ Ⓑ Ⓒ Ⓓ	54 Ⓐ Ⓑ Ⓒ Ⓓ
11 Ⓐ Ⓑ Ⓒ Ⓓ	22 Ⓐ Ⓑ Ⓒ Ⓓ	33 Ⓐ Ⓑ Ⓒ Ⓓ	44 Ⓐ Ⓑ Ⓒ Ⓓ	

ADMINISTRATIVE-SUBORDINATE
RELATIONSHIPS

1 Ⓐ Ⓑ Ⓒ Ⓓ	10 Ⓐ Ⓑ Ⓒ Ⓓ	19 Ⓐ Ⓑ Ⓒ Ⓓ	28 Ⓐ Ⓑ Ⓒ Ⓓ	37 Ⓐ Ⓑ Ⓒ Ⓓ
2 Ⓐ Ⓑ Ⓒ Ⓓ	11 Ⓐ Ⓑ Ⓒ Ⓓ	20 Ⓐ Ⓑ Ⓒ Ⓓ	29 Ⓐ Ⓑ Ⓒ Ⓓ	38 Ⓐ Ⓑ Ⓒ Ⓓ
3 Ⓐ Ⓑ Ⓒ Ⓓ	12 Ⓐ Ⓑ Ⓒ Ⓓ	21 Ⓐ Ⓑ Ⓒ Ⓓ	30 Ⓐ Ⓑ Ⓒ Ⓓ	39 Ⓐ Ⓑ Ⓒ Ⓓ
4 Ⓐ Ⓑ Ⓒ Ⓓ	13 Ⓐ Ⓑ Ⓒ Ⓓ	22 Ⓐ Ⓑ Ⓒ Ⓓ	31 Ⓐ Ⓑ Ⓒ Ⓓ	40 Ⓐ Ⓑ Ⓒ Ⓓ
5 Ⓐ Ⓑ Ⓒ Ⓓ	14 Ⓐ Ⓑ Ⓒ Ⓓ	23 Ⓐ Ⓑ Ⓒ Ⓓ	32 Ⓐ Ⓑ Ⓒ Ⓓ	41 Ⓐ Ⓑ Ⓒ Ⓓ
6 Ⓐ Ⓑ Ⓒ Ⓓ	15 Ⓐ Ⓑ Ⓒ Ⓓ	24 Ⓐ Ⓑ Ⓒ Ⓓ	33 Ⓐ Ⓑ Ⓒ Ⓓ	
7 Ⓐ Ⓑ Ⓒ Ⓓ	16 Ⓐ Ⓑ Ⓒ Ⓓ	25 Ⓐ Ⓑ Ⓒ Ⓓ	34 Ⓐ Ⓑ Ⓒ Ⓓ	
8 Ⓐ Ⓑ Ⓒ Ⓓ	17 Ⓐ Ⓑ Ⓒ Ⓓ	26 Ⓐ Ⓑ Ⓒ Ⓓ	35 Ⓐ Ⓑ Ⓒ Ⓓ	
9 Ⓐ Ⓑ Ⓒ Ⓓ	18 Ⓐ Ⓑ Ⓒ Ⓓ	27 Ⓐ Ⓑ Ⓒ Ⓓ	36 Ⓐ Ⓑ Ⓒ Ⓓ	

ANSWER SHEET FOR
PROBLEMS OF SUPERVISION
AND ADMINISTRATION

1 Ⓐ Ⓑ Ⓒ Ⓓ   17 Ⓐ Ⓑ Ⓒ Ⓓ   33 Ⓐ Ⓑ Ⓒ Ⓓ   49 Ⓐ Ⓑ Ⓒ Ⓓ   65 Ⓐ Ⓑ Ⓒ Ⓓ

2 Ⓐ Ⓑ Ⓒ Ⓓ   18 Ⓐ Ⓑ Ⓒ Ⓓ   34 Ⓐ Ⓑ Ⓒ Ⓓ   50 Ⓐ Ⓑ Ⓒ Ⓓ   66 Ⓐ Ⓑ Ⓒ Ⓓ

3 Ⓐ Ⓑ Ⓒ Ⓓ   19 Ⓐ Ⓑ Ⓒ Ⓓ   35 Ⓐ Ⓑ Ⓒ Ⓓ   51 Ⓐ Ⓑ Ⓒ Ⓓ   67 Ⓐ Ⓑ Ⓒ Ⓓ

4 Ⓐ Ⓑ Ⓒ Ⓓ   20 Ⓐ Ⓑ Ⓒ Ⓓ   36 Ⓐ Ⓑ Ⓒ Ⓓ   52 Ⓐ Ⓑ Ⓒ Ⓓ   68 Ⓐ Ⓑ Ⓒ Ⓓ

5 Ⓐ Ⓑ Ⓒ Ⓓ   21 Ⓐ Ⓑ Ⓒ Ⓓ   37 Ⓐ Ⓑ Ⓒ Ⓓ   53 Ⓐ Ⓑ Ⓒ Ⓓ   69 Ⓐ Ⓑ Ⓒ Ⓓ

6 Ⓐ Ⓑ Ⓒ Ⓓ   22 Ⓐ Ⓑ Ⓒ Ⓓ   38 Ⓐ Ⓑ Ⓒ Ⓓ   54 Ⓐ Ⓑ Ⓒ Ⓓ   70 Ⓐ Ⓑ Ⓒ Ⓓ

7 Ⓐ Ⓑ Ⓒ Ⓓ   23 Ⓐ Ⓑ Ⓒ Ⓓ   39 Ⓐ Ⓑ Ⓒ Ⓓ   55 Ⓐ Ⓑ Ⓒ Ⓓ   71 Ⓐ Ⓑ Ⓒ Ⓓ

8 Ⓐ Ⓑ Ⓒ Ⓓ   24 Ⓐ Ⓑ Ⓒ Ⓓ   40 Ⓐ Ⓑ Ⓒ Ⓓ   56 Ⓐ Ⓑ Ⓒ Ⓓ   72 Ⓐ Ⓑ Ⓒ Ⓓ

9 Ⓐ Ⓑ Ⓒ Ⓓ   25 Ⓐ Ⓑ Ⓒ Ⓓ   41 Ⓐ Ⓑ Ⓒ Ⓓ   57 Ⓐ Ⓑ Ⓒ Ⓓ   73 Ⓐ Ⓑ Ⓒ Ⓓ

10 Ⓐ Ⓑ Ⓒ Ⓓ   26 Ⓐ Ⓑ Ⓒ Ⓓ   42 Ⓐ Ⓑ Ⓒ Ⓓ   58 Ⓐ Ⓑ Ⓒ Ⓓ   74 Ⓐ Ⓑ Ⓒ Ⓓ

11 Ⓐ Ⓑ Ⓒ Ⓓ   27 Ⓐ Ⓑ Ⓒ Ⓓ   43 Ⓐ Ⓑ Ⓒ Ⓓ   59 Ⓐ Ⓑ Ⓒ Ⓓ   75 Ⓐ Ⓑ Ⓒ Ⓓ

12 Ⓐ Ⓑ Ⓒ Ⓓ   28 Ⓐ Ⓑ Ⓒ Ⓓ   44 Ⓐ Ⓑ Ⓒ Ⓓ   60 Ⓐ Ⓑ Ⓒ Ⓓ   76 Ⓐ Ⓑ Ⓒ Ⓓ

13 Ⓐ Ⓑ Ⓒ Ⓓ   29 Ⓐ Ⓑ Ⓒ Ⓓ   45 Ⓐ Ⓑ Ⓒ Ⓓ   61 Ⓐ Ⓑ Ⓒ Ⓓ   77 Ⓐ Ⓑ Ⓒ Ⓓ

14 Ⓐ Ⓑ Ⓒ Ⓓ   30 Ⓐ Ⓑ Ⓒ Ⓓ   46 Ⓐ Ⓑ Ⓒ Ⓓ   62 Ⓐ Ⓑ Ⓒ Ⓓ   78 Ⓐ Ⓑ Ⓒ Ⓓ

15 Ⓐ Ⓑ Ⓒ Ⓓ   31 Ⓐ Ⓑ Ⓒ Ⓓ   47 Ⓐ Ⓑ Ⓒ Ⓓ   63 Ⓐ Ⓑ Ⓒ Ⓓ   79 Ⓐ Ⓑ Ⓒ Ⓓ

16 Ⓐ Ⓑ Ⓒ Ⓓ   32 Ⓐ Ⓑ Ⓒ Ⓓ   48 Ⓐ Ⓑ Ⓒ Ⓓ   64 Ⓐ Ⓑ Ⓒ Ⓓ

ANSWER SHEET FOR
OPERATING EFFICIENCY

1 Ⓐ Ⓑ Ⓒ Ⓓ   24 Ⓐ Ⓑ Ⓒ Ⓓ   46 Ⓐ Ⓑ Ⓒ Ⓓ   69 Ⓐ Ⓑ Ⓒ Ⓓ   92 Ⓐ Ⓑ Ⓒ Ⓓ

2 Ⓐ Ⓑ Ⓒ Ⓓ   25 Ⓐ Ⓑ Ⓒ Ⓓ   47 Ⓐ Ⓑ Ⓒ Ⓓ   70 Ⓐ Ⓑ Ⓒ Ⓓ   93 Ⓐ Ⓑ Ⓒ Ⓓ

3 Ⓐ Ⓑ Ⓒ Ⓓ   26 Ⓐ Ⓑ Ⓒ Ⓓ   48 Ⓐ Ⓑ Ⓒ Ⓓ   71 Ⓐ Ⓑ Ⓒ Ⓓ   94 Ⓐ Ⓑ Ⓒ Ⓓ

4 Ⓐ Ⓑ Ⓒ Ⓓ   27 Ⓐ Ⓑ Ⓒ Ⓓ   49 Ⓐ Ⓑ Ⓒ Ⓓ   72 Ⓐ Ⓑ Ⓒ Ⓓ   95 Ⓐ Ⓑ Ⓒ Ⓓ

5 Ⓐ Ⓑ Ⓒ Ⓓ   28 Ⓐ Ⓑ Ⓒ Ⓓ   50 Ⓐ Ⓑ Ⓒ Ⓓ   73 Ⓐ Ⓑ Ⓒ Ⓓ   96 Ⓐ Ⓑ Ⓒ Ⓓ

6 Ⓐ Ⓑ Ⓒ Ⓓ   29 Ⓐ Ⓑ Ⓒ Ⓓ   51 Ⓐ Ⓑ Ⓒ Ⓓ   74 Ⓐ Ⓑ Ⓒ Ⓓ   97 Ⓐ Ⓑ Ⓒ Ⓓ

7 Ⓐ Ⓑ Ⓒ Ⓓ   30 Ⓐ Ⓑ Ⓒ Ⓓ   52 Ⓐ Ⓑ Ⓒ Ⓓ   75 Ⓐ Ⓑ Ⓒ Ⓓ   98 Ⓐ Ⓑ Ⓒ Ⓓ

8 Ⓐ Ⓑ Ⓒ Ⓓ   31 Ⓐ Ⓑ Ⓒ Ⓓ   53 Ⓐ Ⓑ Ⓒ Ⓓ   76 Ⓐ Ⓑ Ⓒ Ⓓ   99 Ⓐ Ⓑ Ⓒ Ⓓ

9 Ⓐ Ⓑ Ⓒ Ⓓ   32 Ⓐ Ⓑ Ⓒ Ⓓ   54 Ⓐ Ⓑ Ⓒ Ⓓ   77 Ⓐ Ⓑ Ⓒ Ⓓ   100 Ⓐ Ⓑ Ⓒ Ⓓ

10 Ⓐ Ⓑ Ⓒ Ⓓ   33 Ⓐ Ⓑ Ⓒ Ⓓ   55 Ⓐ Ⓑ Ⓒ Ⓓ   78 Ⓐ Ⓑ Ⓒ Ⓓ   101 Ⓐ Ⓑ Ⓒ Ⓓ

11 Ⓐ Ⓑ Ⓒ Ⓓ   34 Ⓐ Ⓑ Ⓒ Ⓓ   56 Ⓐ Ⓑ Ⓒ Ⓓ   79 Ⓐ Ⓑ Ⓒ Ⓓ   102 Ⓐ Ⓑ Ⓒ Ⓓ

12 Ⓐ Ⓑ Ⓒ Ⓓ   35 Ⓐ Ⓑ Ⓒ Ⓓ   57 Ⓐ Ⓑ Ⓒ Ⓓ   80 Ⓐ Ⓑ Ⓒ Ⓓ   103 Ⓐ Ⓑ Ⓒ Ⓓ

13 Ⓐ Ⓑ Ⓒ Ⓓ   36 Ⓐ Ⓑ Ⓒ Ⓓ   58 Ⓐ Ⓑ Ⓒ Ⓓ   81 Ⓐ Ⓑ Ⓒ Ⓓ   104 Ⓐ Ⓑ Ⓒ Ⓓ

14 Ⓐ Ⓑ Ⓒ Ⓓ   37 Ⓐ Ⓑ Ⓒ Ⓓ   59 Ⓐ Ⓑ Ⓒ Ⓓ   82 Ⓐ Ⓑ Ⓒ Ⓓ   105 Ⓐ Ⓑ Ⓒ Ⓓ

15 Ⓐ Ⓑ Ⓒ Ⓓ   38 Ⓐ Ⓑ Ⓒ Ⓓ   60 Ⓐ Ⓑ Ⓒ Ⓓ   83 Ⓐ Ⓑ Ⓒ Ⓓ   106 Ⓐ Ⓑ Ⓒ Ⓓ

16 Ⓐ Ⓑ Ⓒ Ⓓ   39 Ⓐ Ⓑ Ⓒ Ⓓ   61 Ⓐ Ⓑ Ⓒ Ⓓ   84 Ⓐ Ⓑ Ⓒ Ⓓ   107 Ⓐ Ⓑ Ⓒ Ⓓ

17 Ⓐ Ⓑ Ⓒ Ⓓ   40 Ⓐ Ⓑ Ⓒ Ⓓ   62 Ⓐ Ⓑ Ⓒ Ⓓ   85 Ⓐ Ⓑ Ⓒ Ⓓ   108 Ⓐ Ⓑ Ⓒ Ⓓ

18 Ⓐ Ⓑ Ⓒ Ⓓ   41 Ⓐ Ⓑ Ⓒ Ⓓ   63 Ⓐ Ⓑ Ⓒ Ⓓ   86 Ⓐ Ⓑ Ⓒ Ⓓ   109 Ⓐ Ⓑ Ⓒ Ⓓ

19 Ⓐ Ⓑ Ⓒ Ⓓ   42 Ⓐ Ⓑ Ⓒ Ⓓ   64 Ⓐ Ⓑ Ⓒ Ⓓ   87 Ⓐ Ⓑ Ⓒ Ⓓ   110 Ⓐ Ⓑ Ⓒ Ⓓ
                   Ⓔ Ⓕ Ⓖ Ⓗ
20 Ⓐ Ⓑ Ⓒ Ⓓ   Ⓘ Ⓙ Ⓚ Ⓛ   65 Ⓐ Ⓑ Ⓒ Ⓓ   88 Ⓐ Ⓑ Ⓒ Ⓓ

21 Ⓐ Ⓑ Ⓒ Ⓓ   43 Ⓐ Ⓑ Ⓒ Ⓓ   66 Ⓐ Ⓑ Ⓒ Ⓓ   89 Ⓐ Ⓑ Ⓒ Ⓓ

22 Ⓐ Ⓑ Ⓒ Ⓓ   44 Ⓐ Ⓑ Ⓒ Ⓓ   67 Ⓐ Ⓑ Ⓒ Ⓓ   90 Ⓐ Ⓑ Ⓒ Ⓓ

23 Ⓐ Ⓑ Ⓒ Ⓓ   45 Ⓐ Ⓑ Ⓒ Ⓓ   68 Ⓐ Ⓑ Ⓒ Ⓓ   91 Ⓐ Ⓑ Ⓒ Ⓓ

ANSWER SHEET FOR TRAINING

1 Ⓐ Ⓑ Ⓒ Ⓓ   18 Ⓐ Ⓑ Ⓒ Ⓓ   35 Ⓐ Ⓑ Ⓒ Ⓓ   52 Ⓐ Ⓑ Ⓒ Ⓓ   69 Ⓐ Ⓑ Ⓒ Ⓓ

2 Ⓐ Ⓑ Ⓒ Ⓓ   19 Ⓐ Ⓑ Ⓒ Ⓓ   36 Ⓐ Ⓑ Ⓒ Ⓓ   53 Ⓐ Ⓑ Ⓒ Ⓓ   70 Ⓐ Ⓑ Ⓒ Ⓓ

3 Ⓐ Ⓑ Ⓒ Ⓓ   20 Ⓐ Ⓑ Ⓒ Ⓓ   37 Ⓐ Ⓑ Ⓒ Ⓓ   54 Ⓐ Ⓑ Ⓒ Ⓓ   71 Ⓐ Ⓑ Ⓒ Ⓓ

4 Ⓐ Ⓑ Ⓒ Ⓓ   21 Ⓐ Ⓑ Ⓒ Ⓓ   38 Ⓐ Ⓑ Ⓒ Ⓓ   55 Ⓐ Ⓑ Ⓒ Ⓓ   72 Ⓐ Ⓑ Ⓒ Ⓓ

5 Ⓐ Ⓑ Ⓒ Ⓓ   22 Ⓐ Ⓑ Ⓒ Ⓓ   39 Ⓐ Ⓑ Ⓒ Ⓓ   56 Ⓐ Ⓑ Ⓒ Ⓓ   73 Ⓐ Ⓑ Ⓒ Ⓓ

6 Ⓐ Ⓑ Ⓒ Ⓓ   23 Ⓐ Ⓑ Ⓒ Ⓓ   40 Ⓐ Ⓑ Ⓒ Ⓓ   57 Ⓐ Ⓑ Ⓒ Ⓓ   74 Ⓐ Ⓑ Ⓒ Ⓓ

7 Ⓐ Ⓑ Ⓒ Ⓓ   24 Ⓐ Ⓑ Ⓒ Ⓓ   41 Ⓐ Ⓑ Ⓒ Ⓓ   58 Ⓐ Ⓑ Ⓒ Ⓓ   75 Ⓐ Ⓑ Ⓒ Ⓓ

8 Ⓐ Ⓑ Ⓒ Ⓓ   25 Ⓐ Ⓑ Ⓒ Ⓓ   42 Ⓐ Ⓑ Ⓒ Ⓓ   59 Ⓐ Ⓑ Ⓒ Ⓓ   76 Ⓐ Ⓑ Ⓒ Ⓓ

9 Ⓐ Ⓑ Ⓒ Ⓓ   26 Ⓐ Ⓑ Ⓒ Ⓓ   43 Ⓐ Ⓑ Ⓒ Ⓓ   60 Ⓐ Ⓑ Ⓒ Ⓓ   77 Ⓐ Ⓑ Ⓒ Ⓓ

10 Ⓐ Ⓑ Ⓒ Ⓓ   27 Ⓐ Ⓑ Ⓒ Ⓓ   44 Ⓐ Ⓑ Ⓒ Ⓓ   61 Ⓐ Ⓑ Ⓒ Ⓓ   78 Ⓐ Ⓑ Ⓒ Ⓓ

11 Ⓐ Ⓑ Ⓒ Ⓓ   28 Ⓐ Ⓑ Ⓒ Ⓓ   45 Ⓐ Ⓑ Ⓒ Ⓓ   62 Ⓐ Ⓑ Ⓒ Ⓓ   79 Ⓐ Ⓑ Ⓒ Ⓓ

12 Ⓐ Ⓑ Ⓒ Ⓓ   29 Ⓐ Ⓑ Ⓒ Ⓓ   46 Ⓐ Ⓑ Ⓒ Ⓓ   63 Ⓐ Ⓑ Ⓒ Ⓓ   80 Ⓐ Ⓑ Ⓒ Ⓓ

13 Ⓐ Ⓑ Ⓒ Ⓓ   30 Ⓐ Ⓑ Ⓒ Ⓓ   47 Ⓐ Ⓑ Ⓒ Ⓓ   64 Ⓐ Ⓑ Ⓒ Ⓓ   81 Ⓐ Ⓑ Ⓒ Ⓓ

14 Ⓐ Ⓑ Ⓒ Ⓓ   31 Ⓐ Ⓑ Ⓒ Ⓓ   48 Ⓐ Ⓑ Ⓒ Ⓓ   65 Ⓐ Ⓑ Ⓒ Ⓓ   82 Ⓐ Ⓑ Ⓒ Ⓓ

15 Ⓐ Ⓑ Ⓒ Ⓓ   32 Ⓐ Ⓑ Ⓒ Ⓓ   49 Ⓐ Ⓑ Ⓒ Ⓓ   66 Ⓐ Ⓑ Ⓒ Ⓓ   83 Ⓐ Ⓑ Ⓒ Ⓓ

16 Ⓐ Ⓑ Ⓒ Ⓓ   33 Ⓐ Ⓑ Ⓒ Ⓓ   50 Ⓐ Ⓑ Ⓒ Ⓓ   67 Ⓐ Ⓑ Ⓒ Ⓓ   84 Ⓐ Ⓑ Ⓒ Ⓓ

17 Ⓐ Ⓑ Ⓒ Ⓓ   34 Ⓐ Ⓑ Ⓒ Ⓓ   51 Ⓐ Ⓑ Ⓒ Ⓓ   68 Ⓐ Ⓑ Ⓒ Ⓓ

ANSWER SHEET FOR
EMPLOYEE EVALUATION

1 Ⓐ Ⓑ Ⓒ Ⓓ   10 Ⓐ Ⓑ Ⓒ Ⓓ   19 Ⓐ Ⓑ Ⓒ Ⓓ   28 Ⓐ Ⓑ Ⓒ Ⓓ   37 Ⓐ Ⓑ Ⓒ Ⓓ

2 Ⓐ Ⓑ Ⓒ Ⓓ   11 Ⓐ Ⓑ Ⓒ Ⓓ   20 Ⓐ Ⓑ Ⓒ Ⓓ   29 Ⓐ Ⓑ Ⓒ Ⓓ   38 Ⓐ Ⓑ Ⓒ Ⓓ

3 Ⓐ Ⓑ Ⓒ Ⓓ   12 Ⓐ Ⓑ Ⓒ Ⓓ   21 Ⓐ Ⓑ Ⓒ Ⓓ   30 Ⓐ Ⓑ Ⓒ Ⓓ   39 Ⓐ Ⓑ Ⓒ Ⓓ

4 Ⓐ Ⓑ Ⓒ Ⓓ   13 Ⓐ Ⓑ Ⓒ Ⓓ   22 Ⓐ Ⓑ Ⓒ Ⓓ   31 Ⓐ Ⓑ Ⓒ Ⓓ   40 Ⓐ Ⓑ Ⓒ Ⓓ

5 Ⓐ Ⓑ Ⓒ Ⓓ   14 Ⓐ Ⓑ Ⓒ Ⓓ   23 Ⓐ Ⓑ Ⓒ Ⓓ   32 Ⓐ Ⓑ Ⓒ Ⓓ   41 Ⓐ Ⓑ Ⓒ Ⓓ

6 Ⓐ Ⓑ Ⓒ Ⓓ   15 Ⓐ Ⓑ Ⓒ Ⓓ   24 Ⓐ Ⓑ Ⓒ Ⓓ   33 Ⓐ Ⓑ Ⓒ Ⓓ   42 Ⓐ Ⓑ Ⓒ Ⓓ

7 Ⓐ Ⓑ Ⓒ Ⓓ   16 Ⓐ Ⓑ Ⓒ Ⓓ   25 Ⓐ Ⓑ Ⓒ Ⓓ   34 Ⓐ Ⓑ Ⓒ Ⓓ

8 Ⓐ Ⓑ Ⓒ Ⓓ   17 Ⓐ Ⓑ Ⓒ Ⓓ   26 Ⓐ Ⓑ Ⓒ Ⓓ   35 Ⓐ Ⓑ Ⓒ Ⓓ

9 Ⓐ Ⓑ Ⓒ Ⓓ   18 Ⓐ Ⓑ Ⓒ Ⓓ   27 Ⓐ Ⓑ Ⓒ Ⓓ   36 Ⓐ Ⓑ Ⓒ Ⓓ

DELEGATION OF AUTHORITY

1 Ⓐ Ⓑ Ⓒ Ⓓ   6 Ⓐ Ⓑ Ⓒ Ⓓ   11 Ⓐ Ⓑ Ⓒ Ⓓ   16 Ⓐ Ⓑ Ⓒ Ⓓ   21 Ⓐ Ⓑ Ⓒ Ⓓ

2 Ⓐ Ⓑ Ⓒ Ⓓ   7 Ⓐ Ⓑ Ⓒ Ⓓ   12 Ⓐ Ⓑ Ⓒ Ⓓ   17 Ⓐ Ⓑ Ⓒ Ⓓ   22 Ⓐ Ⓑ Ⓒ Ⓓ

3 Ⓐ Ⓑ Ⓒ Ⓓ   8 Ⓐ Ⓑ Ⓒ Ⓓ   13 Ⓐ Ⓑ Ⓒ Ⓓ   18 Ⓐ Ⓑ Ⓒ Ⓓ   23 Ⓐ Ⓑ Ⓒ Ⓓ

4 Ⓐ Ⓑ Ⓒ Ⓓ   9 Ⓐ Ⓑ Ⓒ Ⓓ   14 Ⓐ Ⓑ Ⓒ Ⓓ   19 Ⓐ Ⓑ Ⓒ Ⓓ

5 Ⓐ Ⓑ Ⓒ Ⓓ   10 Ⓐ Ⓑ Ⓒ Ⓓ   15 Ⓐ Ⓑ Ⓒ Ⓓ   20 Ⓐ Ⓑ Ⓒ Ⓓ

ANSWER SHEET FOR
POSITION CLASSIFICATION
AND PERSONNEL ADMINISTRATION

1 Ⓐ Ⓑ Ⓒ Ⓓ   13 Ⓐ Ⓑ Ⓒ Ⓓ   25 Ⓐ Ⓑ Ⓒ Ⓓ   37 Ⓐ Ⓑ Ⓒ Ⓓ   49 Ⓐ Ⓑ Ⓒ Ⓓ

2 Ⓐ Ⓑ Ⓒ Ⓓ   14 Ⓐ Ⓑ Ⓒ Ⓓ   26 Ⓐ Ⓑ Ⓒ Ⓓ   38 Ⓐ Ⓑ Ⓒ Ⓓ   50 Ⓐ Ⓑ Ⓒ Ⓓ

3 Ⓐ Ⓑ Ⓒ Ⓓ   15 Ⓐ Ⓑ Ⓒ Ⓓ   27 Ⓐ Ⓑ Ⓒ Ⓓ   39 Ⓐ Ⓑ Ⓒ Ⓓ   51 Ⓐ Ⓑ Ⓒ Ⓓ

4 Ⓐ Ⓑ Ⓒ Ⓓ   16 Ⓐ Ⓑ Ⓒ Ⓓ   28 Ⓐ Ⓑ Ⓒ Ⓓ   40 Ⓐ Ⓑ Ⓒ Ⓓ   52 Ⓐ Ⓑ Ⓒ Ⓓ

5 Ⓐ Ⓑ Ⓒ Ⓓ   17 Ⓐ Ⓑ Ⓒ Ⓓ   29 Ⓐ Ⓑ Ⓒ Ⓓ   41 Ⓐ Ⓑ Ⓒ Ⓓ   53 Ⓐ Ⓑ Ⓒ Ⓓ

6 Ⓐ Ⓑ Ⓒ Ⓓ   18 Ⓐ Ⓑ Ⓒ Ⓓ   30 Ⓐ Ⓑ Ⓒ Ⓓ   42 Ⓐ Ⓑ Ⓒ Ⓓ   54 Ⓐ Ⓑ Ⓒ Ⓓ

7 Ⓐ Ⓑ Ⓒ Ⓓ   19 Ⓐ Ⓑ Ⓒ Ⓓ   31 Ⓐ Ⓑ Ⓒ Ⓓ   43 Ⓐ Ⓑ Ⓒ Ⓓ   55 Ⓐ Ⓑ Ⓒ Ⓓ

8 Ⓐ Ⓑ Ⓒ Ⓓ   20 Ⓐ Ⓑ Ⓒ Ⓓ   32 Ⓐ Ⓑ Ⓒ Ⓓ   44 Ⓐ Ⓑ Ⓒ Ⓓ   56 Ⓐ Ⓑ Ⓒ Ⓓ

9 Ⓐ Ⓑ Ⓒ Ⓓ   21 Ⓐ Ⓑ Ⓒ Ⓓ   33 Ⓐ Ⓑ Ⓒ Ⓓ   45 Ⓐ Ⓑ Ⓒ Ⓓ   57 Ⓐ Ⓑ Ⓒ Ⓓ

10 Ⓐ Ⓑ Ⓒ Ⓓ   22 Ⓐ Ⓑ Ⓒ Ⓓ   34 Ⓐ Ⓑ Ⓒ Ⓓ   46 Ⓐ Ⓑ Ⓒ Ⓓ   58 Ⓐ Ⓑ Ⓒ Ⓓ

11 Ⓐ Ⓑ Ⓒ Ⓓ   23 Ⓐ Ⓑ Ⓒ Ⓓ   35 Ⓐ Ⓑ Ⓒ Ⓓ   47 Ⓐ Ⓑ Ⓒ Ⓓ   59 Ⓐ Ⓑ Ⓒ Ⓓ

12 Ⓐ Ⓑ Ⓒ Ⓓ   24 Ⓐ Ⓑ Ⓒ Ⓓ   36 Ⓐ Ⓑ Ⓒ Ⓓ   48 Ⓐ Ⓑ Ⓒ Ⓓ

ANSWER SHEET FOR
COMMUNICATIONS, RECORDS,
AND REPORTS

1 Ⓐ Ⓑ Ⓒ Ⓓ	22 Ⓐ Ⓑ Ⓒ Ⓓ	43 Ⓐ Ⓑ Ⓒ Ⓓ	64 Ⓐ Ⓑ Ⓒ Ⓓ	85 Ⓐ Ⓑ Ⓒ Ⓓ
2 Ⓐ Ⓑ Ⓒ Ⓓ	23 Ⓐ Ⓑ Ⓒ Ⓓ	44 Ⓐ Ⓑ Ⓒ Ⓓ	65 Ⓐ Ⓑ Ⓒ Ⓓ	86 Ⓐ Ⓑ Ⓒ Ⓓ
3 Ⓐ Ⓑ Ⓒ Ⓓ	24 Ⓐ Ⓑ Ⓒ Ⓓ	45 Ⓐ Ⓑ Ⓒ Ⓓ	66 Ⓐ Ⓑ Ⓒ Ⓓ	87 Ⓐ Ⓑ Ⓒ Ⓓ
4 Ⓐ Ⓑ Ⓒ Ⓓ	25 Ⓐ Ⓑ Ⓒ Ⓓ	46 Ⓐ Ⓑ Ⓒ Ⓓ	67 Ⓐ Ⓑ Ⓒ Ⓓ	88 Ⓐ Ⓑ Ⓒ Ⓓ
5 Ⓐ Ⓑ Ⓒ Ⓓ	26 Ⓐ Ⓑ Ⓒ Ⓓ	47 Ⓐ Ⓑ Ⓒ Ⓓ	68 Ⓐ Ⓑ Ⓒ Ⓓ	89 Ⓐ Ⓑ Ⓒ Ⓓ
6 Ⓐ Ⓑ Ⓒ Ⓓ	27 Ⓐ Ⓑ Ⓒ Ⓓ	48 Ⓐ Ⓑ Ⓒ Ⓓ	69 Ⓐ Ⓑ Ⓒ Ⓓ	90 Ⓐ Ⓑ Ⓒ Ⓓ
7 Ⓐ Ⓑ Ⓒ Ⓓ	28 Ⓐ Ⓑ Ⓒ Ⓓ	49 Ⓐ Ⓑ Ⓒ Ⓓ	70 Ⓐ Ⓑ Ⓒ Ⓓ	91 Ⓐ Ⓑ Ⓒ Ⓓ
8 Ⓐ Ⓑ Ⓒ Ⓓ	29 Ⓐ Ⓑ Ⓒ Ⓓ	50 Ⓐ Ⓑ Ⓒ Ⓓ	71 Ⓐ Ⓑ Ⓒ Ⓓ	92 Ⓐ Ⓑ Ⓒ Ⓓ
9 Ⓐ Ⓑ Ⓒ Ⓓ	30 Ⓐ Ⓑ Ⓒ Ⓓ	51 Ⓐ Ⓑ Ⓒ Ⓓ	72 Ⓐ Ⓑ Ⓒ Ⓓ	93 Ⓐ Ⓑ Ⓒ Ⓓ
10 Ⓐ Ⓑ Ⓒ Ⓓ	31 Ⓐ Ⓑ Ⓒ Ⓓ	52 Ⓐ Ⓑ Ⓒ Ⓓ	73 Ⓐ Ⓑ Ⓒ Ⓓ	94 Ⓐ Ⓑ Ⓒ Ⓓ
11 Ⓐ Ⓑ Ⓒ Ⓓ	32 Ⓐ Ⓑ Ⓒ Ⓓ	53 Ⓐ Ⓑ Ⓒ Ⓓ	74 Ⓐ Ⓑ Ⓒ Ⓓ	95 Ⓐ Ⓑ Ⓒ Ⓓ
12 Ⓐ Ⓑ Ⓒ Ⓓ	33 Ⓐ Ⓑ Ⓒ Ⓓ	54 Ⓐ Ⓑ Ⓒ Ⓓ	75 Ⓐ Ⓑ Ⓒ Ⓓ	96 Ⓐ Ⓑ Ⓒ Ⓓ
13 Ⓐ Ⓑ Ⓒ Ⓓ	34 Ⓐ Ⓑ Ⓒ Ⓓ	55 Ⓐ Ⓑ Ⓒ Ⓓ	76 Ⓐ Ⓑ Ⓒ Ⓓ	97 Ⓐ Ⓑ Ⓒ Ⓓ
14 Ⓐ Ⓑ Ⓒ Ⓓ	35 Ⓐ Ⓑ Ⓒ Ⓓ	56 Ⓐ Ⓑ Ⓒ Ⓓ	77 Ⓐ Ⓑ Ⓒ Ⓓ	98 Ⓐ Ⓑ Ⓒ Ⓓ
15 Ⓐ Ⓑ Ⓒ Ⓓ	36 Ⓐ Ⓑ Ⓒ Ⓓ	57 Ⓐ Ⓑ Ⓒ Ⓓ	78 Ⓐ Ⓑ Ⓒ Ⓓ	99 Ⓐ Ⓑ Ⓒ Ⓓ
16 Ⓐ Ⓑ Ⓒ Ⓓ	37 Ⓐ Ⓑ Ⓒ Ⓓ	58 Ⓐ Ⓑ Ⓒ Ⓓ	79 Ⓐ Ⓑ Ⓒ Ⓓ	100 Ⓐ Ⓑ Ⓒ Ⓓ
17 Ⓐ Ⓑ Ⓒ Ⓓ	38 Ⓐ Ⓑ Ⓒ Ⓓ	59 Ⓐ Ⓑ Ⓒ Ⓓ	80 Ⓐ Ⓑ Ⓒ Ⓓ	101 Ⓐ Ⓑ Ⓒ Ⓓ
18 Ⓐ Ⓑ Ⓒ Ⓓ	39 Ⓐ Ⓑ Ⓒ Ⓓ	60 Ⓐ Ⓑ Ⓒ Ⓓ	81 Ⓐ Ⓑ Ⓒ Ⓓ	102 Ⓐ Ⓑ Ⓒ Ⓓ
19 Ⓐ Ⓑ Ⓒ Ⓓ	40 Ⓐ Ⓑ Ⓒ Ⓓ	61 Ⓐ Ⓑ Ⓒ Ⓓ	82 Ⓐ Ⓑ Ⓒ Ⓓ	103 Ⓐ Ⓑ Ⓒ Ⓓ
20 Ⓐ Ⓑ Ⓒ Ⓓ	41 Ⓐ Ⓑ Ⓒ Ⓓ	62 Ⓐ Ⓑ Ⓒ Ⓓ	83 Ⓐ Ⓑ Ⓒ Ⓓ	104 Ⓐ Ⓑ Ⓒ Ⓓ
21 Ⓐ Ⓑ Ⓒ Ⓓ	42 Ⓐ Ⓑ Ⓒ Ⓓ	63 Ⓐ Ⓑ Ⓒ Ⓓ	84 Ⓐ Ⓑ Ⓒ Ⓓ	105 Ⓐ Ⓑ Ⓒ Ⓓ

ANSWER SHEET FOR MORALE

1 Ⓐ Ⓑ Ⓒ Ⓓ	5 Ⓐ Ⓑ Ⓒ Ⓓ	9 Ⓐ Ⓑ Ⓒ Ⓓ	13 Ⓐ Ⓑ Ⓒ Ⓓ	17 Ⓐ Ⓑ Ⓒ Ⓓ
2 Ⓐ Ⓑ Ⓒ Ⓓ	6 Ⓐ Ⓑ Ⓒ Ⓓ	10 Ⓐ Ⓑ Ⓒ Ⓓ	14 Ⓐ Ⓑ Ⓒ Ⓓ	18 Ⓐ Ⓑ Ⓒ Ⓓ
3 Ⓐ Ⓑ Ⓒ Ⓓ	7 Ⓐ Ⓑ Ⓒ Ⓓ	11 Ⓐ Ⓑ Ⓒ Ⓓ	15 Ⓐ Ⓑ Ⓒ Ⓓ	19 Ⓐ Ⓑ Ⓒ Ⓓ
4 Ⓐ Ⓑ Ⓒ Ⓓ	8 Ⓐ Ⓑ Ⓒ Ⓓ	12 Ⓐ Ⓑ Ⓒ Ⓓ	16 Ⓐ Ⓑ Ⓒ Ⓓ	

CONFERENCES, MEETINGS, AND INTERVIEWS

1 Ⓐ Ⓑ Ⓒ Ⓓ	7 Ⓐ Ⓑ Ⓒ Ⓓ	13 Ⓐ Ⓑ Ⓒ Ⓓ	19 Ⓐ Ⓑ Ⓒ Ⓓ	25 Ⓐ Ⓑ Ⓒ Ⓓ
2 Ⓐ Ⓑ Ⓒ Ⓓ	8 Ⓐ Ⓑ Ⓒ Ⓓ	14 Ⓐ Ⓑ Ⓒ Ⓓ	20 Ⓐ Ⓑ Ⓒ Ⓓ	26 Ⓐ Ⓑ Ⓒ Ⓓ
3 Ⓐ Ⓑ Ⓒ Ⓓ	9 Ⓐ Ⓑ Ⓒ Ⓓ	15 Ⓐ Ⓑ Ⓒ Ⓓ	21 Ⓐ Ⓑ Ⓒ Ⓓ	27 Ⓐ Ⓑ Ⓒ Ⓓ
4 Ⓐ Ⓑ Ⓒ Ⓓ	10 Ⓐ Ⓑ Ⓒ Ⓓ	16 Ⓐ Ⓑ Ⓒ Ⓓ	22 Ⓐ Ⓑ Ⓒ Ⓓ	28 Ⓐ Ⓑ Ⓒ Ⓓ
5 Ⓐ Ⓑ Ⓒ Ⓓ	11 Ⓐ Ⓑ Ⓒ Ⓓ	17 Ⓐ Ⓑ Ⓒ Ⓓ	23 Ⓐ Ⓑ Ⓒ Ⓓ	29 Ⓐ Ⓑ Ⓒ Ⓓ
6 Ⓐ Ⓑ Ⓒ Ⓓ	12 Ⓐ Ⓑ Ⓒ Ⓓ	18 Ⓐ Ⓑ Ⓒ Ⓓ	24 Ⓐ Ⓑ Ⓒ Ⓓ	

RECRUITMENT

1 Ⓐ Ⓑ Ⓒ Ⓓ	8 Ⓐ Ⓑ Ⓒ Ⓓ	15 Ⓐ Ⓑ Ⓒ Ⓓ	22 Ⓐ Ⓑ Ⓒ Ⓓ	29 Ⓐ Ⓑ Ⓒ Ⓓ
2 Ⓐ Ⓑ Ⓒ Ⓓ	9 Ⓐ Ⓑ Ⓒ Ⓓ	16 Ⓐ Ⓑ Ⓒ Ⓓ	23 Ⓐ Ⓑ Ⓒ Ⓓ	30 Ⓐ Ⓑ Ⓒ Ⓓ
3 Ⓐ Ⓑ Ⓒ Ⓓ	10 Ⓐ Ⓑ Ⓒ Ⓓ	17 Ⓐ Ⓑ Ⓒ Ⓓ	24 Ⓐ Ⓑ Ⓒ Ⓓ	31 Ⓐ Ⓑ Ⓒ Ⓓ
4 Ⓐ Ⓑ Ⓒ Ⓓ	11 Ⓐ Ⓑ Ⓒ Ⓓ	18 Ⓐ Ⓑ Ⓒ Ⓓ	25 Ⓐ Ⓑ Ⓒ Ⓓ	
5 Ⓐ Ⓑ Ⓒ Ⓓ	12 Ⓐ Ⓑ Ⓒ Ⓓ	19 Ⓐ Ⓑ Ⓒ Ⓓ	26 Ⓐ Ⓑ Ⓒ Ⓓ	
6 Ⓐ Ⓑ Ⓒ Ⓓ	13 Ⓐ Ⓑ Ⓒ Ⓓ	20 Ⓐ Ⓑ Ⓒ Ⓓ	27 Ⓐ Ⓑ Ⓒ Ⓓ	
7 Ⓐ Ⓑ Ⓒ Ⓓ	14 Ⓐ Ⓑ Ⓒ Ⓓ	21 Ⓐ Ⓑ Ⓒ Ⓓ	28 Ⓐ Ⓑ Ⓒ Ⓓ	

ANSWER SHEET FOR
FISCAL AND BUDGETARY CONTROL

1 Ⓐ Ⓑ Ⓒ Ⓓ	10 Ⓐ Ⓑ Ⓒ Ⓓ	19 Ⓐ Ⓑ Ⓒ Ⓓ	28 Ⓐ Ⓑ Ⓒ Ⓓ	37 Ⓐ Ⓑ Ⓒ Ⓓ
2 Ⓐ Ⓑ Ⓒ Ⓓ	11 Ⓐ Ⓑ Ⓒ Ⓓ	20 Ⓐ Ⓑ Ⓒ Ⓓ	29 Ⓐ Ⓑ Ⓒ Ⓓ	38 Ⓐ Ⓑ Ⓒ Ⓓ
3 Ⓐ Ⓑ Ⓒ Ⓓ	12 Ⓐ Ⓑ Ⓒ Ⓓ	21 Ⓐ Ⓑ Ⓒ Ⓓ	30 Ⓐ Ⓑ Ⓒ Ⓓ	39 Ⓐ Ⓑ Ⓒ Ⓓ
4 Ⓐ Ⓑ Ⓒ Ⓓ	13 Ⓐ Ⓑ Ⓒ Ⓓ	22 Ⓐ Ⓑ Ⓒ Ⓓ	31 Ⓐ Ⓑ Ⓒ Ⓓ	40 Ⓐ Ⓑ Ⓒ Ⓓ
5 Ⓐ Ⓑ Ⓒ Ⓓ	14 Ⓐ Ⓑ Ⓒ Ⓓ	23 Ⓐ Ⓑ Ⓒ Ⓓ	32 Ⓐ Ⓑ Ⓒ Ⓓ	41 Ⓐ Ⓑ Ⓒ Ⓓ
6 Ⓐ Ⓑ Ⓒ Ⓓ	15 Ⓐ Ⓑ Ⓒ Ⓓ	24 Ⓐ Ⓑ Ⓒ Ⓓ	33 Ⓐ Ⓑ Ⓒ Ⓓ	42 Ⓐ Ⓑ Ⓒ Ⓓ
7 Ⓐ Ⓑ Ⓒ Ⓓ	16 Ⓐ Ⓑ Ⓒ Ⓓ	25 Ⓐ Ⓑ Ⓒ Ⓓ	34 Ⓐ Ⓑ Ⓒ Ⓓ	43 Ⓐ Ⓑ Ⓒ Ⓓ
8 Ⓐ Ⓑ Ⓒ Ⓓ	17 Ⓐ Ⓑ Ⓒ Ⓓ	26 Ⓐ Ⓑ Ⓒ Ⓓ	35 Ⓐ Ⓑ Ⓒ Ⓓ	44 Ⓐ Ⓑ Ⓒ Ⓓ
9 Ⓐ Ⓑ Ⓒ Ⓓ	18 Ⓐ Ⓑ Ⓒ Ⓓ	27 Ⓐ Ⓑ Ⓒ Ⓓ	36 Ⓐ Ⓑ Ⓒ Ⓓ	

PUBLIC RELATIONS

1 Ⓐ Ⓑ Ⓒ Ⓓ	8 Ⓐ Ⓑ Ⓒ Ⓓ	15 Ⓐ Ⓑ Ⓒ Ⓓ	22 Ⓐ Ⓑ Ⓒ Ⓓ	29 Ⓐ Ⓑ Ⓒ Ⓓ
2 Ⓐ Ⓑ Ⓒ Ⓓ	9 Ⓐ Ⓑ Ⓒ Ⓓ	16 Ⓐ Ⓑ Ⓒ Ⓓ	23 Ⓐ Ⓑ Ⓒ Ⓓ	30 Ⓐ Ⓑ Ⓒ Ⓓ
3 Ⓐ Ⓑ Ⓒ Ⓓ	10 Ⓐ Ⓑ Ⓒ Ⓓ	17 Ⓐ Ⓑ Ⓒ Ⓓ	24 Ⓐ Ⓑ Ⓒ Ⓓ	31 Ⓐ Ⓑ Ⓒ Ⓓ
4 Ⓐ Ⓑ Ⓒ Ⓓ	11 Ⓐ Ⓑ Ⓒ Ⓓ	18 Ⓐ Ⓑ Ⓒ Ⓓ	25 Ⓐ Ⓑ Ⓒ Ⓓ	32 Ⓐ Ⓑ Ⓒ Ⓓ
5 Ⓐ Ⓑ Ⓒ Ⓓ	12 Ⓐ Ⓑ Ⓒ Ⓓ	19 Ⓐ Ⓑ Ⓒ Ⓓ	26 Ⓐ Ⓑ Ⓒ Ⓓ	33 Ⓐ Ⓑ Ⓒ Ⓓ
6 Ⓐ Ⓑ Ⓒ Ⓓ	13 Ⓐ Ⓑ Ⓒ Ⓓ	20 Ⓐ Ⓑ Ⓒ Ⓓ	27 Ⓐ Ⓑ Ⓒ Ⓓ	34 Ⓐ Ⓑ Ⓒ Ⓓ
7 Ⓐ Ⓑ Ⓒ Ⓓ	14 Ⓐ Ⓑ Ⓒ Ⓓ	21 Ⓐ Ⓑ Ⓒ Ⓓ	28 Ⓐ Ⓑ Ⓒ Ⓓ	

ANSWER SHEET FOR
STATISTICS AND CHARTS

1 Ⓐ Ⓑ Ⓒ Ⓓ   11 Ⓐ Ⓑ Ⓒ Ⓓ   21 Ⓐ Ⓑ Ⓒ Ⓓ   31 Ⓐ Ⓑ Ⓒ Ⓓ   41 Ⓐ Ⓑ Ⓒ Ⓓ

2 Ⓐ Ⓑ Ⓒ Ⓓ   12 Ⓐ Ⓑ Ⓒ Ⓓ   22 Ⓐ Ⓑ Ⓒ Ⓓ   32 Ⓐ Ⓑ Ⓒ Ⓓ   42 Ⓐ Ⓑ Ⓒ Ⓓ

3 Ⓐ Ⓑ Ⓒ Ⓓ   13 Ⓐ Ⓑ Ⓒ Ⓓ   23 Ⓐ Ⓑ Ⓒ Ⓓ   33 Ⓐ Ⓑ Ⓒ Ⓓ   43 Ⓐ Ⓑ Ⓒ Ⓓ

4 Ⓐ Ⓑ Ⓒ Ⓓ   14 Ⓐ Ⓑ Ⓒ Ⓓ   24 Ⓐ Ⓑ Ⓒ Ⓓ   34 Ⓐ Ⓑ Ⓒ Ⓓ   44 Ⓐ Ⓑ Ⓒ Ⓓ

5 Ⓐ Ⓑ Ⓒ Ⓓ   15 Ⓐ Ⓑ Ⓒ Ⓓ   25 Ⓐ Ⓑ Ⓒ Ⓓ   35 Ⓐ Ⓑ Ⓒ Ⓓ   45 Ⓐ Ⓑ Ⓒ Ⓓ

6 Ⓐ Ⓑ Ⓒ Ⓓ   16 Ⓐ Ⓑ Ⓒ Ⓓ   26 Ⓐ Ⓑ Ⓒ Ⓓ   36 Ⓐ Ⓑ Ⓒ Ⓓ   46 Ⓐ Ⓑ Ⓒ Ⓓ

7 Ⓐ Ⓑ Ⓒ Ⓓ   17 Ⓐ Ⓑ Ⓒ Ⓓ   27 Ⓐ Ⓑ Ⓒ Ⓓ   37 Ⓐ Ⓑ Ⓒ Ⓓ   47 Ⓐ Ⓑ Ⓒ Ⓓ

8 Ⓐ Ⓑ Ⓒ Ⓓ   18 Ⓐ Ⓑ Ⓒ Ⓓ   28 Ⓐ Ⓑ Ⓒ Ⓓ   38 Ⓐ Ⓑ Ⓒ Ⓓ   48 Ⓐ Ⓑ Ⓒ Ⓓ

9 Ⓐ Ⓑ Ⓒ Ⓓ   19 Ⓐ Ⓑ Ⓒ Ⓓ   29 Ⓐ Ⓑ Ⓒ Ⓓ   39 Ⓐ Ⓑ Ⓒ Ⓓ

10 Ⓐ Ⓑ Ⓒ Ⓓ   20 Ⓐ Ⓑ Ⓒ Ⓓ   30 Ⓐ Ⓑ Ⓒ Ⓓ   40 Ⓐ Ⓑ Ⓒ Ⓓ

PART ONE

The Functioning Administrator

ADMINISTRATIVE JUDGMENT

DIRECTIONS FOR ANSWERING QUESTIONS

Each question has four suggested answers, lettered A, B, C, and D. Decide which one is the best answer and on the sample answer sheet (all answer sheets are at the front of the book) find the question number and darken the area, with a soft pencil, which corresponds to the answer that you have selected.

1. When an unusual emergency arises and it would take too long to contact a superior to check the method of handling the situation, the best procedure to follow is to
   (A) act according to your best judgment
   (B) confer immediately with your men on the best action to take and let the majority opinion prevail
   (C) confer with any other supervisor
   (D) make no decision because you have no precedents to follow.

2. Suppose the various jobs under your supervision are frequently delayed because the workers await your arrival to make decisions before proceeding with the work. As a supervisor, the most helpful conclusion for you to draw from this is that
   (A) the workers under your supervision lack initiative and need encouragement
   (B) your orders and instructions may not have been sufficiently clear or complete
   (C) you have incurred the workers' dislike and should look for the cause
   (D) the jobs given to you are generally more difficult than the average.

3. As an administrator, it is advisable for you to keep records of your jobs for future reference. Assume that in reviewing your records you find that whenever a certain worker has been one of those assigned to a job, the job has taken appreciably longer than other similar jobs. In this case, you would do best to

   (A) warn the worker against deliberate slowness so that the individual knows you are aware of the situation
   (B) take this fact into consideration when making up efficiency reports
   (C) give closer supervision to future jobs to which this worker is assigned
   (D) consult your superior on the appropriate disciplinary action to be taken.

4. Supervisors are required to submit written reports of all unusual occurrences promptly. The best reason for such promptness is that
   (A) the report will tend to be more accurate as to facts
   (B) the employee will not be as likely to forget to make the report
   (C) there is always a tendency to do a better job under pressure
   (D) the report may be too long if made at an employee's convenience.

5. The *one* of the following duties of a supervisor which you can most successfully turn over to an employee is that of
   (A) handling discipline of your crew
   (B) checking completed work
   (C) reporting to the chief administrator
   (D) responsibility for the work of your department.

6. An administrator familiar with current economic trends would know that a period of inflation is in

5

general characterized by
- (A) both rising wages and falling prices
- (B) an increase in the purchasing power of money
- (C) a decline in the national income
- (D) a decrease in the purchasing power of money.

7. An employee reporting an accident to the office by phone should request the name of the person receiving the call and note the time. The purpose of this precaution is to fix responsibility for the
- (A) entire handling of the accident thereafter
- (B) recording of the report
- (C) accuracy of the report
- (D) preparation of the final written report.

8. Assume that an unpleasant routine job is to be assigned to one of your workers. Generally the job should be
- (A) assigned to a minor offender as disciplinary action
- (B) rotated among all the workers in your department
- (C) assigned to a junior person until that worker gains seniority
- (D) assigned permanently to one man who would be given special privileges for compensation.

9. A new employee comes to you with a suggestion for changing the method of performing a routine job. As an administrator, you should
- (A) tell him that routine procedures are standardized and cannot be changed
- (B) not consider the suggestion because the new man is not familiar with the work
- (C) tell the man to try out the new method unofficially to see if it works
- (D) discuss the suggestion with the man and determine its value.

10. A newly appointed employee in your department makes blunders apparently regardless of the type of assignments given to him. You should
- (A) recommend his dismissal
- (B) refuse to give him further work assignments until he agrees to be more careful
- (C) ignore the condition since it will ultimately cure itself
- (D) try to determine the cause for the man's poor work before taking further action.

11. The job interest of the employees in your department is best secured by

- (A) requesting their advice on all important matters
- (B) constantly bringing up new matters
- (C) giving good workers special privileges
- (D) creating in each man a sense of his individual importance to the job as a whole.

12. A supervisor criticizes an employee's work by telling him that he is disappointed with it. The supervisor states that the work is completely unsatisfactory, points out the parts that are bad and says that improvement is expected. The supervisor's method of handling this type of a situation is usually considered
- (A) good; the supervisor did not criticize the employee's work in front of other employees
- (B) poor; some favorable comment should have been made at the same time
- (C) good; the employee knows just where he stands, and might resign
- (D) poor; the employee should have been asked why his work was poor.

13. If an administrator finds out that he is definitely disliked by the workers under his supervision, and that the situation is affecting the morale and the efficiency of the department, the best thing the administrator can do is to
- (A) ask the supervisor to talk to the workers
- (B) take stock of oneself to determine if he or she is to blame
- (C) loosen up on the discipline of the department
- (D) supervise the workers more rigidly.

14. If an administrator makes a serious mistake in the details of an order issued to the staff, he or she should
- (A) not attempt to correct it, because the workers will lose their respect for him
- (B) not attempt to correct it, because the workers will eventually correct the error themselves
- (C) correct it in order to show he or she isn't small about such matters
- (D) correct it in order to avoid any costly errors which might result otherwise.

15. A supervisor who has good supervisory ability will have a group of subordinates who
- (A) will continue to function effectively even in his absence
- (B) are certainly capable of performing work outside the scope of their titles

(C) will always have their work done in less than the allotted time

(D) will be constantly asking questions about their work.

16. The one of the following qualities which makes an administrator respected by his employees is that he or she is
    (A) easy to confide in
    (B) fair in all dealings
    (C) easy to please
    (D) of a good disposition.

17. Of the following, the most important reason for investigating the cause of an accident is to
    (A) determine if the employee injured was at fault
    (B) prevent occurrence of the accident again
    (C) determine if the injured employee deserves compensation
    (D) impress on employees the need to be safety-minded.

18. One method an administrator may use to correctly evaluate the ability of his workers is to
    (A) observe their work on varied types of assignments
    (B) find out what the workers think of each other's ability
    (C) gauge their ability by the speed with which they work
    (D) allow them to use their own methods of doing the work.

19. An administrator who pitches in and personally helps out with a rush job would
    (A) lose the respect of his workers
    (B) be able to justify his action to his superiors
    (C) soon find that his employees will expect him to do work on all jobs
    (D) be justified in his action only if it is necessary to prove to his men he is capable.

20. Of the following, the best measurement of a supervisor's ability to do his job is
    (A) a low accident rate
    (B) the opinion of his fellow supervisors
    (C) the opinion of the workers under him
    (D) the work output of his department.

21. The best way for an administrator, to be acquainted with new regulations as soon as possible is to
    (A) study the book of rules

(B) read all bulletins as issued

(C) depend on specific notices by his superiors

(D) be alert to the needs of the department.

22. It would be poor supervision on an administrator's part if he or she
    (A) consulted his or her assistant on unusual problems
    (B) asked for an experienced employee's opinion on the method of doing a special job
    (C) allowed a cooling off period of several days before giving one of his workers a deserved reprimand
    (D) made it a policy to avoid criticizing a worker in front of his co-workers.

23. Of the following, the quality which contributes most toward a good supervisor is
    (A) ability to be considered as "one of the boys"
    (B) ability to keep from worrying
    (C) ability to get the work out
    (D) ability to be forceful.

24. An administrator who does not have all the traits for good leadership should
    (A) change to some other type of work
    (B) determine his or her faults and correct them
    (C) overcome this deficiency by having very few dealings with his employees
    (D) ask the workers for their opinion.

25. From a supervisory viewpoint the most desirable trait which an employee can have, of the following, would be
    (A) the ability to get along with his co-workers
    (B) punctuality of attendance
    (C) excellent knowledge of equipment
    (D) the performance of a good job with little supervision.

26. In accordance with certain plans, the private secretary to a bureau chief is to be assigned to a newly created central stenographic unit. The bureau chief is expected to oppose this move. Of the following, the most appropriate point that should be emphasized in obtaining the bureau chief's cooperation in this matter is that
    (A) the same person will be available at all times to perform his secretarial work
    (B) the absence of a stenographer will not delay urgent or important work

(C) the quality of the work produced by the central stenographic unit will be uniform.

(D) the training of new stenographers will be greatly simplified.

27. On returning from your vacation and resuming your assignment, you learn that the replacement administrator has changed some of your methods and procedures on his own authority. A good way to handle this situation is to
(A) tell the replacement administrator that he had no authority to make any changes
(B) automatically reinstate your previous methods and procedures
(C) compare the merits of the replacement's methods and procedures with yours and then make a choice
(D) accept the new procedures without question.

28. The most productive aid to the administrator in discovering improvements in work procedures is to
(A) allow the workers more time to think
(B) encourage ideas from his workers
(C) make frequent experimental changes in the procedure
(D) implement all suggestions which are submitted.

29. Generally the best procedure for a supervisor to follow to get a planned heavy work load completed is to
(A) explain the necessity and request the worker's cooperation
(B) prod the workers continuously to obtain maximum output
(C) request their immediate supervisor to give the workers a "pep" talk
(D) reduce the lunch period until the work is completed.

30. The administrator best exemplifies leadership ability by
(A) devoting the major portion of his time to supervising subordinates so as to stimulate continuous improvement
(B) formulating a time schedule covering routine duties so as to conserve time for proper performance of his professional duties
(C) delegating responsibility to subordinate officers so as to have time to plan division policies on a long-term basis

(D) setting aside time for self-development and study in order to improve administration.

31. All of the following *except one* are characteristic of a good administrator. That one is
(A) instructing the employees thoroughly
(B) enforcing use of safety measures
(C) directing, personally, each phase of the work
(D) completing details at maximum practical speed.

32. If an administrator is able to admit failures, mistakes, or lack of knowledge, he or she usually
(A) has a sense of security in his own competence
(B) has a lack of authority with subordinates
(C) is incompetent on the job
(D) has been pushed ahead too fast.

33. All but one of the following are considered sound principles to follow in leading workers. The one which is *not* considered a sound principle is
(A) ignoring petty grievances and allowing them to work themselves out
(B) instilling confidence and competition among subordinates
(C) creating a feeling of warmth between supervisor and subordinates
(D) taking prompt action on a decision once it is made.

34. Of the following, the *least* justifiable reason for the establishment of a central unit is that
(A) confidential assignments can be more closely guarded
(B) the quantity of work done can be more easily measured
(C) the work can be more equally distributed
(D) supervisory costs can be decreased.

35. The staff of a unit has been wasteful in the use of stationery, paper, and other office supplies. Of the following, the most desirable action for the supervisor to take to reduce this waste is to first
(A) determine the average quantity of supplies used daily by each staff member and then allot that quantity daily to each staff member
(B) find out which employees have been most wasteful of supplies and reprimand these employees
(C) discuss this matter at a conference with the staff, pointing out the necessity for, and methods of, eliminating waste

(D) issue supplies for an assignment at the time the assignment is made and limit the quantity to the amount needed for that assignment only.

36. Assume that you are the supervisor of a stenographic unit. One of your stenographers, in reviewing her stenographic notes of a letter dictated by a bureau head, discovers that the letter contains an erroneous statement which may cause the bureau head some embarrassment. Since this stenographer had been severely criticised by this bureau head on a previous occasion for having rephrased one of his dictated statements, she is reluctant to make any changes in his dictated material. She refers this problem to you. Under these circumstances, the best action for you to take is to
(A) correct the error and have the stenographer type the letter as corrected, after you have initialed her notebook to show that you have authorized the change
(B) have the stenographer type the letter as it was dictated by the bureau head, but have her attach a note calling his attention to the erroneous statement
(C) have the stenographer transcribe the letter as dictated, except for the erroneous statement; instruct her to leave a blank space for the insertion of a revised statement
(D) call the bureau head's attention to his error and have the stenographer make any change authorized by him.

37. As supervisor of a stenographic unit, you find that an important report prepared and checked for accuracy jointly by two of your stenographers contains a serious, careless mistake. One of the stenographers has a good work record, while the other is known to be a careless worker with a record of low production. Of the following, the most appropriate action for you to take in this matter is to explain to the stenographers the consequences of the mistake and to
(A) urge the more efficient stenographer to be more careful in checking the accuracy of the other stenographer's work
(B) impress the less efficient stenographer with the importance of checking her work thoroughly
(C) make certain that these two stenographers are not assigned to work together in preparing future reports

(D) emphasize to both employees that they must be more careful in their work.

38. The suggestion is made that all the secretaries assigned to the bureau chiefs of a certain agency be transferred to a newly established unit which is to be staffed with stenographers and typists. Of the following, the most probable effect of reassigning these secretaries would be that
(A) the quality of the stenographic and typing work performed by the secretaries would deteriorate
(B) the bureau chiefs would be burdened with much of the routine work that is now performed by their secretaries
(C) typing and stenographic work would be performed less expeditiously and with frequent delays
(D) the development of understudies for bureau chiefs would be greatly hampered.

39. Assume that you are in charge of a unit with 40 employees. The department head requests immediate preparation of a special and rather complicated report which will take about a day to complete if everyone in your unit works on it. After breaking the job into simple components and assigning each component to an employee, should more than one person be instructed on the procedure to be followed on each component?
(A) No; the procedure would be a waste of time in this instance
(B) Yes; it is always desirable to have a replacement available in the event of illness or any other emergency
(C) No; in general, as long as an employee's job performance is satisfactory, there is no need to train an alternate
(D) Yes; the presence of more than one person in a unit who can perform a given task tends to prevent the formation of a bottleneck.

40. A chief staff officer, serving as one of the immediate advisors to the department head, has demonstrated a special capacity for achieving internal agreements and for sound judgment. As a result he has been used more and more as a source of counsel and assistance by the department head. Other staff officers and line officials as well have discovered that it is wise for them to check with this colleague in advance on all problematical matters handed up to the department head. De-

velopments such as this are
  (A) undesirable; they disrupt the normal lines for flow of work in an organization
  ⟶(B) desirable; they allow an organization to make the most of its strength wherever such strength resides
  (C) undesirable; they tend to undermine the authority of the department head and put it in the hands of a staff officer who does not have the responsibility
  (D) desirable; they tend to resolve internal ambiguities in organization.

41. Suppose that a clerk who is employed in a unit under your supervision performs his work quickly but carelessly. He is about to be transferred to another unit in your department. The chief of this other unit asks you for your opinion of this employee's work habits. Of the following, the most appropriate reply for you to make is to
  (A) point out this employee's good qualities only, since he may correct his bad qualities after his transfer is effected
  (B) say nothing good or bad about this employee, thus permitting him to start his new assignment with a clean slate
  ⟵(C) inform the unit chief that this clerk performed his work speedily but was careless
  (D) emphasize this employee's good points and minimize his bad points.

42. Assume that you are in charge of a unit in which employees are frequently required to work in pairs on common tasks. Two of your subordinates frequently engage in heated disputes when they are assigned to work together on such tasks. Of the following actions you may take in handling this problem, the most desirable one for you to take *first* is to
  (A) inform staff, at a staff conference, that quarreling during office hours is not tolerated
  ⟵(B) find out why they quarrel and take the necessary steps to settle the differences
  (C) recommend that one of the employees be transferred to another unit
  (D) warn them that both will be subject to immediate dismissal if further disputes arise between them.

43. A secretary to a division chief is required to take care of all the details relating to a conference of unit heads over which the division chief is to

preside. Of the following, the *least* appropriate action for the secretary to take before the scheduled time of the conference is to
  (A) collect all material that will be needed at the conference
  (B) see that the conference room is in readiness for the conference
  ⟵(C) inform each unit head of the division chief's views on the matters to be discussed
  (D) make sure that each unit head has received notice of this meeting in advance.

44. Of the following factors, the one to which the administrator should give the greatest consideration in planning the training of a new employee is
  ⟵(A) the extent to which the new employee already possesses the skills and knowledge needed for satisfactory job performance
  (B) whether the administrator is to do *the* training or delegate the task to a qualified supervisor
  (C) the desirability of arranging a tour of the various units in the agency to reveal their inter-relationships
  (D) the usefulness of visual aids, such as charts, film slides, and pictures as an aid in training.

45. When subordinates request his advice in solving problems encountered in their work, a certain bureau chief occasionally answers the request by first asking the subordinate what he thinks should be done. This action by the bureau chief is, on the whole
  ⟵(A) desirable, because it stimulates subordinates to give more thought to the solution of problems encountered
  (B) undesirable, because it discourages subordinates from asking questions
  (C) desirable, because it discourages subordinates from asking questions
  (D) undesirable, because it undermines the confidence of subordinates in the ability of their supervisor.

46. Assume that a procedure for handling certain office forms has just been extensively revised. As supervisor of a small unit, you are to instruct your subordinates in the use of the new procedure, which is rather complicated. Of the following, it would be *least* helpful to your subordinates for you to

(A) compare the revised procedure with the one it has replaced

(B) state that you believe the revised procedure to be better than the one it has replaced

— (C) tell them that they will probably find it difficult to learn the new procedure

(D) give only a general outline of the revised procedure at first and then follow with more detailed instructions.

47. Assume that as administrator of a central bureau, you are considering the establishment of a new procedure to check the accuracy of your subordinates' work. Of the following, the most important factor which you should consider before deciding to establish such a procedure is

(A) whether or not your subordinates are likely to resent your use of the new procedure

(B) the frequency with which it will be practicable to check the accuracy of your subordinates' work

(C) the phases of your subordinates' work which will require the greatest amount of review

= (D) whether or not the expected results of the new procedure will justify the time and money spent on using it.

48. A department head insisted that operating officials participate in the development of new procedures along with the planning section. Participation of this type is, on the whole

— (A) desirable; operating realities are more likely to be considered

(B) undesirable; the inclusion of conflicting views before the plan is drawn may result in no plan

(C) desirable; plans will be more flexible and objectives more clearly defined

(D) undesirable; the operating officials should decide to what extent they wish to participate with no pressure from the top.

49. In a division of a department, private secretaries were assigned to members of the technical staff since each required a secretary who was familiar with his particular field and who could handle various routine matters without referring to anyone. Other members of the staff depended for their dictation and typing work upon a small pool consisting of two stenographers and two typists. Because of turnover and the difficulty of recruiting new stenographers and typists, the pool had to be

discontinued. Of the following, the most satisfactory way to provide stenographic and typing service for the division is to

⟶ (A) organize the private secretaries into a decentralized pool under the direction of a supervisor to whom non-technical staff members would send requests for stenographic and typing assistance

(B) organize the private secretaries into a central pool under the direction of a supervisor to whom all staff members would send requests for stenographic and typing assistance

(C) train clerks as typists and typists as stenographers

(D) relieve stenographers and typists of jobs that can be done by messengers or clerks.

50. Suppose that as an administrator, you are considering the establishment of a central transcribing unit to contain the stenographers who have until now been assigned permanently to the various bureaus of the agency. The chief advantage of such a central unit as compared with the present arrangement would be that

⟵ (A) stenographers can be shifted more readily from one assignment to another as the volume of work requires

(B) dictators could make changes more easily in material dictated to stenographers earlier in the day

(C) confidential work would be safeguarded more effectively

(D) closer working relationships would be established between dictators and the stenographers in the unit.

51. Assume that you are the supervisor of a unit that has just been organized in your agency. One of the employees who is being transferred to your unit has been reported as uncooperative in working with her former supervisor and was using unauthorized work procedures rather than following procedures prescribed by her supervisor. Of the following actions, the most appropriate one for you to take *first* when this employee reports to you for work is to

(A) explain to her immediately that you cannot permit her to use procedures other than those that you prescribe for use

(B) display confidence in her by encouraging her to use her judgment as to methods of performing her work

(C) discuss her new assignment with her without referring to her reported uncooperative attitude

(D) indicate that you are aware of her uncooperative attitude but that, nevertheless, you expect her to cooperate fully with you.

52. As a supervisor, you may find it necessary to consult with your superior before taking action on some matters. Of the following, the action for which it is most important that you obtain the prior approval of your superior is one that involves

(A) assuming additional functions for your unit

(B) rotating assignments among your staff members

(C) initiating regular meetings of your staff

(D) assigning certain members of your staff to work overtime on an emergency job.

53. A certain administrator demands that subordinates accept their assigned tasks without question. He refuses to allow them to exercise initiative in carrying out their assignments, and maintains a constant check on their work performance. Suppose that you are to succeed him as chief of this division. The most appropriate of the following policies for you to adopt on becoming the division chief is to

(A) continue to exercise the same rigid controls over the work and the workers in the division since they are accustomed to this type of supervision

(B) discard all strict controls immediately and

give the individual employees complete freedom in determining how to carry out their assignments

(C) develop among your staff a personal loyalty to you which will cause them to think of your reaction before departing from established procedure

(D) remove gradually the controls you consider too strict and provide opportunities for your staff to participate in formulating work plans and procedures.

54. The bureau chiefs of a City agency are each given twenty-four hours within which to prepare and submit an urgent report to the head of their agency. Several bureau chiefs plan to work overtime in order to meet the deadline and request stenographic services during the overtime period. For the chief of the central transcribing unit to ask some of her stenographers to work overtime to supply the requested stenographic services is

(A) desirable, chiefly because it enables the bureau chiefs to meet the deadline

(B) undesirable, chiefly because it creates personnel problems which are often difficult to handle

(C) desirable, chiefly because it enables the bureau chief to determine which of the stenographers are cooperative

(D) undesirable, chiefly because resorting to overtime to meet production requirements indicates poor management.

ANSWER KEY

1. A	12. B	23. C	34. A	45. A
2. B	13. B	24. B	35. C	46. C
3. C	14. D	25. D	36. D	47. D
4. A	15. A	26. B	37. D	48. A
5. B	16. B	27. C	38. B	49. A
6. D	17. B	28. B	39. A	50. A
7. B	18. A	29. A	40. B	51. C
8. C	19. B	30. A	41. C	52. A
9. D	20. D	31. C	42. B	53. D
10. D	21. B	32. A	43. C	54. A
11. D	22. C	33. A	44. A	

EXPLANATORY ANSWERS

1. **(A)** It is part of the administrator's job to make decisions. That is what the administrator is paid to do, and how the work of the agency is accomplished. In an unusual emergency, if the administrator cannot locate his or her superior, the administrator must make the decision, and take responsibility for it.

2. **(B)** This problem arises when the manager has not given clear instructions on how to handle the work. The manager's job is to carefully instruct subordinates so that they know how to handle most situations, and know in what instances to await higher decisions. If instructions are unclear or incomplete, the work is not likely to be completed properly.

3. **(C)** From the data given, you cannot warn the worker about deliberate slowness, consider disciplinary action, or validly consider this information when preparing efficiency reports. All you can do is watch the worker closely on future jobs so that you can determine the degree to which that worker's actions are the cause of any delays, and then correct the situation.

4. **(A)** All unusual occurrences should be reported in writing and as promptly as possible, in order to make sure that the facts are accurate. Few of us have such total recall that the facts will remain accurate if we procrastinate in reporting them.

5. **(B)** Allowing a trained and trusted subordinate to check most completed work frees the supervisor to concentrate on priority items such as planning. Discipline, reporting

to the boss, and the overall responsibility for the unit's work, are legitimate supervisory functions that should not be delegated.

6. **(D)** Inflation results in money being worth less. All other possible answers are incorrect.

7. **(B)** All accidents should be fully and accurately recorded as soon as possible after the occurrence so that the information needed to correct or eliminate the cause of the accident will be known. The worker who reports the action should obtain the name of the person taking the message and the time of the call to make sure that the report has been officially recorded for further follow-up action.

8. **(C)** Assigning an unpleasant job to the worker with the least seniority is the logical choice. In time the individual will gain seniority, and be able to avoid this type of assignment.

9. **(D)** Just because a routine task has always been done one way does not mean the method cannot be changed. A new worker may very likely see a quicker or better way to do the same task, and should be listened to carefully by the supervisor. It is not good administrative practice to tell a new worker to unofficially try out anything new. If you want to try it out, you as the supervisor must bear the consequences.

10. **(D)** The supervisor should train and re-train a new worker. Only after extensive time and effort has been

spent should a supervisor determine that a new worker will never learn to do the work correctly. In the situation presented, the supervisor should try to find out why the new worker makes blunders, and what steps are needed to help him or her.

11. **(D)** The best way to secure employees' interest in the job is to convince them that their work is important, and the individual's role is necessary to the successful achievement of agency objectives. A supervisor wastes time and undermines worker respect if he or she goes to them on all important matters. Job interest is not a matter of always doing something new. Granting special privileges is not a method to maintain worker interest over an extended period of time.

12. **(B)** Workers must believe the supervisor is fair, and to remain fair the supervisor should not only criticize weak points, but also praise good aspects of the worker's performance. This is a fundamental principle of good supervisory/employee relationships.

13. **(B)** The best thing the supervisor can do is examine his or her own behavior. Only after he or she understands the cause for the dislike can discipline be relaxed or tightened, or the superior called in, etc.

14. **(D)** An administrator is primarily responsible for getting the work done as efficiently and as cost-effectively as possible. The mistake should be immediately corrected so that any errors, which would be costly and time-consuming, are caught. Although the administrator who acknowledges a mistake may reap increased worker respect, this is not the primary reason for correcting a wrong order.

15. **(A)** A well-supervised group of workers know the job, and can function effectively without constant direct supervision. They will not necessarily be capable of working at duties above their titles. If they always finish the work in less than the allotted time, possibly too much time has been allotted or too many workers assigned to the work. Incessant asking of meaningless questions may be a sign of poor training by the supervisor.

16. **(B)** A supervisor must be fair in his or her treatment of all situations. Only if workers know that all sides of a problem will be heard and judgment rendered on the basis of what is best for the good of the group and the timely completion of their work will respect be granted to the supervisor. Workers may like a supervisor because he or she has a good disposition, is easy to talk to and is easily pleased, but they will respect only the one who is fair.

17. **(B)** Accidents are costly for both management and worker. It is the supervisor's responsibility to be safety-minded at all times, but when an accident does occur, the supervisor's primary responsibility is to eliminate or correct the cause of it.

18. **(A)** Observation of workers performing their duties is the best means of evaluation.

19. **(B)** All administrators at one time or another have had to deal with rush jobs, and experience has shown that the supervisor who pitches in to help is supported by his or her superiors. If this is the only way to get the job done on time there is nothing wrong with it.

20. **(D)** From a top management point of view, success is measured in output. A supervisor may be liked by subordinates and fellow-supervisors, but unless the assigned work is done well and on time, the supervisor cannot be considered efficient and effective.

21. **(B)** Rules and regulations are made to be observed. An administrator should keep up-to-date on all new changes, deletions, etc., and carry them out as soon as they become effective. The best way to do this is to personally read all bulletins as soon as they are issued, and not wait for notices from superiors.

22. **(C)** Reprimands should be given as soon as possible in order for them to have full effect. Delaying censure lessens the effect, and may cause resentment from the worker who, having not been reprimanded at the time, may understandably think that it was not important enough to receive censure. Prompt censure also prevents the immediate repetition of the actions.

23. **(C)** The supervisor is being paid to get the job done efficiently, and that is the main criteria in judging a person's ability as a supervisor.

24. **(B)** Good leadership is a combination of many traits, a large number of which can be taught. Few leaders are born in complete possession of all of these traits, and any administrator should strive to improve his/her leadership ability. To develop the traits needed, one must determine which traits one lacks, and then work on them.

25. **(D)** Effective supervision is best demonstrated by the worker who is able to function efficiently in the absence of direct supervision. The unit that is able to function well in the absence of the supervisor is well supervised.

26. **(B)** The appropriate way to obtain the chief's cooperation is to assure the chief that his or her important work will continue to be done in a timely manner without the private secretary. Answers C and D are positive points in favor of a central stenographic pool, but neither is going to have a great effect on a bureau chief likely to oppose the centralization. Promising the chief the same person to perform his or her secretarial work at all times negates the purpose of the centralized pool.

27. **(C)** A good administrator knows that he or she is not all-knowing, and changes may be improvements on old methods. The administrator should explore changes, and compare their effectiveness with the previous methods.

28. **(B)** No one has a monopoly on good ideas, and the best administrators encourage workers to come forth with suggestions for improvements because workers are in the best position to know what will and will not work in connection with their own jobs. This does not necessarily mean that every suggestion should be accepted or even seriously considered, or that workers should cease to do their assigned tasks and become part of a "think tank," but rather that an atmosphere should be created where a worker feels free to suggest possible improvements.

29. **(A)** When an unusually heavy work load is contemplated, the good administrator knows that obtaining the full cooperation of the staff is the best way to get the job done. Experience has shown that workers will generally respond in a positive manner if they clearly understand the full nature of the problem and the need for the heavy workload.

30. **(A)** The question asks for the action which best demonstrates leadership quality. All of the possible answers are examples of good actions by an administrator, but the only example of good leadership is stimulating staff improvement by devoting a major portion of time to supervisory endeavors. This is a primary responsibility of a leader.

31. **(C)** The good administrator does not personally direct each work detail, but rather plans for, reviews, and evaluates the resulting product of work directed by others.

32. **(A)** Administrators who admit failures, mistakes, and lack of knowledge, know they are good at their jobs. Otherwise they would be afraid to admit anything. To err is human; to acknowledge error is the sign of a secure individual.

33. **(A)** It is not a good principle to ignore petty grievances. Very often they do not work themselves out, but instead lead to increased disturbances among staff and eventually to major grievances.

34. **(A)** Confidential assignments are most closely guarded when the number of persons involved is kept to a minimum, and the person with the assignment reports only to the administrator or a special assistant. The principal advantages of a central unit are listed in the other answers.

35. **(C)** The thing to do is bring the subject up at a staff meeting, and attempt to make the staff understand the problem and cooperate in reducing waste. Only if this method fails should the other possibilities be considered. A good supervisor tries to have workers understand and cooperate before resorting to orders, reprimands or rationing of supplies.

36. **(D)** The best solution is to bring the error to the attention of the bureau chief. He or she will be grateful to have the error detected. To let it go might be costly and embarrassing.

37. **(D)** The supervisor does not really know why the error was made, and should assume that both stenographers were at fault and therefore treat them both the same.

38. **(B)** In situations when secretaries are reassigned to a clerical/stenographic pool, the individual boss usually finds there is no one to do the routine matters of the office formerly performed by the secretary.

39. **(A)** It would be wasteful to have a worker learn more than his or her specific component of the job since the entire job will be completed in one day. Back-up staff would be needed only if the job were going to take a considerable period of time.

40. **(B)** It is generally good policy for an administrator to utilize the special strengths of immediate advisors in the best possible way, and in the situation presented the administrator has done just that. Note that the special advisor does not undermine the line officials' authority because they are free to accept or reject the advice given them. Similarly, the department head is merely assisted by the staff advisor, and still makes all final decisions.

41. **(C)** A supervisor must remember that he or she is part of a larger organization, and all parts of it must work together to achieve their common goals. In the situation presented, the present supervisor should tell the new unit head the pertinent facts about the transferred worker so that the new supervisor can most effectively work with him or her.

42. **(B)** The *first* action the supervisor should take is to try to find out the cause of the quarrels, and try to settle the differences between the two workers. If that does not solve the problem, other solutions, including the ones offered in the other possible answers, may be used.

43. **(C)** It is not appropriate for a secretary assigned to take care of details concerning a conference of unit heads to tell them the chief's views on the matters to be discussed. It is likely to inhibit the participation of the conference members and is therefore likely to make the conference less productive.

44. **(A)** A formal training unit apparently does not exist. Under these circumstances, the administrator's role is primarily to find out the degree to which formal training is needed. The new worker may already have the skills, knowledge and abilities to enable him or her to do the work after a short orientation course, or may need a more extensive, formal training course. Once this basic information is known, the administrator can determine such matters as who should do the actual training, or whether a tour of the department is needed, etc.

45. **(A)** Experience has shown that a useful training technique is to first have the questioner try to find his or her own answer. This process enables the worker to better utilize the solution in other similar problems, and encourages workers to think for themselves because they will retain the solution better when they find it by themselves. Such a method also builds the worker's self-esteem and interest in the job.

46. **(C)** It is not a good training technique to refer to the difficulties involved in a new complicated procedure, it is discouraging to say the least. The training steps outlined in the other answers are concrete positive steps which the trainer might use.

47. **(D)** Will it pay to do it? Will the time and money spent doing it be worthwhile in the promotion of efficiency?

48. **(A)** Planning cannot be done in a vacuum. Although a planning section has special skills to do this work, the best laid plans must consider operational realities, and this information can only be determined by the participation of line officials in the planning stage. This participation may not result in more flexible or clear procedures, but they will take into consideration the problems that are likely to occur when the procedure is put into effect.

49. **(A)** The best way to provide technical staff with the benefits of private secretaries but still service the rest of the staff is to keep the secretaries working for their technical staff persons, but at the same time make them available for other assignments.

50. **(A)** The principal advantage of using a centralized transcribing pool over assigning stenographers to individual bureaus is that the pool assignment provides that as a particular unit needs typing or stenographic help, it will more easily receive that help. Essentially, it is a technique which conserves, and utilizes, special skills.

51. **(C)** To obtain maximum cooperation and enthusiasm from staff, the supervisor of a new unit should first start from scratch with all employees. Each one must be told his or her duties and responsibilities and what behavior is expected from them. Perhaps the reason for the worker's previous actions was his relationship with his supervisor. There is no point in starting this relationship in a negative manner.

52. **(A)** In general, supervisors should be left free to determine by themselves details that will best meet the needs of their individual units. Supervisors should not add new functions to one's existing responsibilities without prior consultation and approval by a superior. This is the function of the superior, not of the supervisor. It is quite possible that the superior has good reason for not accepting this additional work.

53. **(D)** The type of administrator described in the question is an authoritarian leader. This type of leadership usually insures a certain level of production, but also may result in the stifling of workers. Changes may be indicated, but should not be taken before thoroughly studying the entire situation. If called for, modifications should be made gradually. There may be positive results from employee participation, but on the other hand, the level and demeanor of the workers may have called for this type of supervision. This has not been brought out in the question.

54. **(A)** Since the central transcribing pool is part of the agency's operation, its employees must be concerned with the entire agency's needs. The head of the transcribing pool should comply with the bureau heads' requests because agency work must be completed on time. Whether or not overtime indicates poor management is not the transcribing pool head's concern. Whether it causes personnel problems or helps the transcribing pool head to discover who is or is not cooperative is secondary. The primary goal is to get the work done and to meet deadlines.

ADMINISTRATIVE-SUBORDINATE RELATIONSHIPS

DIRECTIONS FOR ANSWERING QUESTIONS

Each question has four suggested answers, lettered A, B, C, and D. Decide which one is the best answer and on the sample answer sheet (all answer sheets are at the front of the book) find the question number and darken the area, with a soft pencil, which corresponds to the answer that you have selected.

1. As an administrator you find that a supervisor, in his reports to you, did not mention a series of thefts of department property occurring in his unit. Upon questioning, he tells you that he has a plan for dealing with the problem and that he intended to make a complete report when the problem was solved. Of the following, the best course for you to follow is to
   (A) reprimand him for omitting the situation from his reports
   (B) commend him for his initiative in attempting to solve the problem
   (C) explain the necessity for you to have complete reports on all major problems within your jurisdiction
   (D) warn him that he will be held responsible if his plan doesn't succeed.

2. Assume that as division head you find it necessary to inform one of the generally satisfactory supervisors that some aspects of his work are unsatisfactory. The most desirable of the following methods of conducting the interview is for you to call the supervisor to your office and
   (A) tell him that his work is completely unsatisfactory and that you expect better in the future
   (B) start the interview by making, if possible, some favorable comment about his work
   (C) indicate briefly to him what is wrong and close the interview without giving him any chance to comment

   (D) tell him that you don't want him to be upset but that you have received a complaint from the borough commander.

3. A subordinate supervisor, who has quite a following with the workers, disagrees with you as chief supervisor on a certain point in administration. You should
   (A) inform the supervisor that you are the chief administrator and until he is in your position he is to follow your ideas
   (B) try to win him to your way of thinking and thus use his leadership to advantage
   (C) transfer him to a position where he will be unable to interfere with the particular point of administration
   (D) set an example of him by bringing charges of insubordination.

4. When an employee comes to the administrator's office to consult on a personal matter, the administrator should
   (A) inform the employee in a friendly fashion that it is not proper to enter into the private affairs of a subordinate
   (B) listen attentively and tell the employee what to do
   (C) listen attentively, and through guiding questions induce the employee to think through the problem and arrive at a solution
   (D) sympathize with the employee regardless of

the type of problem because that is what the employee wishes to gain from the administrator.

5. The best way for an administrator to get prompt and effective service from his subordinates is
   (A) to try to be popular and be a regular fellow
   (B) to direct them in a superior manner without abusive language, letting them know you are the boss
   (C) to direct them in a just and dignified manner without abusive language
   (D) to direct them in a superior manner, with strong, even profane words.

6. If a newly promoted individual discovers that a subordinate with greater seniority resents him, he or she can best win the respect and cooperation of the subordinate by
   (A) consulting with the subordinate on details with which the subordinate has had a lot of experience
   (B) making quick decisions and adhering to them
   (C) transferring the employee to new work in which he is not experienced
   (D) seeking social contacts with the employee and ignoring the resentment until it disappears.

7. Supervisors were cautioned recently not to try for popularity at the expense of efficiency. This caution is predicated on the assumption that
   (A) "familiarity breeds contempt"
   (B) required actions sometimes cause resentment
   (C) efficiency and popularity don't mix
   (D) cooperative problem-solving may lead to inefficient methods.

8. Of the following statements, the one that is *least* accurate in describing modern concepts of the supervisor-subordinate relationship is that
   (A) reasons for behavior vary and should not be treated similarly
   (B) misunderstandings often underlie job attitudes and behavior
   (C) job problems are often the concern of the supervisor and his or her workers
   (D) members should not participate in solving problems until they understand the causes of such problems.

9. The difference between the ordinary supervisor, concerned only with "getting the work done," and the constructive supervisor, concerned with developing favorable employee attitudes in addition to getting the work done, probably lies in the fact that the
   (A) former is more practical than the latter and will produce more in the long run
   (B) latter refused to be concerned with the details of the job
   (C) latter, more than the former, considers his subordinates as individuals, each with his own problems, interests, and motivations
   (D) constructive superior has the greater ability to use the principles of constructive organization in the management of his job.

10. Supervisors must be careful what they say in the presence of subordinates. The most valid support for this axiom is the fact that
    (A) anything said to one subordinate should be said to all subordinates
    (B) any significant communication between supervisor and subordinate should be in writing
    (C) subordinates characteristically tend to place their own meanings into otherwise meaningless remarks
    (D) the grapevine has no place in a well-run organization.

11. The one of the following circumstances which should indicate most strongly to a supervisor the need for a personal conference with an individual under his supervision is that the subordinate
    (A) seems sufficiently conscientious about the details of work, but rarely volunteers to do extra work
    (B) performs his duties competently but seems aloof and preoccupied
    (C) requests time off for the second time in one month to attend personal business
    (D) asks questions frequently about minor details of procedure.

12. If a subordinate does a good piece of work, the best procedure is to
    (A) say nothing so that the individual will not become conceited
    (B) tell him he has done a good job
    (C) explain how the work could be improved so that the person will not relax his efforts
    (D) tell the individual that he is far better than his

co-workers and would be promoted if there was a vacancy.

13. In making corrections of or criticizing an employee's work, it is *least* desirable to
    (A) choose a quiet and private place
    (B) get all the essential facts
    (C) give the employee a chance to talk
    (D) use the same method for all employees.

14. Suppose an employee makes a suggestion to you that is ridiculous. Of the following, the most proper action by you should be to
    (A) reject the suggestion and reprimand the man for being ridiculous
    (B) bring the suggestion up at a meeting so that the other men can comment on it
    (C) return the suggestion and tell the man that the suggestion, though valuable, is not applicable at this time
    (D) acknowledge the suggestion and explain why it is impractical.

15. You observe a woman performing a task improperly. When you discuss this with her, you are told that her previous superior taught her this method. Of the following, the best action for you to take at this point is to
    (A) tell the woman that she has probably followed her previous supervisor's instructions incorrectly
    (B) relieve this woman of her assignment and give her another job
    (C) indicate why the method she is using is not acceptable
    (D) avoid further comment and permit the woman to continue at this time.

16. An employee "called on the carpet" for poor performance tells his supervisor that his recent behavior has been due to a serious family problem. The supervisor suggests several social agencies which may be able to help him. The supervisor's action was
    (A) bad; the supervisor should not involve himself in the personal affairs of his subordinates
    (B) good; personal problems frequently affect job performance
    (C) good; the discussion with the supervisor will in itself tend to solve the problem
    (D) bad; the employee may consider the supervisor responsible for the action of the social agencies.

17. If you never have any problems reported to you by your subordinates it is most probable that
    (A) you are leading your subordinates so well that there is no room for improvement
    (B) your subordinates do not have the welfare of the department at heart
    (C) your subordinates are probably so self-reliant that they do not need to disturb you
    (D) for some reason you are not making it easy enough to report problems.

18. The direct, immediate guidance and control of subordinates in the performance of their tasks is called
    (A) planning
    (B) coordination
    (C) supervision
    (D) management.

19. Of the following, the *most* significant quality in relation to good supervision is
    (A) the ability of the supervisor honestly to treat subordinates as whole human beings, with all possible combinations of human strengths and weaknesses
    (B) the ability to give and take commands without question
    (C) an understanding that a department is a semi-military organization and that it must be conducted like the U.S. Army
    (D) the ability of the supervisor to understand his or her own personal limitations.

20. In general, when dealing with subordinates, an administrator should adopt
    (A) a strong dominant attitude emphasizing authority
    (B) a conciliatory attitude evidencing willingness to compromise
    (C) a firm friendly attitude designed to evoke cooperation
    (D) an indifferent attitude indicating impartiality.

21. A man under your supervision complains against a decision you have made in assigning staff. You consider the matter to be unimportant but it seems to be very important to him. He is excited and very

angry. The best way to handle this case is to
- (A) tell him to wait a few days and you will do what he wants you to do
- (B) let him talk until "he gets it off his chest" and then explain the reasons for your decision
- (C) show him at once how unimportant the matter is and how absurd his argument is
- (D) refuse to talk to him because of his unwarranted behavior.

22. The best method of handling an employee who is chronically dissatisfied is
- (A) suspension for a period of time
- (B) reprimanding before the staff
- (C) discuss the problem in detail
- (D) transfer the employee to another district.

23. Assume that you have an employee who is extremely efficient but who is continually complaining about the work assigned. You have noticed that the complaints have a bad effect on the other employees. It would usually be best to
- (A) have a talk with the other employees and ask them to overlook the faults because of efficiency
- (B) have a confidential talk with the employee and try to effect a change of attitude
- (C) ask to have the employee transferred
- (D) give him additional work to do leaving no time to complain.

24. When an employee's total work must be criticized, a supervisor can best improve the effect of the criticism by
- (A) mentioning the good points as well as the faults of the employee's work
- (B) pointing out previous instances of similar errors in the employee's work
- (C) holding the employee to a standard of perfection
- (D) comparing the employee's work with the work of a superior officer.

25. Among the problems that particularly confront a new supervisor in relation to his subordinates, the one which requires the exercise of the most unusual degree of skill and diplomacy is
- (A) changing established ideas
- (B) teaching new employees
- (C) calling attention to common errors
- (D) setting an example.

26. In attempting to correct unsatisfactory work of employees, it will be found most effective
- (A) to point out instances of unsatisfactory performance of work and say no more
- (B) to instruct employees in correct performance and make no reference to past inferior work
- (C) to point out instances of unsatisfactory performance of work, show what they signify, what results from them and how to correct them
- (D) to point out instances of unsatisfactory performance of work and reprimand the employee for it.

27. If one of your subordinates does an exceptionally fine piece of work, it would usually be best to
- (A) praise him moderately so that he knows his efforts are appreciated
- (B) say nothing so that he will not become conceited
- (C) tell him that none of his co-workers could have done as fine a job as he did
- (D) explain how the work could have been improved so that he will not become complacent.

28. If a supervisor in the department asks his subordinates for suggestions to solve a particular problem they will usually
- (A) assume that the supervisor lacks sufficient knowledge to occupy his position
- (B) feel that their suggestions make helpful contributions
- (C) resent such a request on the grounds that the supervisor will always take credit for any helpful suggestions
- (D) make no suggestions because the supervisor receives more salary, and should make all suggestions.

29. Of the following, the most valid statement dealing with the relations between supervisors and subordinates in a department is that
- (A) if a supervisor is to maintain the respect of subordinates, he or she should always defend the acts of subordinates against criticism
- (B) when an order which the supervisor knows will make heavy demands on workers is to be read to them, it is a wise policy to preface the reading with some explanatory remarks
- (C) even if a supervisor sees and knows of things that should be done, he or she should never

enforce these details upon workers without orders from a superior

(D) a supervisor should assign the most difficult tasks to the workers with the least service to test their ability.

30. Prior to discussing them with his superior a supervisor often discusses with his subordinates, certain procedures which are under his consideration. Of the following, the principal reason why this technique has been found useful is that
    (A) it prepares the staff for any procedural changes
    (B) the subordinates frequently make worthwhile suggestions
    (C) it gives the supervisors chance to become better acquainted with his staff
    (D) the subordinates appreciate being consulted on the office procedure.

31. From the viewpoint of an administrator, the chief value of authority is its use as a means of
    (A) unifying and coordinating actions
    (B) determining who is responsible if things go wrong
    (C) recognizing ability
    (D) providing social prestige essential for accomplishment of objectives.

32. It is a serious mistake to assume that a weak person in charge of a division can be bolstered by surrounding him with one or more subordinate supervisors who are of known ability. This solution is poor primarily because the
    (A) the administrator exercises control which cannot be delegated regardless of the exigencies of the situation
    (B) the administrator will merely tend to allow these subordinates to take over his responsibility without attempting to assert himself
    (C) level of performance of the division can seldom rise higher than the capacity of the administrator
    (D) administrative control in a decentralized organization relies on unity of command, rather than functional division of responsibility.

33. Normally, operating personnel tend to resist and resent changes or innovations in existing procedures. To the supervisor, the most basic solution to this problem is to

(A) hold the senior employee of each unit responsible for the proper execution of the procedure
(B) develop acceptance by providing information concerning the procedure prior to its establishment
(C) describe the steps in the procedure in terms that will arouse least resentment among subordinates
(D) have the procedure accompanied by an explicit order from higher authority.

34. Suggestions on improving methods of work when submitted by a new employee should be
    (A) disregarded because he is too unfamiliar with the work to submit any worthwhile ideas
    (B) examined only for the purpose of judging the new worker
    (C) ignored because it would make the older employees resentful
    (D) examined for possible merit because the new worker may have a fresh viewpoint.

35. Generally a good way for an administrator to retain the confidence of his subordinates is to
    (A) say as little as possible
    (B) make very infrequent checks on the work
    (C) make no promises unless they will be fulfilled
    (D) never hesitate in giving an answer to any question.

36. Assume that you have a woman in your department who is very conscientious and does more and better work than anyone else. In this case, as her supervisor, you should
    (A) grant her unusual privileges
    (B) persuade her to slow down because others resent a speed-up
    (C) make every effort to show her that her efforts are appreciated
    (D) assign her less work as a reward for her services.

37. "Administrators may find that it is the senior members of the unit who require the most attention on their part." This statement assumes most directly that
    (A) competence in work will increase with experience
    (B) strict supervision may increase the tendency on the part of employee to break minor regulations

(C) the need for supervision may have little relationship to the amount of experience

(D) newer staff members are usually less well acquainted with detailed regulations.

38. If a supervisor has criticized one of his subordinates for making a mistake, the supervisor should
    (A) remind the worker of the error from time to time in order to keep the worker on his toes
    (B) overlook further errors which this worker may make, otherwise this worker may feel he is a victim of discrimination
    (C) impress this worker with the fact that all work will be closely checked from then on
    (D) not dwell on the incident and give the worker an opportunity for redemption.

39. Occasionally some of the men in a department will indulge in active horseplay. This should be
    (A) encouraged because it promotes good fellowship
    (B) permitted as it is a form of relaxation

(C) discouraged because some of the men might not like it

(D) stopped immediately because it is likely to cause accidents.

40. A good way of obtaining high quality work from the department is for the administrator to
    (A) give the employees unusual privileges
    (B) compliment the employees after each job
    (C) maintain a vigorous interest in each job
    (D) individually assist on every job.

41. You notice that one employee stops work an hour before "quitting" time although he produces as much work as his fellow workers. As supervisor you should
    (A) assign the employee to more interesting work
    (B) assign the employee more work than can possibly be done
    (C) inform the employee that you expect one to work until "quitting" time
    (D) do or say nothing to the employee.

ANSWER KEY

1. A	10. C	19. A	28. B	37. C
2. B	11. B	20. C	29. B	38. D
3. B	12. B	21. B	30. B	39. D
4. C	13. D	22. C	31. A	40. C
5. C	14. D	23. B	32. C	41. C
6. A	15. C	24. A	33. B	
7. B	16. B	25. A	34. D	
8. D	17. D	26. C	35. C	
9. C	18. C	27. A	36. C	

EXPLANATORY ANSWERS

1. **(A)** The concept involved in this question is that superiors must be totally informed of important matters. A series of thefts occurring within an administrator's jurisdiction is of great importance because of possible ramifications resulting from these thefts. This is a matter the administrator must know about. It is a serious matter.

2. **(B)** As the question is written, the situation requires a formal interview. To make such interviews successful, both positive and negative aspects of the supervisor's work should be discussed, not just the negative aspects of the supervisor's performance. If possible, the interview should start off on a positive note, and the supervisor given the right to refute charges of unsatisfactory performance. Since the purpose of the interview is to point out to the supervisor how he or she can be a better supervisor, a give-and-take, frank discussion will best help the supervisor profit by the interview.

3. **(B)** The efficient leader is the one who can convince subordinates of the wisdom of his or her decisions so that they will carry them out. In seeking the support of staff the wise administrator uses the strengths of subordinates in the best way possible. In the situation described, the administrator should seek to convince the subordinate of the correctness of the administrator's position, and then use that subordinate's leadership capabilities to bring the matter to a successful conclusion. A good administrator welcomes constructive disagreement, and seeks to win support by winning agreement with his or her opinions.

4. **(C)** The basic principle in dealing with the personal problems of subordinates is the same as that for handling similar situations with anyone. 1. Don't pry into a person's personal life unless your help is requested or unless the consequences of the individual's behavior is adversely affecting your responsibilities as an administrator. 2. Try to help the individual find the answer to the problem himself because this will enforce his belief in the correctness of the solution, will increase self-confidence in his ability to handle his own affairs, and will help him to better cope with the results of the decision he has reached.

5. **(C)** An administrator can expect the best responses to his or her directions to the staff if they are issued in a professional manner, i.e., the order given is fair, calm and straightforward. Trying to be popular and "one of the gang" may result in failure to get the order carried out. Adoption of a superior manner will often be resented, especially by older, experienced workers. The use of profane or even strong language is virtually never effective in the civil service structure and may be strongly resented by some staff members.

6. **(A)** The situation where a newer, and usually younger, person must supervise older, senior employees is a common one, and experience has shown that the best approach the new supervisor should take to lessen the understanderable resentment that may occur is not only to work with the senior employee, utilize his or her knowledge and experience, let him or her know that you appreciate the help, but also stress that you are all working as a team for the common good.

7. **(B)** The assumption behind the cautionary statement is that every supervisor must, at some time, give directions which will not be popular ones. The supervisor must get the job done in the best way possible, and while he or she can try to lessen the inevitable resentment, required actions must take precedence over popularity, even though efficiency and popularity can go hand in hand for many work situations.

8. **(D)** The key word in this question is "least." Answers A, B, and C are modern concepts. It is not necessary, however, according to modern concepts, that subordinates understand the causes for problems in order to help arrive at the solutions to them. Moreover, in many instances it may be undesirable for them to be fully briefed about the underlying reasons for a problem. Helpful contributions may come from many sources. Where a problem exists, information to solve it should be sought from all.

9. **(C)** Both types of supervisors want to accomplish the primary role of the supervisor, i.e., get the work done properly. They may be equally practical, and achieve the same results. The difference between them is that one is more concerned with the need to develop favorable employee attitudes than the other. To develop such attitudes the supervisor must consider staff members as individuals, and consider their individual needs and desires.

10. **(C)** All of us have the tendency to read into a person's remarks something that was not intended, and this is especially true in supervisor/subordinate relationships. Since workers transmit supervisor's remarks through the grapevine, it is very important to think carefully when making a remark which may have repercussions in a subordinate's presence.

11. **(B)** Evidently, it is necessary for the supervisor to become better acquainted with the worker to determine the cause of the worker's attitude and demeanor. There is no problem with work performance, but to permit the worker to continue to act this way may have a deleterious effect on the overall operation. A conference is the best way to get to the root of this problem.

12. **(B)** Everyone likes to receive praise when praise is due, so that complimenting a subordinate for a job well done is appropriate. If a subordinate does everything well, it may be unnecessary and even counter-productive to continue with the compliments, especially if a tangible reward (promotion, raise, etc.) is not possible. Too much praise and false promises of promotion, especially in the Civil Service structure, are inappropriate and dangerous to a continued amicable relationship between supervisor and subordinate.

13. **(D)** When criticizing an employee the factors given in Answers A, B, and C are appropriate. It is least desirable to use the same method to criticize each employee. One person profits by direct statements, with little need for comments or suggestions for improvement; another must be carefully told exactly what is wrong and how to correct it; another must be handled gently because he or she tends to become emotionally disturbed, etc. People react differently to criticism, and a good supervisor handles each corrective interview differently.

14. **(D)** If a worker makes a suggestion in good faith, he or she deserves the courtesy of careful consideration and an explanation of the reasons why it is unacceptable. Antagonizing the employee by making him feel ridiculous by reprimands or by ridicule in a general meeting will result in his refusal to submit future suggestions, some of which may be very useful. It is important the worker know why the suggestion is a bad one so that he or she will submit more thoughtful ideas in the future.

15. **(C)** A worker should not be permitted to follow an incorrect method of performing work. In order to accept a method which is different from the one a worker has been using, he or she needs to fully appreciate why changes are needed and the previous method not acceptable. This is especially true in the situation described—when a new supervisor is rejecting the procedure acceptable to the previous one.

16. **(B)** A supervisor must be aware that personal or family problems may adversely affect job performance, and must be prepared to offer help with the problem. From the facts given, the supervisor is aware that the individual may need professional help from a social agency, and should recommend that the worker seek such help.

17. **(D)** In every work situation problems arise that are the supervisor's responsibility to try to solve. If none are reported to you, something is wrong and very probably your workers for some reason are not bringing problems to your attention. Your biggest problem then is to find out why they are not being reported. Perhaps workers fear your anger, or mistrust your judgment, or are so self-reliant they mistakenly think they can handle every problem. Whatever the reason(s), the supervisor must examine the situation, and make sure the staff understands that it is the supervisor's role to know and try to solve problems affecting the work of the unit.

18. **(C)** The essential elements for good supervision involve, working directly with subordinates, guiding them, and controlling their work. The preamble of this question defines supervision.

19. **(A)** The best supervisor is the one who successfully uses the strengths and weaknesses of each staff member to most effectively get the job done. To utilize staff in this manner, the most significant quality the supervisor requires is the ability to truly understand and appreciate that each of us differs from others, and has a set of characteristics which are uniquely ours. Every worker, including supervisors, must understand his or her own personal limitations in order to be successful (answer D), but this is not a particularly significant quality to distinguish a good supervisor from the poor one.

20. **(C)** The best way to administer any organization is to develop team spirit and the conviction of staff that if they work together the job will be concluded successfully. The administrator's role is to adopt an approach or attitude which will foster that spirit. The authoritarian leader often finds himself obeyed, but will not have a creative staff who does more than what they are ordered to do. A conciliatory or indifferent attitude on the part of

the administrator will frequently result in loss of respect from staff and failure to use the best way possible for doing a job. This is because the existing way or easiest way is preferred by staff, and the administrator is uninterested or unwilling to assume the firm direction needed to change the methods being used.

21. **(B)** When dealing with any person it is important to realize that what seems important to you may not be as important to others, and vice versa. In the situation described, the best policy is to hear the subordinate out, and thus defuse his or her anger. When the worker has been given the chance to air his or her views, he or she will then be able and willing to rationally listen and understand the reasons for your decisions. Although he or she may still not agree, they can at least accept your decisions. Listening to staff's point of view and attempting to convince them of the wisdom of your decisions is an important part of good administration. Agreeing to change a decision, no matter how trivial, just because it will satisfy a worker and not because your decision was wrong, however, is poor administrative practice, as is belittling the importance of a matter which an employee thinks to be highly important.

22. **(C)** The chronically dissatisfied employee very often does not perform adequately. Moreover, since dissatisfaction can be as "catching" as chicken pox, he or she may be a negative factor in attempting to manage a unit. The best way to handle the problem is to discuss the matter directly with the employee, to learn the source of the dissatisfaction, and, if possible, to find a way to correct it. Public reprimands, suspension or punitive measures will not make him or her less dissatisfied, and transferring the employee to another district only transfers the problem unless, in fact, the cause of the dissatisfaction is the present work location itself.

23. **(B)** Like the situation in question 22 above, this employee is dissatisfied, but in this case you know the source and know it is adversely affecting others. Moreover, you are told that the employee is efficient. The solution is much the same as in question 21. The supervisor must talk to the employee, and try to change his or her attitude to a more positive one. What about the work is causing dissatisfaction? Too little work? Too monotonous? Too difficult? No supervisor likes to lose a good worker, so if you can change the present negative attitude by pinning down the exact reasons for it and find a solution, you will have fulfilled your role as a sincere, interested, caring supervisor.

24. **(A)** To be effective, criticism must be accepted by the employee, and experience has shown that he or she must be in a suitable frame of mind to accept it. The discussion should include mention of the worker's good points so that an atmosphere is created in which the worker knows the supervisor is being fair, and trying to advise the employee for both his own good and the good of the entire work force. To dwell on previous errors, hold the worker to impossible standards of perfection, or compare the worker to other employees will not improve his or her performance.

25. **(A)** Experience has shown that the most difficult staff problem facing a new supervisor is attempting to change established work patterns and ideas. A staff accustomed to the ideas and ways of doing things under the previous supervisor will normally resist change unless the new one can convince them of the advantages of such changes. Skill and diplomacy are essential because staff will resent implications that a newcomer knows better than they or the previous supervisor.

26. **(C)** In the attempt to correct unsatisfactory performance it is not sufficient to point out errors, nor to just show the employee the correct way to do the work. Experience has shown that the only way a worker will improve performance is if he or she fully understands the nature of the errors, the reasons why the performance is bad, the consequences of the bad performance, and its impact on the unit's other activities. When this is fully understood, the worker knows how to correct the unsatisfactory performance.

27. **(A)** All workers appreciate praise when it is due. However, it can be overdone. It becomes meaningless when it is overdone, but when it is limited to deserving occasions and is delivered in a rational manner it will be appreciated.

28. **(B)** None of us are perfect—everyone can use a little help, and the good supervisor knows that staff suggestions can be a great boon to getting a unit's work done in the best way possible. Employees generally welcome the opportunity to give suggestions towards solving a problem or improving a procedure. The most effective work force is the one where each person feels he or she is part of a team effort, and when a supervisor asks his team for suggestions. This tends to enhance team spirit, and the individual feels that he or she is making a meaningful contribution to team success.

29. **(B)** Workers generally respond in a positive fashion to heavy demands made on them only if they understand the need for such demands. When a supervisor reads such an order to staff, full voluntary cooperation can be obtained only if the supervisor prefaces the order with an explanation of the reasons why this extraordinary situation has occurred. The supervisor's role is to explain management's needs to subordinates, and attempt to convince staff of the necessity of the order and the special demands it involves.

30. **(B)** The main purpose of prior discussion with staff before discussing a possible procedure with your supervisor is to make sure that your proposal is workable, and is the best one possible. It is always a good idea to discuss a proposal with the people who are going to have to carry it out, for they are in the best position to know if it is workable and how it can be improved. Another less important advantage is the enhancement of team cooper-

ation, but the principal reason is to produce a better procedure.

31. **(A)** From an administrator's viewpoint, authority is the means to direct separate actions into a unified whole. With authority goes the responsibility for errors, but since this is a negative value it is not the purpose for which authority is given to do a job.

32. **(C)** Rarely does an organization rise above the ability of its top executive. Attempts in industry and government to surround a weak executive with strong subordinate assistants have failed, and will always fail. For one reason or another the organization always reflects the ability of the chief executive. In other words, a strong organization is never headed by a weak chief executive. This is also true in professional sports when weak baseball teams have resulted from having a "weak" manager surrounded by "strong" coaches.

33. **(B)** The best way to obtain staff acceptance is to give them full information about the new procedure. This provides time for them to raise questions about specific points in the procedure, accustoms them to the changes and what they mean in terms of actual daily work, and fosters acceptance of the new procedure which is so essential to success in its utilization.

34. **(D)** Since a good supervisor is open to all suggestions for improving procedures, a new employee may have ideas which he or she brings to the job which may be very useful. A new employee also sees problems with new eyes, and can offer suggestions which workers accustomed to a routine for many years may not perceive.

35. **(C)** It is good administrative practice never to promise anything you are not certain you can fulfill. At best, you will have to apologize if you find you can not keep it, and at worst will foster discontent, dissatisfaction, and a serious loss of confidence in your ability as a leader. Confidence of workers is not fostered when the supervisor remains silent, just when he or she remains competent, fair and honest in relations with subordinates. Nor does a good administrator give hasty, ill-thought out answers which will soon lose him the respect and confidence of the staff.

36. **(C)** Although a few continue to do their best in all situations, most people need a little recognition of good intentions and good work if they are to continue to do their best. A supervisor usually can not grant unusual privileges, certainly can not afford to let the good worker do less than he or she has done before, and should not urge him to slow up or do less efficient work.

37. **(C)** In this question you are asked for the assumption underlying the sentence, which states that the senior members of the staff may require the most attention of administrators. Of the possible correct answers only answer C notes that need for supervision. The other answers make different assumptions from the one indicated in the question.

38. **(D)** There is nothing in the question to indicate that criticism will not have positive results. Therefore, the supervisor should accept the fact that his criticism was an unintentional error. No ultimate good will come from the supervisor's dwelling on the matter.

39. **(D)** "Active horseplay" implies physical activity among workers in a good natured manner. Unfortunately, this kind of activity all too often results in accidents with time lost from work and bitterness among the recipients of this good intentioned, well meaning activity. Very often the results are disastrous. When it exists it should be stopped.

40. **(C)** The best way for an administrator to obtain good quality work from the staff is to have everyone in the organization interested in the work, proud of successes by the group, and working as a team toward fulfilling the agency's functions. The administrator should lead the way by personally maintaining awareness of, and interest in, all the activities of the agency. This does not mean active participation by the administrator in the actual daily work of the department. The administrator's role is to plan, coordinate and direct activities, to oversee its operations, and to be on top of all the various jobs that are being handled within the agency.

41. **(C)** The employee is obviously a faster worker. There is no indication in the question of a lack of quality or quantity of production. This worker must be motivated to produce more than the work standards call for and should be put in a frame of mind to do so willingly.

PROBLEMS OF SUPERVISION AND ADMINISTRATION

DIRECTIONS FOR ANSWERING QUESTIONS

Each question has four suggested answers, lettered A, B, C, and D. Decide which one is the best answer and on the sample answer sheet (all answer sheets are at the front of the book) find the question number and darken the area, with a soft pencil, which corresponds to the answer that you have selected.

1. An important responsibility that you have as an administrator is to make certain that all required work is completed on time. Of the following procedures, the one which is most likely to lead to accomplishing this aim is for you to
   (A) require every subordinate to submit a daily work report
   (B) schedule the work and keep track of its progress
   (C) impress your subordinates with the importance of getting work done on time
   (D) hold a weekly conference during which the work of the organization is discussed.

2. Listed below are several administrative duties and a method of accomplishing each duty. While the duties are all correct, only one method of performing the duty is correct. It is
   (A) to see that discipline is maintained by adhering to a set of rules without deviation of any kind in any case
   (B) to see that there is unity of command by making every person directly responsible and answerable to the chief
   (C) to see that there is competent and vigorous management of the department by means of clear lines of authority and distinct statements of duties
   (D) to see that everything is subject to proper control by personally making all decisions both general and detailed.

3. Under the best administrative conditions, "authority" becomes a problem of
   (A) responsibility and leadership
   (B) the scientific issuance of orders
   (C) the determination of the relative worth of existing rules and regulations
   (D) constructive criticism.

4. Of the following, the *least* desirable procedure for an administrator to follow is to
   (A) be flexible in planning and carrying out assignments
   (B) organize his work before taking responsibility for helping others in theirs
   (C) avoid schedules or routines when busy
   (D) secure the support of subordinates in carrying out responsibilities.

5. "Subordinates must obey orders without delay or question, but at the same time the administrator takes on a definite responsibility." Of the following, the most acceptable statement concerning such responsibility is that the administrator should
   (A) issue orders in a positive and decisive manner
   (B) explain to the staff the reason for each order issued
   (C) avoid issuing orders except as a last resort
   (D) issue only those orders which can be justified.

6. A sound organization may be said to exist when
   (A) there is a division in lines of authority

(B) executive authority and responsibility are co-equal
(C) lines of authority are left undefined to encourage initiative
(D) an administrator has many subordinates reporting directly.

7. When one exceeds the "span of control" in a department, it is almost inevitable to have
(A) over-disciplined work
(B) delineation of responsibility
(C) over-specialization
(D) undisciplined work.

8. The major function of all administrators with regard to the departmental policies is to
(A) review them critically to uncover obsolete or unworkable items
(B) transmit all statements of policy to subordinates without comment
(C) interpret policy to subordinates
(D) make the decision as to policy whenever subordinates point out conflicting provisions.

9. In supervising a new employee, the one of the following which is not generally accepted as a good basic principle is to
(A) allow the employee to take immediate responsibility for some assigned work
(B) prevent any temporary dependence on the supervisor
(C) allow the employee to make mistakes, without any advance instructions, and to learn by experience, because he or she will be more sure to remember the right way
(D) hold the employee to the perfect execution of every rule of the department until he or she learns all the policies.

10. Although it is not necessary to list and define every supervisory responsibility, it is essential for an individual placed in a supervisory position first to
(A) clarify lines of authority to himself and to subordinates
(B) learn to adjust to the particular managerial group
(C) assume responsibility for the errors of subordinates
(D) delegate work to others to conserve time for handling complicated cases.

11. The most basic of the following duties of a supervisor is that of
(A) seeing that the departmental rules are enforced
(B) properly delegating authority to qualified individuals
(C) seeing that each man adequately performs the work assigned to him
(D) getting along well with the subordinates.

12. On being promoted to a supervisory position, an individual should recognize that the position is primarily one of
(A) security
(B) power
(C) responsibility
(D) authority.

13. The supervisor has a reputation as a "conscientious officer." The best example of this statement is that such officer
(A) feels obligated to do what he or she believes is right
(B) frequently makes suggestions for improvement in procedure
(C) has good personal relationships with superiors and subordinates
(D) is accustomed to hard work.

14. A supervisor is indefinite in assigning responsibilities for various phases of work. This action is most likely to result in
(A) valuable training of subordinates in using their own initiative
(B) the assuming of authority by those who are most willing to do so
(C) friction, misunderstanding and ineffective work
(D) the work being done by the most capable of doing it.

15. "An administrator should be a leader whom his men will follow with enthusiasm." A competent administrator should realize that this type of leadership is most effectively based upon
(A) close observance of precisely formulated rules and regulations
(B) diligent study by both subordinates and administrators
(C) respect and confidence of the subordinates
(D) strict and invariable discipline.

16. "Every supervisor who has had occasion to teach his subordinates how to operate a new piece of equipment has seen trial-and-error learning, in which the worker fumbles about until he strikes upon the proper procedure by accident." Of the following, the most accurate statement concerning trial-and-error learning in training is that
    (A) trial-and-error learning should be reduced by the supervisor through proper guidance
    (B) the supervisor will find it most effective to allow trial-and-error learning to precede specific training
    (C) trial-and-error learning is more efficient per unit time than any other type of learning
    (D) interference with natural trial-and-error learning is likely to be wasteful and time-consuming.

17. If an administrator must use authority to obtain acceptance of an idea, the cause most probably is that
    (A) subordinates have little respect for a supervisor who fails to use authority
    (B) discipline depends upon subordinates' recognition of the supervisor's absolute authority
    (C) the introduction of new ideas is solely the administrator's responsibility
    (D) the idea may not warrant acceptance on its own merit.

18. The recommendation has been made that interviews with dissatisfied employees be discontinued and that grievances be received and replied to in writing only. This recommendation is
    (A) desirable primarily because employees will not be able to keep changing their arguments as objections are pointed out to them
    (B) undesirable primarily because there is no point in encouraging needless correspondence when a short interview may settle the matter
    (C) undesirable primarily because it will tend to dehumanize a procedure in which human values may be receiving insufficient consideration
    (D) desirable primarily because the amount of time that administrators spend on grievances will be decreased.

19. Impartiality is considered to be one of the most important qualifications of an administrator. This is so mainly because

    (A) the administrator should rotate responsible assignments among the members of his staff
    (B) an administrator should be able to train subordinates to be impartial
    (C) impartiality and intellectual honesty are closely related
    (D) staff cooperation tends to deteriorate when an administrator shows favoritism.

20. "A common difference among executives is that some are not content unless they are out in front in everything that concerns their organization, while others prefer to run things by pulling strings, by putting others out in front and by stepping into the breach only when necessary." Generally speaking, an advantage this latter method of operation has over the former is that it
    (A) results in a higher level of morale over a sustained period of time
    (B) gets results by exhortation and direct stimulus
    (C) makes it unnecessary to calculate integrated moves
    (D) makes the personality of the executive felt further down the line.

21. The statement has been made, "An individual who is a top-notch executive in one organization would make a top-notch executive in any other organization, even if the organizations are as diverse as a sales agency and a research foundation." This statement is, in general,
    (A) correct; the characteristics required for a good executive are invariant with respect to organization
    (B) not correct; there is no way of predicting how a good executive in one organization would be in any other
    (C) correct; while the characteristics required for a good executive vary from organization to organization, the common core requirements are great enough to insure similar performance
    (D) not correct; although some prediction can be made, different types of organizations require different types of executives.

22. The head of a unit is responsible for the quality and accuracy of the work performed by his staff. In handling errors made by members of his or her staff, the unit head should be concerned chiefly with
    (A) determining how best to reprimand the persons responsible for the errors

(B) finding out who is ultimately responsible for the errors

(C) recording each error made by a staff member in that staff member's personal record

(D) preventing such errors from being made again.

23. The supervisor of a large central typing bureau is responsible for the accuracy of the work performed by her subordinates. Of the following procedures which she might adopt to insure the accurate copying of long reports from rough draft originals, the most effective one is to

(A) examine the rough draft for errors in grammar, punctuation, and spelling before assigning it to a typist to copy

(B) glance through each typed report before it leaves her bureau to detect any obvious errors made by the typist

(C) have another employee read the rough draft original to the typist who typed the report, and have the typist make whatever corrections are necessary

(D) rotate assignments involving the typing of long reports equally among all the typists who volunteer to type them.

24. "Administrators must learn to farm out essential functions to unintegrated agencies, but to organize all responsibilities in unified but decentralized hierarchies." A problem which an administrator may be expected to face if he has not learned this is that

(A) the organization fails to develop administrators capable of independent action

(B) issues will not be posed at the level where decisions should be made

(C) relationships with the public will not be satisfactory

(D) it will be difficult to achieve administrative control or get agreement on departmental action.

25. "So important to good administration is effective leadership that some administrators who are well equipped in this respect have compensated for deficiencies in other qualities." On the basis of this quotation, the most accurate of the following statements is that

(A) administrative ability is the most valuable attribute a leader can have

(B) effective leaders are generally deficient in other administrative qualities

(C) other administrative qualities may be substituted for leadership ability

(D) good leaders may make good administrators even though lacking in other administrative qualities.

26. "The successful administrator wins victories through preventive rather than through curative action." The one of the following which is the most accurate statement on the basis of this quotation is that

(A) success in supervision may be measured more accurately in terms of errors corrected than in terms of errors prevented

(B) anticipating problems makes for better supervision than waiting until these problems arise

(C) difficulties that cannot be prevented by the supervisor cannot be overcome

(D) the solution of problems in supervision is best achieved by scientific methods.

Questions 27 to 30 are to be answered solely on the basis of the information contained in the following paragraph:

"Good personnel relations of an organization depend upon mutual confidence, trust, and good will. The basis of confidence is understanding. Most troubles start with people who do not understand each other. When the organization's intentions or motives are misunderstood, or when reasons for actions, practices, or policies are misconstrued, complete cooperation from individuals is not forthcoming. If management expects full cooperation from employees, it has a responsibility of sharing with them the information which is the foundation of proper understanding, confidence, and trust. Personnel management has long since outgrown the days when it was the vogue to 'treat them rough and tell them nothing.' Up-to-date personnel management provides all possible information about the activities, aims, and purposes of the organization. It seems altogether creditable that a desire should exist among employees for such information which the best-intentioned executive might think would not interest them and which the worst-intentioned would think was none of their business."

27. The above paragraph implies that one of the causes of the difficulty which an organization might have with its personnel relations is that its employees

(A) have not expressed interest in the activities, aims, and purposes of the organization

(B) do not believe in the good faith of the organization

(C) have been able to give full cooperation to the organization

(D) do not recommend improvements in the practices and policies of the organization.

28. According to the above paragraph, in order for an organization to have good personnel relations, it is *not* essential that
    (A) employees have confidence in the organization
    (B) the purposes of the organization be understood by the employees
    (C) employees have a desire for information about the organization
    (D) information about the organization be communicated to employees.

29. According to the paragraph, an organization which provides full information about itself to its employees
    (A) understands the intentions of its employees
    (B) satisfies a praiseworthy desire among its employees
    (C) is managed by executives who have the best intentions toward its employees
    (D) is confident that its employees understand the motives.

30. The one of the following which is the most suitable title for the paragraph is
    (A) The Foundations of Good Personnel Relations
    (B) The Consequences of Employee Misunderstanding
    (C) The Development of Personnel Management Practices
    (D) The Acceptance of Organizational Objectives

31. "A line supervisor can play an important role in helping his subordinates to make healthy mental, emotional, and social adjustments." The one of the following which would *not* be considered to be a part of the supervisor's role in helping his subordinates to make these adjustments is to
    (A) ascertain which subordinates are likely to develop maladjustments
    (B) recognize indications of these types of maladjustments

(C) refer subordinates displaying signs of maladjustments that he or she cannot handle to specialists for assistance

(D) create a work environment that will tend to minimize his subordinates' preoccupations with personal problems.

32. You are an Administrator in charge of a unit of clerical employees. One of your subordinates, Mr. Smith, has not seemed to be his usual self in the past several weeks, but, rather, has seemed to be disturbed. In addition, he has not been producing his usual quantity of work and has been provoking arguments with his colleagues. He approaches you and asks if he may discuss with you a problem which he believes has been affecting his work. As Mr. Smith begins to discuss the problem, you immediately realize that, although it may be disturbing to him, it is really a trivial matter. Of the following, the *first* step that you should take in this situation is to
    (A) permit Mr. Smith to continue to describe his problem, interrupting him only when clarification of a point is needed
    (B) tell Mr. Smith that his becoming unduly upset about the problem will not help to solve it
    (C) point out that you and your subordinates have faced more serious problems and that this one is a relatively minor matter
    (D) suggest that the problem should be solved before it develops into a serious matter.

33. Assume that a supervisor praises subordinates for satisfactory aspects of their work only when he or she is about to criticize them for unsatisfactory aspects of their work. Such a practice is undesirable primarily because
    (A) his subordinates may expect to be praised for their work even if it is unsatisfactory
    (B) praising his subordinates for some aspects of their work while criticizing other aspects will weaken the effects of the criticisms
    (C) subordinates would be more receptive to criticism if it were followed by praise
    (D) subordinates may come to disregard praise and wait for criticism to be given.

34. Following a recent promotion, an employee becomes very irritable and frequently loses his temper. Of the following, the most advisable action of

the employee's supervisor to take *first* is to
(A) have the employee take a supervisor training course
(B) suggest that the employee get counseling or similar help
(C) try to determine the reason for the employee's irritability
(D) warn the employee that he may be demoted to his former position.

35. "Interest is essentially an attitude of continuing attentiveness, found where activity is satisfactorily self-expressive. Whenever work is so circumscribed that the chance for self-expression or development is denied, monotony is present." On the basis of this quotation, it is most accurate to state that
(A) tasks which are repetitive in nature do not permit self-expression and therefore create monotony
(B) interest in one's work is increased by financial and non-financial incentives
(C) jobs which are monotonous can be made self-expressive by substituting satisfactory working conditions
(D) workers whose tasks afford them no opportunity for self-expression find such tasks to be monotonous.

36. "The improvement in skill and the development of proper attitudes are essential factors in the building of correct work habits." Of the following, the most valid implication of this quotation for a supervisor is that
(A) the more skillful an employee is, the better will be his attitude toward his work
(B) developing proper attitudes in subordinates toward their work is more time-consuming for the supervisor than improving their skill
(C) the improvement of a worker's skill is only part of the supervisor's job
(D) correct work habits are established in order to either improve the skill of workers or develop in them a proper attitude toward their work.

37. Of the following, the greatest work incentive that a supervisor should recognize is that
(A) everyone has a desire for approval or recognition
(B) fear may drive persons to do better work
(C) rivalry is a spur to effort
(D) constant watching will produce better work.

38. If an intelligent employee assigned to a routine job is inclined to be restless, a supervisor could most probably correct this situation by
(A) transferring or recommending the transfer of the employee to a more challenging job if it were possible
(B) praising the employee's work before the other workers
(C) explaining to the employee that not everyone in the job can be freed from routine duties
(D) offering constructive criticism and urging the employee to take more interest in his job.

39. In order to maintain the best morale in his or her staff, a supervisor preferably should
(A) tell the inefficient worker to "get busy"
(B) praise the good worker in the presence of the staff
(C) maintain fairness and impartiality consistently
(D) give sarcastic criticism to the slow worker whenever the occasion demands.

40. If an employee is emotionally upset when he comes to a supervisor with a problem, the supervisor should, in most instances
(A) inquire into the employee's personal problems for the cause of the emotional disturbance
(B) refuse to meet with the employee until the employee has regained self control
(C) give an immediate decision satisfactory to the employee
(D) help the employee to become calmer before discussing a solution.

41. Of the following responsibilities of a supervisor, the most important is
(A) becoming acquainted with the personal problems of each of the subordinates
(B) assigning and evaluating work
(C) keeping a daily record of work completed by each subordinate
(D) smoothing out personal frictions and jealousies among the subordinates.

42. The chief task of a supervisor of a trained clerical staff with the normal work load to perform is to
(A) give continual direction to each employee
(B) keep up potential or intensity of group effort
(C) revise rules and regulations in order to impress the staff with his autocratic rights

(D) criticize the work of each employee regularly in order to show his superior knowledge.

43. The immediate task of a supervisor of a clerical staff, augmented by an increase in temporary employees to put out an increased volume of work in accordance with a well-established routine, is to
(A) assign and train the new subordinates
(B) develop written instructions covering every detail of the procedure and outlining the responsibility
(C) develop and maintain high morale
(D) keep exact records of the work production (quantity and quality) of each employee.

44. If a subordinate makes a work suggestion that would give better service but would result in gain by some persons and in loss by others, the supervisor should
(A) agree to put over the employee's wishes at once
(B) discuss the suggestion fully with the employee and tell him it will receive due consideration
(C) thank the employee for the suggestion and tell him you will discuss it at a later date
(D) tell the employee that the suggestion will be filed for reference.

45. Often a staff wastes time doing unproductive work as part of a particular routine or in traveling about while working. The first possibility a supervisor should investigate as the cause of this situation is
(A) lack of interest in the work
(B) poor working conditions
(C) improper work habits caused by inadequate supervision
(D) poor planning and organization.

46. Of the following ways in which a supervisor may expect to obtain conformance among the employees to the rules and regulations of office conduct in an organization, ordinarily the most effective would be for him to
(A) post the rules and regulations in a conspicuous place
(B) discuss instances of nonconformity in staff meetings
(C) delegate to the employees the responsibility for seeing that rules and regulations are observed
(D) observe the rules and regulations himself.

47. A supervisor can best develop an employee's understanding of a job and his skill in performing it by
(A) insisting on high standards
(B) thorough, patient teaching
(C) encouraging trial and error on the part of the learner
(D) constantly "driving" the learner.

48. If it becomes necessary for a supervisor to hold a corrective interview with a worker, good practice dictates that the reprimand should be given
(A) in private, in an authoritative manner
(B) informally, in the presence of other workers
(C) by publicly centering attention on the person rather that on the work
(D) in private, in a firm, decisive manner.

49. In teaching a procedure to any member of staff, which method is the most desirable for a supervisor to follow? To teach the procedure by
(A) giving the worker the written procedure and having the worker learn by doing the work
(B) "absorption," through the constant observation of another worker until the procedure is mastered
(C) telling the worker "how" to do the task, and then criticize every time an error is made
(D) assigning the worker to work with an experienced employee until he or she learns the techniques used by the experienced employee.

50. When arguments arise between employees over the advantage of seating arrangements to give the best light, of the following, the best procedure for a supervisor to follow to deal with the situation efficiently and fairly is to
(A) issue a memorandum explaining the correct way such arguments should be handled
(B) reprimand the offenders before the entire staff and explain to all the way such matters should be handled
(C) arbitrarily change the seating arrangement
(D) arrange the seating so that the light is good for the greatest number according to the type of work requiring the best lighting.

51. In attempting to improve the work habits of the

staff, a supervisor's chief concern should be to
(A) assume that correct work habits will develop from employees observing the good habits of others in the group
(B) make scientific time studies of the workmanship of all employees before attempting to correct any work habits
(C) permit each employee to use individuality in performing his assigned tasks so as not to stifle initiative
(D) teach and re-teach the employees to use properly and consistently the methods and tools at hand.

52. In order to properly design a form for office use, of the following, which consideration should come first?
(A) the limit to the number of items to be included
(B) the purpose the form is to fulfill
(C) the expense involved
(D) the necessity for the form.

53. What principle of proper supervisory relationship to his subordinates is suggested to the supervisor by the old saying:
    "Twice I did well, and that I heard never
    "Once I did ill, and that I heard ever!"
(A) to make a continuous fuss over a fault or error
(B) to give credit when due
(C) to make an example of the inefficient worker
(D) to use the inefficient as instruments to spur the efficient to greater effort.

54. When a worker comes to you with an unusual emergency, and you as the supervisor are unable to consult your superior on the handling of the emergency, the best procedure to follow is to
(A) handle the case according to your own judgment without bringing the case to the attention of your superior
(B) tell the worker directly involved to use his or her best judgment in handling the matter
(C) take a particular action and prepare a memorandum to your superior on the case, stating what action has been taken and that you have tried unsuccessfully to get an interview
(D) delay action until your superior can give the matter his attention.

55. If, as a supervisor, you find yourself in a position where your authority is not clear and well defined, the first thing you should do is to

(A) take hold hard and supervise the work and workers strictly
(B) take it easy, regardless of output, in order to be on good terms with the other employees
(C) make an outline of your responsibilities and submit it to your superior for approval
(D) "keeping an eye on the work" until indefiniteness in assigning and announcing your responsibilities is cleared up by your superior.

56. Competent supervisors are "leaders, not ordering but serving their subordinates." The most important proof that a supervisor is carrying out leadership functions in dealing with subordinates is that he or she
(A) maintains complete production records of all subordinates
(B) reminds subordinates of his or her authoritative powers
(C) considers every employee as an important individual and helps him or her to develop in the job
(D) compares the successes and failures of the subordinate with the others with whom he or she works.

57. You are a supervisor in charge of a department. An employee fails to report for work, and the department is exceedingly short of workers. You should first
(A) operate short until other arrangements can be made
(B) notify your supervisor by telephone, and be given advice
(C) hold the entire staff, and notify the Chief Administrator
(D) require everyone to work overtime.

58. If a supervisor has an employee who is willing and tries hard but has consistently proved to be incompetent, the best of the following things to do is to
(A) pay no attention to the case
(B) report the case to superiors
(C) encourage the employee by assigning light duties
(D) continue to give the employee regular work and call him down when he or she fails.

59. Suppose you have just been promoted to administrator in an organization that has been running well. The best way to attain your aims and gain the

good-will of the men working under you would be by initially

(A) trying to instill in each employee an idea of what true efficiency is

(B) ask each employee confidentially what was wrong with the previous administration

(C) continuing the policies of your predecessor, gradually introducing needed changes

(D) immediately revamp the entire department along the proper lines.

60. Suppose that a newly appointed administrator is finding it difficult to organize his work. Of the following, the most appropriate suggestion that could be made in this situation is that the administrator should first

(A) review his workload with a view to simplifying and condensing it

(B) immediately allocate some of his tasks to employees

(C) break the total job into its component parts and plan the time needed for each part

(D) allow an equal amount of time for each required task.

61. Suppose that you have the task of formulating a plan for the purpose of making more efficient the operation of a particular activity. In general, you should pay *least* regard to the

(A) length of time which is consumed in the activity

(B) degree of prestige which will accrue to you resulting from the activity

(C) desirability of providing work schedules for the participants in the activity

(D) number of persons involved in the activity.

62. If a situation arises which to you is not clearly covered by rules and regulations, you should

(A) use your best judgment in the matter

(B) refer the matter to your superior

(C) do as the majority of your subordinates think best

(D) visit your superior and consult with him.

63. For five years a supervisor has been successful in performing his duties. A new employee makes a suggestion concerning a change in procedure. The supervisor should

(A) tell the employee that, in view of the present smooth operations, no changes are necessary

(B) tell the employee that any changes must be made by you the supervisor

(C) give careful consideration to the proposed change

(D) make the change but hold the employee responsible if it works out badly.

64. It comes to the administrator's attention that a particular employee went to his supervisor to discuss a seemingly trivial personal matter. Later the supervisor, who thought the situation humorous, told others in his department about it

(A) the administrator should do nothing, since most of the men enjoyed the joke

(B) the administrator should do nothing since this is the supervisor's business and he or she is in charge of the men

(C) the administrator should do nothing, because the employee should use discretion about the type of thing with which he bothers the supervisor

(D) the administrator should call this situation to the supervisor's attention as violation of supervision in breaking any confidence, no matter how small, which was placed in the supervisor by a subordinate.

65. Occasional outbursts of temper

(A) should be excused in a supervisor

(B) are inexcusable in a supervisor

(C) are to be expected from all employees

(D) are an effective supervisory technique.

66. If you are asked a technical question by one of your subordinates and do not know the answer, you should

(A) attempt to answer it the best you can

(B) tell the worker you do not know the answer but that you will get the information for him

(C) tell the worker that you are too busy to explain at the moment

(D) suggest that the worker not bother you with things he or she can find out for himself or herself.

67. Suppose that an administrator, in reviewing the progress of a probationary employee, tells you that the man does his work well and seems adaptable, but that he just does not seem to cooperate with older staff members. Of the following, the most constructive suggestion that should be made to the administrator at this time is that the

(A) administrator analyze the inadequacies in orientation of the new employee

(B) employee be advised of the desirability of mutual respect among staff members

(C) older members be asked to try to understand the drives and insecurity of a probationary employee

(D) desirability of a transfer of the new man to another department be considered.

68. One of the factors making it difficult for administrators to introduce new methods which will alter procedures that have been in existence for some time is
(A) the tendency of people to dislike something old because it is old
(B) the feeling of distrust which people have for the ideas of "experts"
(C) the nearly universal tendency of all people to dislike change
(D) the tendency of people to change rapidly their likes and dislikes.

69. When presenting a completely new idea to a group of employees the most important principle of learning to be observed is
(A) to relate the new idea to some familiar idea or activity previously learned
(B) to point out how difficult the new idea is to learn
(C) to give the employee printed material to read on the new idea
(D) to break down the new principle into constituent parts before presenting the whole.

70. A new division head, after studying an inspection procedure which has been in use for a long time decided that it was unsatisfactory. He thereupon recommended to the supervisor of the department that the procedure be discontinued and that a new inspection procedure be instituted which made no use of present personnel and ignored the existing procedure. This recommendation is, in general
(A) satisfactory; procedures which have been used for a long time tend to lose their value
(B) unsatisfactory; procedures which have been used for a long time have obviously stood the test of time
(C) satisfactory; when new procedures are instituted it is best to leave no stone unturned
(D) unsatisfactory; plans should make as much use as possible of existing procedures and personnel before requesting new resources.

71. Assume that you have been appointed a supervisor. Of the following, the best justification for learning from the Bureau Chief as much as possible about the subordinates whom you are to supervise is that
(A) personality problems usually disappear with knowledge of individual differences
(B) knowledge of individual characteristics of the workers often aids in the effective handling of them
(C) no supervisor can be effective in his work unless he has a cooperative relationship with his superior
(D) such knowledge will provide the basis for mutual understanding between the supervisor and his subordinates.

72. If an employee's performance is poor, the supervisor should first
(A) tell the entire department about it
(B) record all errors, and recommend dismissal
(C) call attention privately to errors and offer suggestions for improvement
(D) assign only menial tasks involving no responsibility.

73. Of the following the direct way to make it easier for a new employee to remember how a specific piece of work is to be done, the supervisor should
(A) watch the newcomer until there is no possibility of making an error
(B) ask the new employee if he has any questions concerning the work
(C) explain the reasons for doing the work in the manner specified
(D) refer the new worker to selected books on the general subject of the work being done.

74. To settle a dispute or conflict between two employees, which one of the following actions should you take?
(A) have both present their points of view and arguments in a written memorandum and on this basis make your decision
(B) require that the two individuals settle the case between themselves
(C) call each separately, and after hearing their cases presented, decide the issue
(D) bring both in for a conference at the same time and make the decision in their presence.

75. If a supervisor learns that some member of the staff has been given orders by supervisors of other

branches of the department, the best of the following procedures for him to take would be to
- (A) preserve department morale by disregarding the occurrences
- (B) discuss the matter with his or her supervisor
- (C) tell the members of his or her staff to disregard the orders
- (D) tell the supervisors who issued the orders to confine their authority to those under their jurisdiction.

76. When a new employee under your supervision makes an error in his work, it is best to correct the employee
- (A) a few days later
- (B) immediately
- (C) after the same error has been repeated several times
- (D) at the next general meeting of your subordinates without mentioning names.

77. You are in charge of an office in which each member of the staff has a different set of duties, although each has the same title. No member of the staff can perform the duties of any other member of the staff without first receiving extensive training. Assume that it is necessary for one member of the staff to take on, in addition to his regular work, an assignment which any member of the staff is capable of carrying out. The primary consideration which would have the most weight in determining which staff member is to be given the additional assignment is the

- (A) quality of the work performed by the individual members of the staff
- (B) time consumed by individual members of the staff in performing their work
- (C) level of difficulty of the duties being performed by individual members of the staff
- (D) relative importance of the duties being performed by individual members of the staff.

78. Investigation of the high employee turnover in an office reveals that a principal cause of this turnover is the arrogant attitude of the supervisor. The supervisor is otherwise very competent and his office always does a superior job. Of the following, the most advisable course of action for the department to take is to
- (A) assign somebody to assist the supervisor
- (B) have the supervisor brought up on charges
- (C) transfer the supervisor to another office
- (D) try to change the supervisor's attitude.

79. One section has not been able to keep up with the rest of the agency in getting its work out. It is discovered that an employee in that section does very little work. The other employees resent it since it means they have an increased workload. The section head sits in a private office and is not aware of what is going on. Of the following, the most advisable action for the agency to take is to
- (A) arrange for the employees to get more supervision
- (B) discharge the employee who is at fault
- (C) reorganize the entire agency
- (D) transfer the supervisor.

ANSWER KEY

1. B	17. D	33. D	49. A	65. B
2. C	18. C	34. C	50. D	66. B
3. A	19. D	35. D	51. D	67. B
4. C	20. A	36. C	52. B	68. C
5. D	21. C	37. A	53. B	69. A
6. B	22. D	38. A	54. C	70. D
7. D	23. C	39. C	55. C	71. B
8. C	24. D	40. D	56. C	72. C
9. A	25. D	41. B	57. A	73. C
10. A	26. B	42. B	58. B	74. D
11. C	27. B	43. A	59. C	75. B
12. C	28. C	44. B	60. C	76. B
13. A	29. B	45. D	61. B	77. B
14. C	30. A	46. D	62. A	78. D
15. C	31. A	47. B	63. C	79. A
16. A	32. A	48. D	64. D	

EXPLANATORY ANSWERS

1. **(B)** By scheduling work, the administrator knows when to expect completion of each portion of the job, and can take appropriate action if the schedule is not met. This may involve changes in personnel, equipment or procedures, or even the need to revise the schedule in order to meet the absolute deadline. Daily work reports, weekly conferences, or staff realization of the importance of deadlines are not helpful without a pre-determined schedule.

2. **(C)** Competent and vigorous management is possible only if each employee understand exactly what is expected of him or her. When referral to higher authority is needed, staff should know to whom the referral should be made. Discipline is not correctly maintained by slavish adherence to rules which may not be good ones or are inappropriate in certain situations. Unity of command achieved by everyone reporting directly to the chief is impractical. Administrative control is maintained by means of review of reports and inspections of decisions made at lower levels.

3. **(A)** Under the best administrative conditions the problem of the person in authority is to provide the leadership needed to attain the results desired and accept the responsibility for errors made. The administrator may use scientific methods to issue orders, may examine existing rules and regulations for their worth, and may constructively criticize certain procedures and actions, but these are all tools, not the basic problem inherent in the assumption of authority.

4. **(C)** In this question you are asked to indicate the least desirable procedure for an administrator to follow. Avoiding schedules or routines when busy is often neither efficient nor productive because you may be overlooking an essential element of the work.

5. **(D)** An administrator should give an order only after fully considering the consequences, and be prepared to justify the order to superiors, officials in related organizations, and to concerned individuals in the general public if necessary.

6. **(B)** A sound organizational structure exists when the individuals given authority to make decisions are also held responsible for those decisions.

7. **(D)** Span of control refers to the number of persons reporting to one superior. If too many persons report to the same supervisor, an inevitable result is that some work will not be supervised at all, and no one except the supervisor can be held responsible. In organizations where each person specializes in a particular activity, the span of control of the supervisor may rightly be larger

than ordinary because a specialist will probably need less supervision.

8. **(C)** With respect to departmental policies, an administrator's principal role is to make sure that all staff understand and carry out policy uniformly. To do this, the administrator must interpret the policy to staff. An administrator may on occasion review and criticize existing policy, and may be empowered to decide in the case of conflicting policy statements, but these are subordinate to interpreting policy to staff.

9. **(A)** Holding an employee responsible for work done is justified only after the worker is fully trained and has demonstrated proficiency in the assigned tasks.

10. **(A)** The key word in this question is first. A supervisor must first define his or her own position in relation to superiors, subordinates and peers, and to make sure that subordinates know to whom and when they report.

11. **(C)** The most basic duty of any supervisor is to see that the work gets done by making sure that each worker does the portion assigned in a correct and timely fashion. A supervisor should see that rules are enforced, delegate authority judiciously, and attempt to establish and maintain good relations with subordinates, but these are secondary to the correct answer.

12. **(C)** Good administration requires that a supervisor be held responsible for successful completion of a unit's work. It is most important that the promoted appointee recognize this as the chief purpose of the appointment, and accept the fact that the position carries with it the obligation to assume responsibility.

13. **(A)** A ''conscientious supervisor'' is one who believes in the worth of the action he or she takes or the decision made. A good supervisor may work hard, suggest procedural improvements, and get along well with both supervisors and staff, but unless the supervisor is willing to do what he or she believes to be the right thing regardless of possible adverse reactions, the title ''conscientious supervisor'' is not appropriate.

14. **(C)** When a supervisor fails to give each subordinate clear and definite assignments for which the worker will be held responsible, the most likely result will be catastrophe. Workers will quarrel over who does what task, some tasks will be duplicated and others neglected, and work will generally be ineffective because no one will feel responsible for its correctness.

15. **(C)** The leader whose subordinates follow enthusiastically is the one who has earned that enthusiasm. He or she finds remedies for factors causing poor morale, e.g., eliminates unnecessary routine work, has employees understand and participate if possible in making decisions, stresses the importance of the work, shows fairness in his decisions, etc. Enthusiasm cannot be taught to a worker—he or she must absorb it from the leader,

and can be generated only when the supervisor has earned his or her respect and confidence.

16. **(A)** Trial-and-error learning is time-consuming, wasteful, and less efficient than other learning techniques. It may take the worker an excessively long time to arrive at a solution, and this may not be the best, or even a desirable one. It may result in accidents to the worker and damage to the machinery. For these reasons it is best that the supervisor carefully guide the worker towards the desired solution if the trial-and-error method is being utilized.

17. **(D)** The administrator who has to use the force of his authority in order to have staff carry out an idea should re-examine it very carefully because it is highly unlikely that the idea merits acceptance without changes. The best administrator has carefully thought through all the ramifications of his or her ideas, and is able to convince subordinates of the wisdom of the plan because they accept the idea as a good one.

18. **(C)** Grievances and dissatisfaction occur in virtually all agencies, and correct handling of them goes a long way towards administering a unit successfully. The cause is usually inter-personal, and requires a give-and-take between the supervisor and worker. De-humanizing the procedures by requiring only written grievances will often result in making the situation worse. The best way to handle a worker's grievance is to work with him or her to arrive at a solution acceptable to both sides.

19. **(D)** Experience has shown that where an administrator shows favoritism for one or more workers over others, the staff ceases to have respect for, and does not give the supervisor the cooperation, support and team-effort necessary to successfully complete the work.

20. **(A)** The executive who advocates that subordinates make decisions which affect their own work and which they are capable of making, and permits subordinates to participate in planning and other administrative functions finds that this permissiveness tends to generate a higher level of morale in an organization than the executive who leaves little for the subordinates to do or decide other than the actual work performance.

21. **(C)** Basically, studies have determined that most executives can function equally well in most organizations, even those performing diverse functions. With this in mind many municipalities and government agencies have implemented the rotation of executive staff.

22. **(D)** The primary responsibility of any executive is to get the job done correctly and in a timely fashion. As such, a unit head must see that the same errors do not crop up again. Locating and reprimanding the person who made the errors are secondary responsibilities. Recording each worker's errors in their personnel record is a questionable personnel practice and may well be counterproductive.

23. **(C)** Of the possible correct answers the only reasonable solution given is to have another employee read the rough copy, and have the typist make the needed corrections on the final copy. For the supervisor to read the rough copy detracts from the larger responsibilities of supervision. Glancing through rough copy catches only obvious errors. Rotating assignments among volunteers doesn't ensure that the work will be done correctly.

24. **(D)** Administrators may be forced to decentralize activities extensively but must keep in mind that these activities must be controlled and coordinated so that desired end results can be achieved.

25. **(D)** Since leadership is the most desirable quality of an administrator, it is this which ranks uppermost in the minds of his or her superiors when choosing one. The quotation does not say that administrative ability is the supervisor's most valuable asset. It does not imply that good leaders generally lack other administrative qualities, nor that anything can be substituted for the lack of leadership ability.

26. **(B)** An effective administrator must be able to anticipate problems before they occur and must be more or less ready with solutions when they do. In this way many problems can be avoided by the proper timely corrective action.

27. **(B)** The paragraph concerns the problem of good personnel relations which in a large part depends upon an open communication between administration and the rank and file. In the absence of communication of information concerning an agency's activities the rank and file will tend to lose faith in the organization.

28. **(C)** The important thing implied in this passage is that essential information should be made available whether or not the staff expresses a desire for it.

29. **(B)** The reason for the transition towards a more open policy of information stems from administrative realization that a well informed employee is an efficient employee. A worker who wants to know more about the intentions and motives of his or her organization displays a praiseworthy attitude. The absence of information will breed an attitude of mistrust among the workers.

30. **(A)** The basic thrust of the paragraph is to explain how mutual confidence, based on understanding, is the foundation of good personnel relations.

31. **(A)** A supervisor is not usually trained to ascertain who is likely to develop maladjustments, and it is not his or her function to do so. Moreover, such policy may create problems which may never have existed.

32. **(A)** The question asks for the first step to be taken. Mr. Smith must first be given the opportunity to explain the whole matter. A supervisor should not assume after

hearing only part of the problem that he knows it is a trivial matter. Further, giving Mr. Smith the opportunity to fully explain encourages him to believe you are genuinely interested in helping to solve his problem.

33. **(D)** A supervisor who only praises when he or she criticizes negates the value of the praise. A good supervisor knows that employees appreciate praise when it is due, and accept criticism when it is justified. Both praise and criticism are generally given at the same time in the course of an evaluation of total performance and is good supervisory technique, but in the regular course of a unit's activities, the good supervisor should judiciously give praise by itself.

34. **(C)** First the supervisor must find out why the employee is irritable. Only when the cause of the behavior is known can corrective action be taken.

35. **(D)** You are asked to interpret the quotation given. Answers A, B, and C may be true, but they are not indicated by the quotation because all it says is that where tasks afford no chance for self-expression, they become monotonous.

36. **(C)** The quotation states that improvement and the development of proper attitudes are essential attitudes. This implies that improving the worker's skills is only part of the supervisor's job in developing good work habits.

37. **(A)** The desire for approval and recognition for competence is virtually universal and generally accepted as the greatest incentive for producing good work. Use of the techniques of instilling fear, encouraging rivalry, and constantly watching employees work may be the correct procedure to follow in motivating some employees, but they are not universally correct. Each worker is an individual and must be motivated in the best way possible depending upon his or her individual characteristics.

38. **(A)** Employees must understand that all jobs have routine aspects, but if a job is totally routine in nature, the intelligent and interested employee should be given work that will retain his or her interest, and give the agency the benefit of his or her intelligence and interest.

39. **(C)** In order to maintain good morale of all staff members, a supervisor must be counted on by subordinates for the fairness and lack of partiality in all judgments. Chastising inefficient workers and sarcastic criticism, does not boost morale; praising a good worker in front of others improves that worker's morale, but not necessarily that of others.

40. **(D)** A visibly upset employee who comes to the supervisor should first be helped to calm down so that the worker and supervisor together can rationally discuss the cause of the agitation and jointly try to resolve the problem. Refusal by the supervisor to discuss the matter until the worker is calm may cause resentment, and lead

the worker to find an unsatisfactory solution in other ways. Nothing in the question indicates that the personal life of the worker is the cause of the lack of emotional control. Immediately deciding the matter in the way the employee favors is unwise since it may not be the correct solution.

41. **(B)** The most important task of any supervisor is to get the work done well and on time, and to do this work must be properly assigned and must be followed up to see that it is done correctly. The other possible answers can help him or her to fulfill that primary responsibility.

42. **(B)** A supervisor in the situation of having a trained staff with a normal workload finds that the chief task is to maintain the interest of staff in their work and the quality and quantity of work to be completed. Giving continual directions to staff, revising rules needlessly, and criticizing staff unnecessarily may have counterproductive results.

43. **(A)** Under the circumstances, the immediate need is to assign new workers, and have them receive the training needed to do the work. Immediate is the key word in the question. Building and maintaining morale is an ongoing task of the supervisor, and is not an immediate need brought about by the addition of staff.

44. **(B)** Work-related suggestions submitted by employees are a sign of the staff's interest and enthusiasm, and should generally be considered as soon as feasible. In the situation presented, the worker's suggestion has both good and bad points, and merits full consideration and possibly discussions with your superiors. It therefore should first be fully discussed with the employee so that you are sure you know what he or she is suggesting, and the worker is assured that you are fully considering the idea.

45. **(D)** The good supervisor first examines his or her own activities. Has the supervisor failed to organize the steps in the procedures correctly? Has the supervisor organized the office layout in a way that wastes time in getting the work from one worker to the next? Only when a supervisor is sure that the routine set up is correct should he or she investigate other possible reasons for the wasted time.

46. **(D)** The supervisor cannot follow the axiom, "Do as I say and not as I do." Many techniques can be used to insure compliance with regulations, but unless the supervisor leads the way, there can be little assurance that staff will obey them.

47. **(B)** Of the possible answers, only thorough, patient teaching will help develop a worker's understanding of the job and skill in performing it. Insisting on high standards, using "trial and error", and "driving the learner" will not help understanding.

48. **(D)** Corrective interviews are best given in private to avoid embarrassing the reprimanded worker and other

employees . The supervisor should adopt a firm manner, tell the worker what is wrong, why it is wrong, and how it should be corrected. Most workers will accept criticism and profit by it, if the reasons are valid, and the supervisor carefully explains that the corrections are for the purpose of improving the unit's work.

49. **(A)** The best way to teach an employee a new procedure is to let him or her read the details of the new procedure, make sure it is understood, and then allow the worker to try to follow it under your supervision and review. Watching others, even an experienced worker, may result in either failure to really understand the procedure, or the worker picking up wrong methods. In addition, the experienced worker employs "shortcuts" which the learner will not really understand or be able to apply judiciously when on his own. A worker can only truly learn by doing.

50. **(D)** The supervisor's responsibility is to arrange office seating in the best possible manner for accomplishing the unit's work while considering individual desires and needs of employees. If arguments occur over the arrangement of seats, the supervisor should settle the matter in as fair a manner as possible. In this situation, the seating should be arranged to give the best light to the workers who need it most, and at the same time provide as much light to as many workers as possible.

51. **(D)** For a supervisor to improve work habits of subordinates, it is necessary to teach them to use proper methods at all times. It is also necessary to periodically follow up to make sure they are correctly using tools and following designated procedures, and retraining workers who have not used designated procedures or have fallen into bad habits. Correct work habits must be taught; they cannot be absorbed by watching how others do a job.

52. **(B)** The first thing to consider is the purpose for which the form will be used. Number of items needed, cost factors, and necessity of the form are later considerations, based on the purpose for which the form is needed.

53. **(B)** The quotation laments the worker never praised for good work, but always criticized for poor work. The basic supervisory principle involved is that credit should be given when due. The wrong answers are concerned with the opposite situation—handling inefficiency.

54. **(C)** Handling emergency situations as soon as they occur is the responsibility of the supervisor. In most cases the advice of a superior is necessary or desirable, and the superior should always be advised of the occurrence if available. The best procedure in this instance is to make a decision regarding the action to be taken, take the action, and then fully inform your supervisor in writing, including the fact that you had been unable to obtain his or her advice before making the decision.

55. **(C)** No supervisor can correctly carry out the job unless the full extent of his or her authority is clear. If the

authority is not clear, the most responsible thing to do is attempt to make it clear as soon as possible, that is, outline what you think to be your duties and responsibilities, and bring it to your supervisor for approval.

56. **(C)** A competent leader who serves his or her subordinates is the one who helps them to understand their duties and teaches them the best way to do their jobs. Such a leader knows and appreciates that each of us is different, with different needs and goals, different learning skills and duties, and instructs based on these individual characteristics.

57. **(A)** In these circumstances a supervisor is expected to do as best he or she can with what is at hand. So, as a short term solution, the supervisor is expected to function with the personnel available.

58. **(B)** A supervisor is responsible for seeing that the work gets done properly, and that all employees contribute to the unit's success. It does no good to ignore the employee's inability to handle the work, assign the employee to lighter duties while not adjusting his pay accordingly, or fruitlessly chastise a well-meaning employee who is incompetent and obviously in the wrong job. The only choice is the difficult one of reporting the matter to your superior, who should handle the matter in the manner which will best help the agency fulfill its responsibilities.

59. **(C)** A newly appointed administrator who takes over an existing organizational unit should maintain the status quo until he or she has fully studied the situation, and gained the employees' confidence. Making major changes right off the bat may result in unnecessary or undesirable changes, will confuse employees accustomed to the existing way of doing things, and perhaps cause them to mistrust your motives and cause them to fear for their jobs. When you have gained full knowledge and have earned the support of your subordinates, you can institute changes slowly.

60. **(C)** The best way for a new administrator to organize his or her work is to first determine just what the work consists of, break the total work down into its components, and determine how much time is needed to accomplish each part. After this is accomplished, the administrator can review the work in detail, and assign the priority of each task.

61. **(B)** You should consider the time element of the activity, the need for work schedules for each participant, and the number of persons needed for the activity. The degree of prestige you may acquire should not be an important part of your thinking because you are merely doing the job to which you were assigned.

62. **(A)** Sometimes a supervisor must act on his or her own using his or her best judgment. The use of judgment is an integral part of the job of a supervisor. There are no rules or regulations to tell the supervisor when to step in and use his or her best judgment.

63. **(C)** No matter how successful an operation has been, there is always room for improvement, and no one has a monopoly on good ideas. Since most successful supervisors look to their subordinates for constructive ways to improve existing activities, a new employee often has the "fresh eyes" to see the need or desirability for change in a particular activity. Once the new idea has been accepted, it becomes the supervisor's responsibility to accept the consequences if the new idea fails to work out well.

64. **(D)** A supervisor must respect the confidentiality of personal matters discussed with subordinates, whether or not the matter appears trivial to the supervisor. What appears trivial to one person may be a serious matter to another. An administrator who learns of a breach of confidentiality by a lower-ranking supervisor would be remiss in his responsibilities if he or she failed to point this out to the erring supervisor.

65. **(B)** A supervisor should make every effort to never lose his or her temper. A supervisor who is even tempered gains the respect of subordinates and furthermore, an even demeanor will encourage subordinates to act in a similar manner. One of the most important qualities of leadership is temperament. Note that choices A and B are direct opposites. When there are two choices directly opposite almost invariably one of these choices is correct.

66. **(B)** A subordinate who comes to you with a technical question is entitled to an answer. A good supervisor has trained staff to first seek to find the correct answer themselves, and if they still cannot solve a problem to come to you. If you do not know the answer, say so, and say you will try to find out the answer. Staff will appreciate your frankness and willingness to learn. No one has the answers to everything.

67. **(B)** As the situation is described, the problem is with the probationer, for there is no indication that the older employees are unwilling to cooperate with him. The best recommendation you can make is to have the probationer advised of the positive advantages of teamwork and mutual respect in accomplishing a unit's activities. The probationer should be shown the advantages that will accrue to him by learning from more experienced workers. You do not want to lose the services of an otherwise good employee by transferring the individual to another part of the agency, where his attitude towards older workers will continue to hamper his effectiveness. The transfer will not solve the basic problem.

68. **(C)** Almost all workers dislike and distrust any changes whether they are instituted by regular staff or by newly established procedures. This fact makes it difficult to institute any change even if it makes the worker's job easier.

69. **(A)** People learn a new idea more easily if they can relate it to something they have previously learned. This

is the cardinal principle to follow when attempting to teach workers a new idea.

70. **(D)** The fact that a procedure has been in effect for a long period of time does not mean it is the best procedure or even a truly effective one. A new division head has the right and the duty to examine existing procedures and look to improve them. When a procedure has been working and staff become trained to use it, however, a supervisor would be in error to dismiss the entire procedure and institute wholesale changes. Parts of the existing procedure may still be effective.

71. **(B)** The good supervisor understands the individual characteristics of each staff member, and uses this information to get the best possible performance from each of them. This knowledge will not change an individual's behavior, but it will help the supervisor deal with it. Obtaining this information may or may not affect the supervisor's relationship with the superior, and will not provide subordinates with a corresponding knowledge of the supervisor's personality, but it may help superiors avoid pitfalls in handling situations with staff.

72. **(C)** When an employee's performance is poor, the supervisor should try to have the situation corrected. The first thing to do is to have a private conversation with the worker. The best criticism is constructive in nature, where errors are pointed out and suggestions for correction are discussed. Stronger methods may be necessary if this solution fails to result in improved performance.

73. **(C)** The best way to help subordinates remember how to do a specific piece of work is to make sure they understand why the work should be done, why it is easier, safer, faster, etc. Watching the worker do it correctly does not guarantee that it will always be done that way, and may be an inefficient waste of the supervisor's time. Answers B and D are just training devices or techniques that may aid the learning process, but only if the worker fully understands why a procedure should be done.

74. **(D)** The better writer may profit from the decision if both presented written memoranda. To have them settle it themselves is avoiding the issue. Since each worker is likely to exaggerate the facts, it is likely that the true facts of the situation would not come to light if both parties were not present when their cases were presented.

75. **(B)** One of an administrator's primary tasks is to clearly define and limit the extent of responsibility and authority assigned to each supervisor. In the situation presented there may be a failure by higher authorities to successfully outline to each supervisor the extent of his or her individual responsibilities and authority. Your best action is to bring the matter to the attention of your superior.

76. **(B)** A supervisor should correct the errors of new employees as soon as they are spotted. The employee is learning the job and errors and unsatisfactory ways of doing things should be corrected at the beginning rather than after they have become part of his or her work pattern. Individual errors by new workers should be pointed out to them in person, not presented in a generalized way or at staff meetings where the new worker may not realize it is his or her error that is being discussed.

77. **(B)** It is strictly a matter of assigning the work to the individual who has the time to do it because all other considerations are equal.

78. **(D)** As a long term matter, an attempt should be made to change the supervisor's attitude. Organizations should grow, and the supervisor's attitude will hamper this growth. You as the supervisor's superior must change the attitude of the supervisor.

79. **(A)** The section head is at fault for not knowing what is going on under his supervision. This must be changed at once even if it takes moving the supervisor out of his private office. A supervisor who is not fully aware of the activities of his subordinates is ineffective.

OPERATING EFFICIENCY

Each question has four suggested answers, lettered A, B, C, and D. Decide which one is the best answer and on the sample answer sheet (all answer sheets are at the front of the book) find the question number and darken the area, with a soft pencil, which corresponds to the answer that you have selected.

1. Eliminating slack in work assignments is
   (A) speed-up
   (B) time study
   (C) motion study
   (D) efficient management.

2. Suppose that you have been directed to submit a recommendation as to the advisability of having your department utilize computing machines, to be operated by office appliance operators, for work now performed manually by clerks. Of the following, the factor which should be least influential in determining the nature of the recommendation to be made by you is the
   (A) initial and operating costs of the machines
   (B) adequacy with which the clerks displaced by the office appliance operators can be assigned to other work
   (C) seniority rights of the clerk
   (D) relative accuracy of the two methods.

3. Suppose that you have the task of formulating a plan for the purpose of making more efficient the operation of a particular activity. In general, you should pay least regard to
   (A) the length of time which is consumed in the activity
   (B) the degree of prestige which will accrue to you
   (C) the value of the end product resulting from the activity
   (D) the desirability of providing work schedules for the participants in the activity.

4. In developing a system for controlling the production of a bureau, the bureau chief should give consideration to reducing the fluctuations in the bureau's work load. Of the following, the technique that is generally *least* helpful in reducing fluctuations in work load is
   (A) staffing the bureau so that it can handle peak loads
   (B) maintaining a controlled backlog of work
   (C) regulating the timing of work routed to the bureau
   (D) changing the order of steps in work processes.

5. As part of his program to simplify clerical procedures, the chief of the records management division had decided to make an analysis of the forms used by his agency and to establish a system of forms control. The chief has assigned the assistant bureau chief to perform the bulk of the work in connection with this project. This assistant will receive part-time help from four subordinate employees. Of the following actions the bureau chief may take in planning the work on this project, the most appropriate one is for the chief to
   (A) have the plans drawn up by the assistant and then submitted for final approval to the four part-time subordinates before work on the project is begun
   (B) have the assistant work with the chief in drawing up the plans and then present the plans to the four part-time subordinates for their comments
   (C) join with the five employees as a committee to formulate the plans for the project
   (D) personally prepare the plans and then submit the plans for approval to all five employees who are to work on the project.

6. Suppose that you are in charge of a stenographic bureau composed of ten stenographers and typists. The bureau's average daily output consists of N pages with a daily total of K lines. Of the following, the most accurate statement is that the average
   (A) daily output in number of words equals the product of N times K
   (B) daily output in number of words equals the product of K times N
   (C) number of lines per page equals the quotient of K divided by N
   (D) number of lines typed per five-day week equals the product of N times K times 5.

7. "Functional centralization is the bringing together of employees doing the same kind of work and performing similar tasks." Of the following, the one which is not an important advantage flowing from the introduction of functional centralization in a large city department is that
   (A) inter-bureau communication and traffic is reduced
   (B) standardized work procedures are introduced more easily
   (C) inequalities in working conditions are reduced
   (D) adjustment of work flow to employee vacation or absence is facilitated.

8. You are called upon to submit suggestions with regard to the reorganization of the bureaus in your department so that the business of the department can be carried on more smoothly. Of the following, the chief organizational principle in accomplishing such a purpose is that
   (A) the widest degree of latitude must be given each bureau chief in his own bureau
   (B) the mailing, filing and supply bureaus must be centrally located in relation to the other bureaus
   (C) each bureau, while distinct, must be able to work in harmony with the others so as to attain common objectives
   (D) there should be an inverse relationship between the number of bureaus and the number of departmental functions.

9. Of the following, the least likely to help in achieving coordination between several bureau units is

   (A) a study of the flow through the units, of work on the various materials and problems handled by the department
   (B) time and motion studies of the operations of the employees in the bureau
   (C) monthly reports of each unit on the work performed and the work on hand remaining to be done
   (D) a periodic conference of the heads of all the units on their problems in coordinating the work of the department.

10. "The data prove that an increase in the number of clerks performing filing work results in an increased cost per item filed." On the basis of these data, we can be certain that
    (A) if filing costs per item filed increase, it is caused by an increase in the number of clerks filing
    (B) if filing costs per item filed decrease, the number of clerks filing cannot be increasing
    (C) if the number of clerks filing is changed, the unit cost of filing will change
    (D) if the number of clerks filing is decreased, the cost per item filed will decrease.

11. "Each unit either has sufficient space assigned to it or it has not. No unit which has insufficient space assigned to it has neglected to ask for additional space." From these data we can state
    (A) units with sufficient space have not asked for additional space
    (B) only units which have sufficient space may not have asked for additional space
    (C) nothing about the relationship between the need for additional space and requests made for additional space
    (D) all units which have requested additional space have insufficient space.

12. Of the following types of work, the one for which a manual process is most usually to be preferred over a mechanized process is one in which the transactions are very
    (A) numerous
    (B) similar
    (C) dissimilar
    (D) predictable.

13. The one of the following which does *not* require definition when setting up a work measurement system is the

(A) level of work accomplishment at which to measure
(B) work unit in which to measure
(C) time unit by which to measure
—(D) acceptable quota for each activity.

14. During a discussion of the time unit that would be appropriate to measure employee-time in a work measurement program in a city department, the man-day was suggested. This unit is
 (A) satisfactory; record keeping will be kept to a minimum
 (B) unsatisfactory; it will be difficult to verify the unit against official time records
 (C) satisfactory; it will be easy to verify the unit against official time records
 —(D) unsatisfactory; its use will unnecessarily complicate record keeping.

15. As part of a space layout survey, an administrator instructed his subordinates to study the flow of work and sequence of operating procedures. The administrator's major purpose in doing this was to determine
 —(A) the physical distribution and movement of personnel, material and equipment
 (B) the amount of space which is available and the amount of space which will be required
 (C) the order in which the component steps in the different procedures are performed
 (D) how the distribution of personnel to various organization units is related to their space requirements.

16. Assume that you have broken a complex job into simpler and smaller components. After you have assigned a component to each employee, should you proceed to teach employee a number of alternative methods for doing this job?
 (A) Yes; the more methods for performing a job an employee knows, the more chance there is that he will choose the one best suited to his abilities
 (B) No; experienced employees should be permitted to decide how to perform the jobs assigned to them
 —(C) No; a single method for each job should be decided upon and taught
 (D) Yes; the employees will have greater interest in their jobs.

17. "The first few times a procedure is carried through, a close check should be kept of all work times." The primary reason for this is to
 —(A) permit revision of schedules
 (B) determine if the employees understand the procedure
 (C) evaluate the problems which may have been presented by the new procedure
 (D) determine the efficiency of the employees.

18. The new head of a central filing unit, after studying a procedure in use, decided that it was unsatisfactory. He thereupon drew up an entirely new procedure which made no use of and ignored the existing procedure. This plan of action is, in general
 (A) satisfactory; a new broom sweeps clean
 —(B) unsatisfactory; any plan should use available resources to the utmost before resorting to new creation
 (C) satisfactory; it is usually less time-consuming to construct a new plan than to remedy an old one
 (D) unsatisfactory; before deciding that the existing procedure was unusable he should have requested that an independent, unbiased agency study the problem.

Answer question 19 on the basis of the following paragraph:

"Production planning is mainly a process of synthesis. As a basis for the positive act of bringing complex production elements properly together, however, analysis is necessary, especially if improvement is to be made in an existing organization. The necessary analysis requires customary means of orientation and preliminary fact gathering—with emphasis, however, on the recognition of administrative goals and of the relationship among work steps."

19. The entire process described is primarily one of
 — (A) taking apart, examining and recombining
 (B) deciding what changes are necessary, making the changes and checking on their value
 (C) fact finding so as to prove the necessary orientation
 (D) discovering just where the emphasis in production should be placed and then modifying the existing procedure so that it is placed properly.

20. The one of the following which is *not* an essential element of an integrated reporting system for work-measurement is a
    (A) uniform record form for accumulating data and instructions for its maintenance
    (B) procedure for routing reports upward through the organization and routing summaries downward
    (C) looseleaf revisable manual which contains all procedural materials that are reasonably permanent and have a substantial reference value
    (D) method for summarizing, analyzing and presenting data from several reports.

21. The type of data which would be most useful in determining if an increase in the length of rest periods is followed by an increased rate of production is data which would indicate that
    (A) decrease in the total production never follows an increase in the length of the rest period
    (B) increase in the total production never follows an increase in the length of the rest period
    (C) increase in the rate of production never follows a decrease in the length of the rest period
    (D) decrease in the total production may follow a decrease in the length of the rest period.

22. In a division of a department, private secretaries were assigned to members of the technical staff since each required a secretary who was familiar with his particular field and who could handle various routine matters without referring to anyone. Other members of the staff depended for their dictation and typing work upon a small pool consisting of two stenographers and two typists. Because of turnover and the difficulty of recruiting new stenographers and typists, the pool had to be discontinued. Of the following, the most satisfactory way to provide stenographic and typing service for the division is to
    (A) organize the private secretaries into a decentralized pool under the direction of a supervisor to whom non-technical staff members would send requests for stenographic and typing assistance
    (B) organize the private secretaries into a central pool under the direction of a supervisor to whom all staff members would send requests for stenographic and typing assistance
    (C) train clerks as typists and typists as stenographers
    (D) relieve stenographers and typists of jobs that can be done by messengers or clerks.

23. "A reorganization of the bureau to provide for a stenographic pool instead of individual unit stenographers will result in more stenographic help being available to each unit when it is required, and consequently will result in greater productivity for each unit. An analysis of the space requirements shows that setting up a stenographic pool will require a minimum of 400 square feet of good space. In order to obtain this space, it will be necessary to reduce the space available for technical personnel, resulting in lesser productivity for each unit." On the basis of the above discussion, it can be stated that in order to obtain greater productivity for each unit
    (A) a stenographic pool should be set up
    (B) further analysis of the space requirement should be made
    (C) it is not certain as to whether or not a stenographic pool should be set up
    (D) a stenographic pool should not be set up.

24. Assume that you are studying the results of mechanizing several hand operations. The type of data which would be most useful in proving that an increase in mechanization is followed by a lower cost of operation is data which show that
    (A) in some cases a lower cost of operation was not preceded by an increase in mechanization
    (B) in no case was a higher cost of operation preceded by a decrease in mechanization
    (C) in some cases an increase in mechanization was followed by a decrease in cost of operation
    (D) in no case was a higher cost of operation preceded by an increase in mechanization.

25. Suppose that you have broken a complex job into its smaller components before making assignments to the employees under your jurisdiction. Of the following, the least advisable procedure to follow from that point is to
    (A) give each employee a picture of the importance of his work for the success of the total job

(B) establish a definite line of work flow and responsibility

(C) post a written memorandum of the best method for performing each job

(D) teach a number of alternative methods for doing each job.

26. Some organizations attempt to keep a constant backlog of work. This procedure is usually
    (A) undesirable; reports are not ready when they are needed
    (B) desirable; it tends to insure continuity of work flow
    (C) undesirable; it tends to keep the employees under constant pressure
    (D) desirable; it tends to keep the employees under constant pressure.

27. A supervisor, in assigning a worker to the job, generally follows the policy of fitting the worker to the job. This procedure is
    (A) undesirable; the job should be fitted to the worker
    (B) desirable; primary emphasis should be on the work to be accomplished
    (C) undesirable; the policy does not consider human values
    (D) desirable; setting up a definite policy and following it permits careful analysis.

28. "The flow of work in an organization may be divided and channeled according to either a serial method or a parallel method. Under the serial method, the work moves through a single channel with each job progressing step by step through various work stations where a worker at each station completes a particular step of the job. Under the parallel method, the jobs are distributed among a number of workers, each worker completing all the steps of a job." The most accurate of the following statements regarding these two methods of dividing the flow of work is that
    (A) the training or break-in time necessary for workers to acquire processing skills is generally shorter under the parallel method
    (B) the serial method enables the workers to obtain a fuller understanding of the significance of their work
    (C) the parallel method tends to minimize the need for control devices to keep track of individual jobs in process

(D) flexibility in the use of available staff is generally increased under the serial method.

29. "Some subdivision of work is imperative in large-scale operation. However, in subdividing work the supervisor should adopt the methods that have the greatest number of advantages and the fewest disadvantages." The one of the following that is most likely to result from subdivision of work is
    (A) measuring work performed by employees is made more difficult
    (B) authority and responsibility for the performance of particular operations are not clearly defined
    (C) standardizing work processes is made more difficult
    (D) work is delayed in passing between employees and between operating units.

30. "Savings of 20 per cent or more in clerical operating costs can often be achieved by improvement of the physical conditions under which office work is performed." In general, the most valid of the following statements regarding physical conditions is that
    (A) conference rooms should have more light than mail rooms
    (B) the tops of desks should be glossy rather than dull
    (C) noise is reflected more by hard-surfaced materials than by soft or porous materials
    (D) yellow is a more desirable wall color for offices receiving an abundance of sunlight.

31. "An important aid in good office management is knowledge on the part of subordinates of the significance of their work." The possession of such knowledge by an employee will probably least *affect* his or her
    (A) interest in his work
    (B) understanding of the relationship between the work of his/her unit and that of other units
    (C) willingness to cooperate with other employees
    (D) ability to undertake assignments requiring special skills.

32. Before discussing a proposed office layout, the administrative officer stated, "We intend to have a minimum number of private offices. We will

assign private offices only where quiet is deemed essential or confidential conferences are required.'' The one of the following which is usually the most valid reason for this rule is that it
(A) permits proper placing of employees who deal with the public
(B) makes clerical supervision easier
(C) tends to ensure that the work of each unit will flow continually forward within itself
(D) allows placing complementary units close together.

33. Assuming that dictating equipment is not available, of the following, the situation in which it would be most desirable to establish a central stenographic unit is one in which the unit would serve
(A) ten correspondence clerks assigned to full-time positions answering correspondence of a large government department
(B) seven members of a government Commission heading a large department
(C) seven heads of bureaus in a government department consisting of 250 employees
(D) fifty investigators in a large department.

34. A statement concerning the vari-type machine which is true is
(A) it can be set to space out each line so that both margins are perfectly square and even, just as in a book
(B) it is much easier for a good typist
(C) it is something like a linotype, since it takes molten metal and converts it into lines of type for printing purposes
(D) letters and other types or ordinary correspondence cannot be done on this machine.

35. You are given a new assignment and are put in charge of a reproducing unit in a large department. Many expensive reproducing machines are used in your unit. Upon study of your breakage reports, you note that serious breakages are constantly occurring. You believe that the employees may not realize the expense involved and have a tendency to be careless. Of the following, it is best for you first to
(A) bring up on charges the person or persons responsible for the next few breakages which occur
(B) call a staff meeting and reprimand strongly the individuals responsible for the breakages

(C) gradually turn your staff over by transferring the old employees and bringing in new people
(D) put a small plate on each machine giving the cost of the machine, such as "This machine costs $2100. Its careful use will be appreciated.''

36. If you wanted to check on the accuracy of the filing in your unit, you would
(A) check all the files thoroughly at regular intervals
(B) watch the clerks while they were filing
(C) glance through filed papers at random
(D) inspect thoroughly a small section of the files at random.

37. The automatic system of filing is a combination of the
(A) alphabetic and numerical systems
(B) alphabetic and subject systems
(C) numerical and subject systems
(D) chronological and geographical systems.

38. Of the following, the least desirable office layout is
(A) obsolete office equipment should be placed in the rear of the office
(B) not more than two desks should be placed side by side
(C) files should be placed against walls and railings
(D) heavy safes should be located close to the walls or columns to eliminate as much strain as possible on the beams.

39. "Instead of directing his attention solely toward devising new systems and procedures for performing established clerical operations, the alert office manager carefully studies these operations with a view to determining the value that accrues to the organization from their performance.'' Of the following, the most valid implication of this quotation is that
(A) established clerical operations may not be of sufficient benefit to the organization to justify their continuance
(B) devising new systems of performing clerical operations is no longer the function of the office manager
(C) the performance of established clerical op-

erations usually brings little or no direct benefit to an organization

(D) devising better ways of performing a necessary clerical task may be of no value to an organization.

40. The competent supervisor realizes that procedures which have been followed for a considerable length of time can frequently be reconstructed and improved. He knows that charts, or diagrams, are often of inestimable value in bringing out forcibly and visibly the outstanding defects in a procedure. Of the following types of charts, the one which would ordinarily be of most value to a supervisor making a study of the clerical procedures in his unit is

(A) an organization chart

(B) a circle or pie chart

(C) a flow or process chart

(D) a bar or column chart.

41. Suppose that the employees in your unit are required to perform a great deal of computation involving a large amount of addition and subtraction. Since accuracy is more important than speed in the work of your unit, employees are required to check all the figures used in the computations before turning in their work. Of the following machines, the one which would be most practicable for the work of your unit is a

(A) listing adding machine

(B) comptometer

(C) punch card tabulating machine

(D) billing machine.

42. Suppose that the supplies code in your office has been mislaid. However, you know that the following codes mean the indicated machines and locations

Xa—typewriter in the Secretary's office

Yb—computing machine in the office of the Chief Clerk

Zd—mimeograph machine in the Printing Division

Wb—calculating machine in the office of the Chief Clerk

From the information given above, you can determine that the proper code for a typewriter in the Printing Division is (Note there are twelve options to this question.)

(A) Xa

(B) Xd

(C) Yb

(D) Za

(E) Zd

(F) Wb

(G) Xb

(H) Ya

(I) Yd

(J) Zb

(K) Wa

(L) Wd

43. "Carbon copies of correspondence should always remain attached to the original letter until the letter is signed. They will then be distributed to the proper places." Such a procedure as described in this quotation is

(A) wise because each carbon copy should be signed before filing

(B) wise because it minimizes the danger of filing copies of correspondence which never were approved and mailed

(C) unwise because it is unnecessary for every carbon copy of a letter to be signed

(D) unwise because such a procedure forces an unnecessary delay in the filing of correspondence.

44. Natural illumination is least necessary in

(A) an executive office

(B) storage room

(C) a central stenographic bureau

(D) a conference room.

45. You are assigned to review the procedures in an office in order to recommend improvements to the Commissioner directly. You go into an office performing seven routine operations in the processing of one type of office form. The question you should first ask yourself in your study of any one of these operations is

(A) Can it be simplified?

(B) Is it necessary?

(C) Is it performed in proper order or should its position in the procedure be changed?

(D) Is the equipment for doing it satisfactory?

46. "Analysis and simplification of office procedures are functions that should be conducted in all offices and on a continuing basis. These functions may be performed by the line supervisor, by staff methods specialists, or by outside consultants on methods analysis." An appraisal of these three methods of assigning responsibility for improving office procedures reveals that the *least* accurate of the following statements is that

(A) outside consultants employed to simplify office procedures frequently bring with them a vast amount of previous experience as well as a fresh viewpoint

(B) line supervisors usually lack the special training which effective procedure analysis work requires

(C) continuity of effort and staff cooperation can better be secured by periodically employed consultants than by a permanent staff of methods analysts

(D) the reason many line supervisors fail to modernize procedures is that the supervisor is too often over-burdened with operating responsibilities.

47. "An important aid in good office management is knowledge on the part of subordinates of the significance of their work." The possession of such knowledge by an employee will probably *least* affect his

(A) interest in his work

(B) understanding of the relationship between the work of his unit and that of other units

(C) willingness to cooperate with other employees

(D) ability to undertake assignments requiring special skills.

48. "In planning the layout of office space, the office supervisor should bear in mind that one large room is a more efficient operating unit than the same number of square feet split up into smaller rooms." Of the following, the least valid basis for the preceding statement is that in the large room

(A) better light and ventilation are possible

(B) flow of work between employees is more direct

(C) supervision and control are more easily maintained

(D) time and motion studies are easier to conduct.

49. The principles of scientific office management are most frequently applied by government office supervisors in

(A) maintaining flexibility in hiring and firing

(B) developing improved pay scales

(C) standardizing clerical practices and procedures

(D) revising organizational structure.

50. The one of the following factors to which the bureau head should attach *least* importance in deciding on the advisability of substituting machine for manual operations in a given area of office work is the

(A) need for accuracy in the work

(B) relative importance of the work

(C) speed with which the work must be completed

(D) volume of work.

51. Of the following wall colors, the one which will reflect the greatest amount of light, other things being equal, is

(A) buff

(B) light gray

(C) light blue

(D) brown.

52. The number of foot-candles of illumination usually considered best for general office work is

(A) 10

(B) 30

(C) 60

(D) 90.

53. The most desirable relative humidity in an office is

(A) 30%

(B) 50%

(C) 70%

(D) 90%.

54. When several pieces of correspondence are filed in the same folder they are usually arranged

(A) according to subject

(B) numerically

(C) in the order in which they are received

(D) alphabetically.

55. Of the following, the least desirable method for a bureau head to use in handling letter responses to inquiries is to

(A) answer letters in order of their receipt

(B) refer briefly in the reply to the letter being answered

(C) use mimeographed forms for answering questions frequently asked

(D) vary the length of the reply according to the circumstances.

56. Suppose that a departmental officer wanted advice from you on how to reduce the possibility of errors in the preparation of the departmental payroll. Of the following, the technique that is not only likely to be effective but is practicable as well is to
    (A) have two clerks independently prepare the payrolls, and have a third person compare the work of the first two
    (B) have one person prepare the payroll and have a second person check in every detail the work of the first
    (C) look over the payroll to ascertain whether entries appear reasonable and spot check those points which are most likely to be diagnostic of errors
    (D) have the same person prepare the payroll twice, and compare his two copies.

57. As an administrative officer in a large department, you wish to recommend to your superior that a postage meter be installed in the central mailing office to replace manual methods. Of the following, the least acceptable reason for acquiring a postage meter is that it would
    (A) reduce the possibility of diversion of postage to personal use by employees
    (B) automatically assist in an accurate accounting of the cost of mailing
    (C) increase efficiency in the handling and dispatch of mail
    (D) avoid the necessity of advising the mailing department beforehand concerning extraordinarily large mailings.

58. You are called upon to suggest a reorganization of your department's office layout to make room for expanding functions. Of the following, the *least* important principle to be remembered is that
    (A) a minimum amount of time should be lost in inter-office business
    (B) there should be no inconvenience to the public
    (C) the physical surroundings of the employees should be as pleasant as possible
    (D) location should not incur employee resentment.

59. In the bureau in which you are serving, it is necessary to establish some systematic policy for the removal and destruction of old correspondence. Of the following, the best method for you to recommend for this purpose is to
    (A) file all material; when the available room is filled, destroy the oldest material to make room for the new
    (B) file all material, but mark material of temporary value in some fashion; at regular intervals, destroy temporary material
    (C) file all material; when the available room is filled, go through the files and remove all useless material
    (D) file all material; when the available room is filled, destroy a sufficiently large representative sampling to allow reasonable room for future correspondence.

60. It is a standard operating procedure in an office which receives several thousand forms each week to have the file clerk accumulate a week's receipts before filing them. The forms will not be examined for a period of one month after receipt. In comparison with daily filing, this procedure is, in general
    (A) less satisfactory; it tends to build up an unnecessary backlog of work
    (B) more satisfactory; it tends to reduce filing time
    (C) less satisfactory; all information should be placed in a safe storage place as soon as possible
    (D) more satisfactory; it tends to eliminate the prefiling period.

61. Of the following, a major purpose of numbering invoices, complaints, orders or other key forms in order of receipt or issuance is to
    (A) facilitate their orderly maintenance and ready location when needed
    (B) keep track of the number of forms of any particular type that are used
    (C) reveal any discrepancy between the material or the complaint received and the record on hand
    (D) serve as a check on the date when a particular form was used.

62. Of the following, the chief advantage of rotating the qualified staff among various job assignments is the
    (A) development of versatility in staff members

(B) ability for a worker to catch errors made by previous employees

(C) establishment of bases upon which to formulate work norms

(D) lessening of the undesirable trend toward increasing specialization.

Questions 63 to 65 are to be answered solely on the basis of the information contained in the following quotation: ''The office was once considered as nothing more than a focal point of internal and external correspondence. It was capable only of dispatching a few letters upon occasion and of preparing records of little practical value. Under such a concept, the vitality of the office force was impaired. Initiative became stagnant and the lot of the office worker was not likely to be a happy one. However, under the new concept of office management, the possibilities of waste and mismanagement in office operation are now fully recognized, as are the possibilities for the modern office to assist in the direction and control of business operations. Fortunately, the modern concept of the office as a centralized service-rendering unit is gaining ever greater acceptance in today's complex business world, for without the modern office, the production wheels do not turn and the distribution of goods and services is not possible.''

63. According to the above quotation, the fundamental difference between the old and the new concept of the office is the change in the
  (A) accepted functions of the office
  (B) content and the value of the records kept
  (C) office methods and systems
  (D) vitality and morale of the office force.

64. According to the above quotation, an office operated today under the old concept of the office most likely would
  (A) make older workers happy in their jobs
  (B) be part of an old thriving business concern
  (C) have a passive role in the conduct of a business enterprise
  (D) attract workers who do not believe in modern methods.

65. Of the following, the most important implication of the above quotation is that a present day business organization cannot function effectively without the
  (A) use of modern office equipment
  (B) participation and cooperation of the office

(C) continued modernization of office procedures

(D) employment of office workers with skill and initiative.

Questions 66 to 68 are to be answered on the basis of the information contained in the following quotation: ''The need for the best in management techniques has given rise to the expression 'scientific management.' Within reasonable limits management can be scientific, but it will probably be many decades before it becomes truly scientific either in the factory or in the office. As long as it is impossible to measure accurately individual performance and to equate human behavior, so long will it be impossible to develop completely scientific techniques of office management. There is a likelihood, of course, that management might be reduced to a science when it is applied to inanimate objects which facilitate operations, such as machinery, office equipment and furnishings, and forms. The limiting factor, therefore, is the human element.''

66. The above quotation is concerned primarily with the
  (A) value of scientific office management
  (B) methods for the development of scientific office management
  (C) need for the best office management techniques
  (D) possibility of reducing office management to a science.

67. According to the above quotation, the realization of truly scientific office management is dependent upon the
  (A) expression of management techniques
  (B) development of accurate personnel measurement techniques
  (C) passage of many decades, most probably
  (D) elimination of individual differences in human behavior.

68. According to the above quotation, the scientific management of inanimate objects
  (A) occurs automatically because there is no human factor
  (B) cannot occur in a factory, but can occur in an office
  (C) could be achieved without the concurrent achievement of truly scientific office management

(D) has no bearing on the development of scientific methods of office management.

69. Of the following, the chief value of a flow of work chart to the management of an organization is its usefulness in
   (A) locating the causes of delay in carrying out an operation
   (B) training new employees in the performance of their duties
   (C) determining the effectiveness of the employees in the organization
   (D) determining the accuracy of its organization chart.

70. Being in charge of a large clerical force, you wish to initiate an intensive study of the rate of clerical production in order to reduce costs and increase efficiency. Of the following, the most important point to consider in executing your plan is that the
   (A) cooperation of a competent psychologist should be secured, at least in an advisory capacity
   (B) study should be conducted for at least one budgetary period
   (C) work of all employees under your supervision, rather than a sample, should be analyzed
   (D) confidence of the employees should be gained through thorough publicizing and discussion of the plan.

71. Assume that a procedure for handling certain office forms has just been extensively revised. As supervisor of a small unit, you are to instruct your subordinates in the use of the new procedure, which is rather complicated. Of the following, it would be *least* helpful to your subordinates for you to
   (A) compare the revised procedure with the one it has replaced
   (B) state that you believe the revised procedure to be better than the one it has replaced
   (C) tell them that they will probably find it difficult to learn the new procedure
   (D) give only a general outline of the revised procedure at first and then follow with more detailed instructions.

72. Normally, operating personnel tend to resist and resent changes or innovations in existing procedures. To the supervising officer, the most desirable solution to this problem is to
   (A) hold the senior officer of each unit responsible for the proper execution of the procedure
   (B) plan the procedure so that it interferes least with current procedures
   (C) develop acceptance by providing information concerning the procedure prior to its establishment
   (D) have the procedure accompanied by an explicit order from higher authority.

73. In determining the type and number of records to be kept, the governing principle should be that records are primarily
   (A) aids in attaining the objectives of the agency rather than objectives in themselves
   (B) means of determining areas of administration which require change or improvement
   (C) raw material for statistical analysis and therefore invaluable
   (D) tangible evidence of the types of activities in which the agency is engaged.

74. In undertaking a long-range program directed toward simplification of the records of an agency, the *first* of the following steps should be the study of the
   (A) administrative structure of the organization
   (B) mechanics by which the current record system operates
   (C) record requirements expected for the immediate future
   (D) records systems of similar organizations.

75. The effective "span of control" in the administration varies *least* with the
   (A) accessibility and efficiency of a central records system
   (B) level of responsibility
   (C) necessary degree of supervision and direction
   (D) type of work supervised.

76. A unit supervisor has devised a plan which he believes will increase the efficiency of his unit. He has sufficient authority to put the plan into effect. The best of the following procedures for him to use is to
   (A) call a meeting of his subordinates in order to explain the plan and to direct that it be put into effect

(B) hold a conference with his subordinates in order to explain and discuss the plan, and put it into effect after its feasibility has been substantially agreed upon

(C) write a memo to his subordinates explaining the plan and ordering that it be put into effect

(D) write a memo to his subordinates explaining the plan and ordering that it be put into effect, but authorizing any subordinate who finds any weakness in the plan to discuss it with the supervisor prior to instituting it.

77. Assume that the head of your agency has appointed you to a committee that has been assigned the task of reviewing the clerical procedures used in a large bureau of the agency and of recommending appropriate changes in the procedures where necessary. Of the following, the first step that should be taken by the committee in carrying out its assignment is to

(A) survey the most efficient procedures used in comparable agencies

(B) study the organization of the bureau and the work it is required to do

(C) evaluate the possible effects of proposed revisions in the procedures

(D) determine the effectiveness of existing procedures.

78. Assume that your supervisor has placed you in complete charge of an important project and that several clerks have been assigned to assist you. You have been given authority to establish any new procedures or revise existing procedures in order to complete the project as soon as possible. Just before you begin work on the project, one of the clerks suggests a change in the procedure which you realize at once would result in completion of the project in about half the time you expected to spend on it. Of the following, the most effective course of action to take is to

(A) adopt the suggestion immediately to expedite the completion of the project

(B) discuss the suggestion with your superior to obtain his consent to the change

(C) point out to the clerk that an adequate procedure has already been established, but that his suggestion may be used in future projects of this type

(D) encourage the other clerks to make further suggestions.

79. "In order to promote efficiency and economy in an agency, it is advisable for the management to systematize and standardize procedures and relationships in so far as this can be done; however, excessive routinizing which does not permit individual contributions or achievements should be avoided." On the basis of this quotation, it is most accurate to state that

(A) systematized procedures should be designed mainly to encourage individual achievements

(B) standardized procedures should allow for individual accomplishments

(C) systematization of procedures may not be possible in organizations which have a large variety of functions

(D) individual employees of an organization must fully accept standardized procedures if the procedures are to be effective.

80. "A methods improvement program might be called a war against habit." The most accurate implication of this statement is that

(A) routine handling of routine office assignments should be discouraged

(B) standardization of office procedures may encourage employees to form inefficient work habits

(C) employees tend to continue the use of existing procedures, even when such procedures are inefficient

(D) procedures should be changed constantly to prevent them from becoming habits.

81. Suppose that it has been found that the present method of performing a task is inadequate. Of the following, the *first* action to be taken in planning a new method is to

(A) determine the probable cost of the proposed new method

(B) convince your supervisors and control personnel of the need for the new method

(C) ascertain the exact method of doing the job at present

(D) work out your new method in conjunction with those who will perform the operation.

82. A supervisor who wants to be sure work is completed on time should

(A) assign additional employees before any bottlenecks appear

(B) keep the workers under continuous observation to make sure that they are working up to capacity

(C) plan the work and keep informed of its progress

(D) step in and do as much of the work as possible.

83. The principles of good office layout have been applied most properly to the layout of a central transcribing unit when
(A) the transcribing typists face the windows when working
(B) a private office has been set aside for the unit supervisor
(C) unavoidable sources of distraction have been placed in back of the staff members and at a distance from them
(D) the desks of the transcribing staff are so arranged that employees work face to face.

84. The *least* important factor to be considered in planning the layout of an office is the
(A) relative importance of the different types of work to be done
(B) convenience with which communication can be achieved
(C) functional relationships of the activities of the office
(D) necessity for screening confidential activities from unauthorized persons.

85. Organizations that occupy large, general, open-area offices sometimes consider it desirable to build private offices for the supervisors of large bureaus. The one of the following which is generally *not* considered to be a justification of the use of private offices is that they
(A) lend prestige to the person occupying the office
(B) provide facilities for private conferences
(C) achieve the maximum use of office space
(D) provide facilities for performing work requiring a high degree of concentration.

86. "A supervisor whose unit has a good production record is usually found to be more occupied with the functions associated with leadership than with the performance of the same functions as his subordinates." The most valid implication of this quotation is that

(A) a supervisor whose unit has a good production record usually is not as competent in performing routine tasks as are his subordinates
(B) ability to lead and competence in performing the day-to-day tasks of his subordinates are the requirements of a successful supervisor
(C) a supervisor who spends more time on planning and organizing the work of his unit than on performing the routine tasks of his subordinates will find that his unit's production record will be good
(D) a supervisor whose unit has a good production record usually places less emphasis on performing the day-to-day tasks of his subordinates than on planning the work of his unit.

87. "In any public agency, the top administrative officials are concerned largely with the work of overall creative planning with respect to the anticipated progress of the agency. The first-line supervisors, on the other hand, are concerned largely with the control of current action for the execution of current jobs." On the basis of this quotation, a first-line supervisor would be chiefly responsible for
(A) increasing or decreasing the responsibilities of his unit to reflect changes in the policies of the agency
(B) modifying the work assignments of his present staff to handle a seasonal variation in the activities of the unit
(C) revising the procedure that is used for transmitting instructions from the head of the agency to the unit heads
(D) raising and lowering the production goals of his unit as often as necessary to adjust them to the abilities of his subordinates.

88. The flow of work in a public agency may be impeded by a number of factors. Some of the factors impeding the flow of work may be controlled or corrected more easily than others. Of the following, the factor impeding flow of work which is most difficult for a public agency to control is
(A) a lack of adequate standards of performance
(B) unexpected changes in the volume of work
(C) unforeseen vacation requests by employees
(D) assignment of employees without considering their abilities.

89. "The work production of typists is sometimes measured by the number of strokes typed per unit of time." This method of work measurement is
    (A) desirable because the total number of strokes counted may disclose improper use of the space bar
    (B) undesirable because the total number of strokes may be counted incorrectly if a typist is typing too slowly or too quickly
    (C) desirable when subjective, as well as objective, factors must be taken into account
    (D) undesirable when there is wide variation in the complexity of the material typed.

90. In undertaking to improve the method of performing a certain job or operation, the new office manager should first ascertain the
    (A) present method of performing the job
    (B) purpose of the job
    (C) number and titles of employees assigned to the job
    (D) methods used by other agencies to perform the same kind of job.

91. "The use of standard practices and procedures in large organizations is often essential in order to insure a smooth, efficient, and controlled flow of work. A strict adherence to standard practices and procedures to the extent that unnecessary delay is created is known, in general, as 'red tape'." On the basis of this quotation, the most accurate of the following statements is that
    (A) although the use of standard practices and procedures promotes efficiency, it also creates unnecessary delays and "red tape"
    (B) in order to insure a smooth, efficient and controlled plan of work, "red tape" should be eliminated by a strict adherence to standard practices and procedures
    (C) "red tape" is a necessary evil which invariably creeps into any large organization which uses standard practices and procedures
    (D) "red tape" exists when delay takes place as a result of a too rigid conformity with standard practices and procedures.

92. Mr. Stone, who has been recently placed in charge of a clerical unit staffed with ten employees, plans to institute several radical changes in the procedures of his unit. Of the following actions he may take before adopting any of the revisions, the most desirable is for Mr. Stone to
    (A) distribute to each staff member a memorandum describing the revised procedures and requesting the staff's cooperation in giving the revised procedures a fair trial
    (B) issue to each staff member a memorandum describing the proposed changes and inviting him to submit his written criticism of these proposed changes
    (C) issue to each staff member a memorandum describing the proposed changes and notifying him of the time and date of a staff conference to be held on the merits of the proposed changes
    (D) discuss the proposed changes with each staff member independently and obtain his opinion of the proposed changes.

93. "The improvement in skill and the development of proper attitudes are essential factors in the building of correct work habits." Of the following, the most valid implication of this quotation for a supervisor is that
    (A) the more skillful an employee is, the better will be his attitude toward his work
    (B) developing proper attitudes in subordinates toward their work is more time-consuming for the supervisor than improving their skill
    (C) the improvement of a worker's skill is only part of a supervisor's job
    (D) correct work habits are established in order to either improve the skill of workers or develop in them a proper attitude toward their work.

94. Assume that you are the supervisor of a unit which performs routine clerical work. For you to encourage your subordinates to make suggestions for increasing the unit's efficiency is
    (A) undesirable; employees who perform routine work may resent having additional duties and responsibilities assigned to them
    (B) desirable; by presenting criticism of each other's work, the employees may develop a competitive spirit and in this way increase their efficiency
    (C) undesirable; the employees may conclude that the supervisor is not capable of efficiently supervising the work of the unit

(D) desirable; increased interest in their assignment may be acquired by the employees,
and the work of the unit may be performed
more efficiently.

95. The one of the following which is the most accurate statement regarding routine operations in an
office is that
(A) routine assignments should not last more
than two or three days each week
(B) methods for performing routine work should
be standardized as much as is practicable
(C) routine work performed by one employee
should be checked by another employee
(D) changes in the procedures of a unit should
not affect the existing routine operations of
the unit.

96. As part of a space layout survey, an administrator
instructed his subordinates to study the flow of
work and sequence of operating procedures. His
major purpose in doing this was to determine
(A) the physical distribution and movement of
personnel, material and equipment
(B) the amount of space which is available and
the amount of space which will be required
(C) how the distribution of personnel to various
organization units is related to their space
requirements
(D) what future requirements will be, based on
observable present trends.

97. "No routine will automatically bring itself into
proper relation with changing conditions." Of
the following situations, the one which most
nearly exemplifies the truth of this quotation is
(A) a change in the rules governing the submis-
sion of reports by employees working in the
field is found to be impractical and the previous procedure is reinstituted
(B) a long established method of filing papers in
a bureau is found to be inadequate because
of changes in the functions of the bureau
(C) a long established method of distributing
orders to the staff is found to work effectively when the size of the staff is considerably increased
(D) a change in the rules governing hours of
attendance at work proves distasteful to
many employees.

98. "Interest is essentially an attitude of continuing
attentiveness, found where activity is satisfactorily self-expressive. Whenever work is so circumscribed that the chance for self-expression or
development is denied, monotony is present."
On the basis of this quotation, it is most accurate
to state that
(A) tasks which are repetitive in nature do not
permit self-expression and therefore create
monotony
(B) interest in one's work is increased by financial and non-financial incentives
(C) jobs which are monotonous can be made
self-expressive by substituting satisfactory
working conditions
(D) workers whose tasks afford them no opportunity for self-expression find such tasks to
be monotonous.

99. Data relating to the operation of any unit should
be accumulated and periodically summarized
and analyzed, primarily in order to
(A) point out the most efficient and least efficient workers
(B) determine the relative value of each procedure
(C) locate the elements of an operation which
are usually efficient or inefficient
(D) evaluate the importance of maintaining operating records and quotas.

100. Assume that one of the units under your jurisdiction has 40 typists. Their skill ranges from 15 to
80 words a minute. The most feasible of the
following methods to increase the typing output
of this unit is to
(A) study the various typing jobs to determine
the skill requirements for each type of work
and assign to each typist tasks commensurate with his or her skill
(B) assign the slow typists to clerical work and
hire new typists
(C) assign such tasks as typing straight copy to
the slower typists
(D) reduce the skill requirements necessary to
produce a satisfactory quantity of work.

101. "If independent functions are separated, there is
an immediate gain in conserving special skills. If
we are able to make optimum use of the abilities
of our employees, these skills must be con-

served.'' Assuming the correctness of this statement, it follows that

(A) if we are not making optimum use of employee abilities, independent functions have not been separated

(B) we are making optimum use of employee abilities if we conserve special skills

(C) we are making optimum use of employee abilities if independent functions have been separated

(D) we are not making optimum use of employee abilities if we do not conserve special skills.

102. Studies in human behavior have shown that an employee in a work group who is capable of producing substantially more work than is being produced by the average of the group generally

(A) will tend to produce substantially more work than is produced by the average member of the group

(B) will attempt to become the informal leader of the group

(C) will tend to produce less work than he is capable of producing

(D) will attempt to influence the other members of the group to increase their production.

103. The work distribution chart is a valuable tool for an office supervisor to use in conducting work simplification programs. Of the following questions, the one which a work distribution chart would generally be *least* useful in answering is

(A) What activities take the most time?

(B) Are the employees doing many unrelated tasks?

(C) Is work being distributed evenly among the employees?

(D) Are activities being performed in proper sequence?

104. The dimensions of an office are 25 feet by 15 feet. It is to be fitted with desks 4 feet by 3 feet. The distance between the front of one desk and the rear of another should be 3 feet while the distance between the sides of 2 desks should be 4 feet. Assuming that no desk is placed closer than one foot from any wall, the optimum number that can be placed in the office is

(A) 6
(B) 8
(C) 10
(D) 12.

105. The one of the following for which Frank B. Gilbreth is *best* known is his work on

(A) communications
(B) executive development
(C) forms analysis
(D) time and motion.

106. The simo-chart is ordinarily used in

(A) equipment utilization analysis
(B) flow analysis
(C) micromotion study
(D) organization study.

107. The *first* step in installing a work count system is to

(A) check the accuracy of your measurement
(B) follow the item to its completion
(C) identify measurable items
(D) measure rejects against cost of prevention.

108. Time and motion study is usually associated with the

(A) flow chart
(B) form distribution chart
(C) operation chart
(D) work count.

109. The sound-level meter records the amount of noise in terms of

(A) cycles
(B) decibels
(C) octaves
(D) wave lengths.

110. In securing space for a ''public contact'' agency, the most desirable location would usually be

(A) any floor of a building with frequent elevator service
(B) any floor above traffic noises
(C) one flight up
(D) the street level.

ANSWER KEY

1. D	23. C	45. B	67. B	89. D
2. C	24. D	46. C	68. C	90. B
3. B	25. D	47. D	69. A	91. D
4. A	26. B	48. D	70. D	92. C
5. B	27. B	49. C	71. C	93. C
6. C	28. C	50. B	72. C	94. D
7. A	29. D	51. A	73. A	95. B
8. C	30. C	52. B	74. A	96. A
9. B	31. D	53. A	75. A	97. B
10. B	32. B	54. C	76. B	98. D
11. B	33. D	55. A	77. B	99. C
12. C	34. A	56. C	78. A	100. A
13. D	35. D	57. D	79. B	101. D
14. D	36. D	58. D	80. C	102. C
15. A	37. A	59. B	81. C	103. D
16. C	38. A	60. B	82. C	104. B
17. A	39. A	61. A	83. C	105. D
18. B	40. C	62. A	84. A	106. C
19. A	41. A	63. A	85. C	107. C
20. C	42. C	64. C	86. D	108. C
21. A	43. B	65. B	87. B	109. B
22. A	44. B	66. D	88. B	110. D

EXPLANATORY ANSWERS

1. **(D)** Efficient management requires that there be as little wasted time as possible. Speed-up means just what it says—to complete the work more quickly. Time and motion studies measure the time it takes to do a job and the motions or physical activities involved.

2. **(C)** The question posed is what factor is least important. Seniority rights of clerks is essentially a personnel matter, and should be handled after the decision to mechanize has been made. No one has a right to a job for which they are not qualified, and if the job has to be done by office machine clerks and not by clerks, that change must be made.

3. **(B)** The least important factor is the degree of prestige which you will accrue. Your job is to formulate plans— that's what you are being paid to do. All other possible answers are important considerations in formulating the plan.

4. **(A)** In order to reduce fluctuations in workload, it is not helpful to staff the bureau so that it can handle peak loads. One of the chief purposes of reducing fluctuating work loads is to prevent or lessen the occurrence of peak periods when additional staff may be needed.

5. **(B)** You are told that the assistant chief will perform the bulk of the actual work involved, and will have the part-time help of four subordinates. Planning is a management function and should be done by the chief and the assistant chief who will carry out the major part of the work. The comments of subordinates will help work out details and give them an understanding of the job, but their approval of the plan is not called for under the circumstances given.

6. **(C)** For many people the best way to tackle a question of this type is to substitute figures for the letters given, e.g., the average daily output is 10 pages of 100 lines of work. It can then easily be seen that the only possible answer is

that the number of lines per page is 10 lines, or the quotient of K divided N. No clue is given regarding the number of words produced daily. The number of lines typed per five equals K times 5, not N times K times 5.

7. **(A)** Functional centralization will not appreciably cut inter-bureau communication and traffic, and may actually increase it. Thus, for example, if all typists in an agency are centralized, there will be considerably more traffic and communication between the typing pool and the various offices and bureaus which previously had their own typists.

8. **(C)** The basic organizational principle to be followed in organizing bureaus for smoother departmental operations is that each separate bureau must be able to work with other bureaus in a harmonious fashion. The degree of latitude given to each chief is dependent upon other variables than organizational principles. The location of mailing, filing and supply facilities is important, but not of major organizational importance.

9. **(B)** In order to achieve coordination between several units of a bureau it is not usually necessary to conduct time and motion studies of the work of employees in each bureau. Those studies would only assist in determining the best methods to use to complete the work assigned to each worker, not to study coordination between units.

10. **(B)** You are asked to determine what logically follows from the quotation. The only thing you can conclude from the data is that if the per item cost decreases, there cannot be an increase in the number of clerks who are engaged in filing the material.

11. **(B)** You are asked to interpret what the quotation is really saying. It does state that all units with insufficient space have asked for more space. We cannot say some units with enough space have not asked for more space (answers A and D). We know there is a relationship between those with insufficient space and those requesting for more space.

12. **(C)** Usually a manual process is preferred over a mechanized process when the transactions are so dissimilar that a mechanized approach is impractical. Numerous, similar, and predictable transactions can be mechanized satisfactorily.

13. **(D)** A work measurement system is a device to measure or report on the output of a worker or unit. There is no need to establish an acceptable quota for each activity before setting up the system. On the contrary, the information obtained from the reporting system can be used to set up acceptable quotas for each activity.

14. **(D)** Man-hours would be more meaningful and would simplify the process. If a worker produced 160 units in a day, we would have to know how much time the worker was employed that day. If we were told the worker

produced 20 units in one hour, no further questions would be necessary.

15. **(A)** The study of the flow of work and the sequence of operating procedures as part of a space layout survey primarily serves to determine where workers, material, and equipment are needed for each operation and for moving the work from one operation to the next. From this data the layout of space needed for each operation and the best location of each operation can be developed.

16. **(C)** In breaking down a complex job into smaller, simpler components, it is preferable to find out the best method to accomplish each component, and teach only that method to the worker. Variations in methods of performance result in variations in accuracy and time taken to do a component, and thus makes scheduling more difficult.

17. **(B)** The schedules set would then tend to be more realistic.

18. **(B)** To institute a completely new procedure rather than revise the existing procedure consumes unnecessary time, may be wasteful of existing machines, equipment, and supplies, and may harm morale since it implies that the former supervisor was incompetent. There is always at least some good in even some of the most inefficient operations.

19. **(A)** Essentially stated in the first sentence of the passage.

20. **(C)** An integrated reporting system for work measurement does not necessarily involve referral to the procedure manual needed to do the job. It does need all the forms and procedures referred to in the three other answers. The procedural manuals would be needed if the work measurement reports themselves showed a possible need to revise these procedures.

21. **(A)** If production does not decrease when the length of the rest periods are increased, why not increase the length of the rest periods? This is a valid argument for doing it. The other choices do not contain arguments that could support a proposal to lengthen the rest periods.

22. **(A)** This is the only manner in which the special skills of the involved stenographers can be conserved and the secretarial work of the division be performed.

23. **(C)** On the one hand, you are told the advantages of a stenographic pool includes increased productivity. On the other, you are told that the space needed for establishing the pool will cut the space available for technical staff, and thus decrease work productivity. Therefore, there is not any way to tell whether establishing a stenographic pool will justify the decrease in productivity of the technical staff.

24. **(D)** This answer is the course of action that could "sell" the mechanization of a function. The cost of operation will not increase and there is a possibility of increased efficiency and maybe even a monetary saving. Note that the phrase "in some cases" will not "sell" a superior on anything. A proposal must be stronger than that.

25. **(D)** There is no point in teaching alternative methods for doing each job. Training is an expensive operation in any organization, and the necessity for alternative methods may never become a reality.

26. **(B)** Maintaining a constant backlog of work helps ensure that there is no idle time when workers must be paid to do nothing, and no useful work is accomplished. Maintaining such a backlog does not mean scheduled work is not done on time because the work schedule should be formulated so that the backlog remains constant and available to be done if staff is ahead of schedule.

27. **(B)** A superior always keeps in mind that his or her primary duty is to get the work done correctly and on time. To do this it is good policy to look at the job to be done, and then find the worker who can do it most expeditiously and correctly.

28. **(C)** Under the serial method where each worker does only a specific part of the entire job, controls must be set up for each specific part of the job in order to be able to keep track of the progress of the job toward its completion.

29. **(D)** The subdivision of work is most likely to result in a degree of delay both as a worker completes his or her portion of the work and passes it onto the next worker, and also when the work passes from one unit to another. Subdivision of work calls for coordination, more communication, etc. These processes take time.

30. **(C)** The only true statement is that noise is reflected more by hard-surfaced materials than by soft or porous materials. Thus, ceilings of porous material are more helpful in reducing noise than are plastered and painted ones.

31. **(D)** A worker's knowledge of the significance of his or her work will least affect his or her ability to tackle assignments where he or she does not possess the special skills needed to do the job. It will affect his or her interest in the job, understanding of its relationship to other jobs and willingness to work well with other employees.

32. **(B)** Supervision of clerical workers is made easier if the supervisor is in a position to constantly observe subordinates and to be available immediately for consultations. For these reasons it is a rare occasion indeed when a first-line supervisor of clerical workers is assigned a private office.

33. **(D)** Investigators generally interview people, examine data and then dictate reports on individual cases, or in batches of individual cases. They can dictate to any stenographer who is available. If no investigator has cases to dictate, the stenographers can still be productively employed in taking dictation from other staff members. Since correspondence clerks use stock paragraphs to answer a good portion of governmental correspondence, a stenographer would not be needed. Members of a government commission need private secretaries, since much of their work is of a specialized confidential nature. Bureau heads in a small agency would generally be best served by either private secretaries or bureau secretaries who are sufficiently familiar with the bureau's specific work to make dictation easier, and perform many of the routine activities of the bureau.

34. **(A)** Candidates should know that a vari-type machine can be set up to space out each line to give justified or even left hand and right hand margins.

35. **(D)** You should remind employees of the expense involved in buying or repairing reproduction equipment. This can be done by simply reminding the workers of the cost of each machine and that careful use would be appreciated. This "soft" approach is preferable to the stronger remedies given in the other answers because you are new to the job, and don't really know who or what is responsible for the damage.

36. **(D)** The chances are good that a thoroughly inspected section of files picked at random will be typical of all sections. To check all the files at regular intervals wastes time. To glance through filed papers at random will not guarantee that all the files are kept in the same manner. To simply watch the clerks while they are filing is meaningless.

37. **(A)** Each document automatically adopts its location in the files either alphabetically or numerically. Material to be filed does not need to be coded.

38. **(A)** Obsolete office equipment should not be kept in the office. It takes up space which could be utilized more efficiently.

39. **(A)** The quotation says in effect, that an alert office manager does not just try to improve established clerical operations, but also studies whether the operations themselves are worthwhile. The most valid implication from this is that established clerical operations may not be worth continuing.

40. **(C)** A flow or process chart reveals the outstanding defects in a procedure because it shows duplication of work, incorrect placement of personnel and/or equipment, and the wrong order of steps taken in the procedure, etc.

41. **(A)** The listing adding machine will be most helpful for the purpose of checking figures used in computational work including addition and subtraction.

42. **(C)** From the data given you know that the Initial Caps refer to individual machines (X = typewriter, Y = computing machines), and the small letters refer to the location (a = secretary's office, b = chief clerk's office). The code for a typewriter in the Printing Division is therefore Xd.

43. **(B)** Very often the person who is going to sign the letter wants changes made before he or she will sign it, or decides that the letter is not to be sent out or sent at a later date. Although carbons do not have to be signed, some offices initial the carbons to indicate that it has been mailed.

44. **(B)** Natural light is least needed in a storage room because it is used infrequently and when it is used, it is used for short periods of time.

45. **(B)** If the processing of one type of office form involves seven routine operations, quite possibly some of these operations are not necessary. In reviewing the procedure for possible improvement, the first question to ask is whether each of the individual operations is needed, and then, if the answer is positive, to consider the other answers.

46. **(C)** You are asked for the least accurate statement. The continuity of effort and staff cooperation is generally better secured by utilizing a permanent staff of method analysts rather than periodically employed outside consultants. The staff frequently resents "outside interference" of consultants who must often "learn from scratch" the whole operation before they can begin to recommend improvements. Outside consultants are usually needed when large scale or fundamental changes are needed.

47. **(D)** Knowledge by each worker of the importance of his or her specific job deepens the worker's interest in the job, the understanding of the relationship of the worker's activities to the work of fellow employees, and strengthens his or her willingness to cooperate with other employees. It does not help that worker to take on work which requires skills he or she does not possess.

48. **(D)** One large room generally provides better light and ventilation for all workers, allows for a more direct flow of work, and helps supervise and control work. It does not affect the conduct of time and motion studies, although the results of such studies may possibly point to the need for change in office layout.

49. **(C)** Scientific office management techniques are frequently applied to standardize clerical practices and procedures, but not to such personnel activities as hiring, firing or determining pay scales. A revised organizational structure may result in the need to use principles of scientific office management, but these principles are not applied to revise the structure itself.

50. **(B)** The relative importance of the work itself has little or no bearing on whether a manual or machine operation is used because either way, the finished work should be correct and fully usable.

51. **(A)** This is the most reflective of the colors given.

52. **(B)** This has been proven the ideal amount of light for performing close work.

53. **(A)** This is the most comfortable degree of humidity for work purposes.

54. **(C)** Correspondence filed in a folder should generally relate to the same topic, and therefore be arranged in the order in which they are received. If the folder contains unanswered correspondence, those letters should also be filed in order of receipt, even though they are often not answered in order of receipt.

55. **(A)** Although it is not good practice to unnecessarily delay answering letters, some require research and thus cannot be answered in the order that the letters are received.

56. **(C)** The best method to reduce the possibility of errors in preparing a department payroll is to first peruse the entire payroll, and determine if it appears reasonable when compared to previous payrolls and with changes you know to have been made during the previous payroll period.

57. **(D)** The mail room should always be advised beforehand if an extraordinarily large mailing is going to be necessary, and whether or not a postage meter will be installed, since the mail room supervisor must adjust for handling the large mailing.

58. **(D)** Any change in office layout is likely to create a degree of resentment because it is virtually impossible to make everyone happy. Someone has to occupy the least desirable space. The other possible answers are important principles to follow in reorganizing an office layout.

59. **(B)** Useless correspondence clutters up files and makes it difficult to find correspondence that is needed. The best policy to establish to systematize the removal and destruction of useless, old correspondence, is to mark all material which is known to be of temporary nature in some fashion so that all such material will be removed from the files at regular intervals. Destroying old material, just because it is old or destroying a "representative sample of material" is very poor practice.

60. **(B)** The file clerk will not have to go to the place of filing on a daily basis. The file clerk can let the material collect for a month, put them in order, and file them in batches rather than singularly.

61. **(A)** The major purpose of numbering key forms in order of receipt or issuance is to locate a particular form more easily or to know that the form was issued. There would be no need to number the forms in this fashion if all that is wanted is a record of the total number of each form issued. Answers C and D are not information that can be obtained from numbering each form issued or received.

62. **(A)** The chief advantage of rotating qualified staff is to develop the ability of each worker to handle many types of assignments so that he or she can be used wherever the needs of the unit dictate.

63. **(A)** The quotation refers primarily to the changed consideration of the office as merely the focal point for correspondence to that of a central service rendering unit.

64. **(C)** The quotation states that the modern office assists in the direction and control of business operations. It is therefore logical that an office operated today under the old office concept would probably have a passive role in the conduct of the business.

65. **(B)** Based on the quotation, it can be implied that present day business organizations need the participation and cooperation of the office in order to function effectively. None of the other possible answers can be inferred from the quotation.

66. **(D)** The chief thrust of the paragraph is the discussion of the possibility that office management can be reduced to a science. The other possible answers are only concerned briefly, or not at all, with data in the quotation.

67. **(B)** The quotation clearly indicates that completely scientific office management is impossible until or unless it becomes possible to "measure accurately individual behavior and to equate human behavior."

68. **(C)** The quotation clearly indicates that scientific techniques can and are applied to inanimate objects, but that truly scientific office management also involves the measurement of individual behavior and the ability to equate human behavior has not yet been accomplished.

69. **(A)** A flow of work depicts an operation precisely—showing steps, movement, and type of operation, etc. Thus, one can discover bottlenecks, and unnecessary transfer operations, etc.

70. **(D)** Workers must understand, through discussion and publicizing of the plan, that the purpose of the study is not to subsequently institute speed-up tactics and is not a "union-busting" activity, but is rather an attempt to find better ways to get the work done—ways that will benefit the worker and the organization. Without worker confidence, no study of this type can be completely successful.

71. **(C)** To tell them they will probably find it difficult to learn the new procedure is to discourage trainees before they start.

72. **(C)** The best way to overcome resistance to changes in existing procedure is to inform staff of what is involved in the projected changes prior to making the changes so that they will have a chance to understand and accept them. They will also feel that they had a hand in the changes.

73. **(A)** The primary and all-encompassing reason to maintain records is to help the administration to reach the goal and objectives of the agency. The three incorrect answers are just useful parts or means to reach the primary objective, which is not to keep records but get the work done.

74. **(A)** The administrative structure of an organization dictates what and the amount of records to be kept. The question must be asked what records and what information must every unit in the organization have to function properly.

75. **(A)** The span of control, i.e., the number of workers reporting to one supervisor, is not affected by the accessibility and efficiency of a central records system. It is affected by the level of responsibility of the supervisor and workers, the degree of supervision by the workers, and the type of unit supervised, plus other factors.

76. **(B)** The advantages of this course of action are twofold. First, the subordinates will be made to feel that they had a hand in the formulation of the plan; and second, they may have some very valuable suggestions concerning it and may be able to point out apparent flaws not visible to the supervisor.

77. **(B)** The committee should first study the organization of the bureau and the work assigned to the bureau and its component parts. Only when this is known can committee members begin to study the existing procedures designed to carry out the required work of the bureau, determine the bureau's effectiveness compared with that of other bureaus doing similar work, and propose revisions and evaluate the possible effects of their proposals.

78. **(A)** In the situation presented, you have sufficient authority to adopt the suggestion immediately and should do so.

79. **(B)** In effect, the quotation says that systemization and standardization of procedures and relationships are good, but can be overdone and should not be allowed to make individual contributions and achievements impossible or even difficult.

80. **(C)** The quotation implies that once a procedure has been established, there is a tendency to continue to follow it religiously even if it is no longer the best procedure possible. It does not mean that good proce-

dures and good routines should be changed just for the sake of change, but rather that once established, a procedure should be reevaluated as times and conditions change to determine its continued effectiveness. This is the purpose of a methods improvement program.

81. **(C)** The first action to be taken in planning for a new method is to look at the present method carefully to know just exactly how the job is being done. Only then can a new method be worked out, the cost of the new method be determined, and the new method "sold" to superiors.

82. **(C)** In order to make sure work is completed on time, the good supervisor must plan how the work is to be done, the steps involved, assign specific workers to do each step, and set the projected dates of completion and the method to control the timely completion of the project.

83. **(C)** Good office layout of a central transcribing unit requires that staff members not be disturbed by unnecessary equipment or personnel in their immediate area. Thus, for example, a duplicating machine used by many people should be placed in the back of the room where it will not distract typists, and telephones should not usually be kept on the typists' desks.

84. **(A)** A secretary's desk is very often in the most favored position because of receptionist duties, whereas the professional working with his or her own staff can be placed in a less favorable spot.

85. **(C)** Private offices naturally take up more room than if the space is kept open. Partitions and walls are space consuming.

86. **(D)** An efficient and effective supervisor spends a majority of his or her time in planning, training, and directing of the work and spends a minimum of time if any on the actual work of the unit, that is the work that can and should be performed by the staff.

87. **(B)** Based on the quotation, the supervisor would be concerned with modifying assignments made necessary by seasonal variations in the unit's work. The first line supervisor would not generally be responsible for increasing or decreasing his or her unit's work responsibilities, or revising procedures where the head of the agency is involved, or raising or lowering production goals. All these activities require higher level authority, as indicated in the quotation.

88. **(B)** In a public agency the unexpected changes in the volume of work present the most difficult problems. If, for example, Congress passes a law to provide added benefits and added criteria for receiving these benefits, the anticipated workload may suddenly and dramatically change for an agency. An agency should be able to control the situations presented in the other possible answers.

89. **(D)** If all typists in a unit are typing routine reports or correspondence containing no difficult charts, statistics or unfamiliar terms, the method of measuring work production described in the question might be useful. If the material to be typed is not similar, the method of measurement will not be usable.

90. **(B)** The purpose of an operation must be thoroughly understood before any office manager undertakes the job of improving its method of performance. In the absence of this knowledge the office manager might erroneously label a unit of the operation useless when actually it is necessary and valuable.

91. **(D)** Adherence to standard practices and procedures is not seen in the quotation as an evil unto itself. Indeed, these are necessary to make a unit run smoothly. Inflexible or "kneejerk" adherence to procedures, however, does cause red tape.

92. **(C)** The workers will be more able to judge whether the changes are practical than a new supervisor, and their participation will help the supervisor obtain both their respect and cooperation. The other possible answers contain methods that are less desirable because they would not give the supervisor the benefit of a group situation which serves to unite the group behind the supervisor, and will probably come up with better solutions than from individual workers unwilling to put their ideas in writing. In addition, a group conference usually results in the elimination or change of unworkable ideas, whereas one worker might hesitate to criticize a new supervisor's proposal.

93. **(C)** The quotation states that both improving skill and developing proper attitudes are essential in building correct work. It follows then that improving a worker's skill is only one part of a supervisor's job.

94. **(D)** The supervisor who encourages subordinates to make suggestions is performing a desirable function since he or she encourages interest and development of new and possibly good methods to increase efficiency and productivity. Workers appreciate being part of a cooperative effort to get things done in a better fashion. Note that positive efforts to improve a unit's work does not mean workers should be allowed to criticize other individuals' performance. That function rightfully must be done by the supervisor.

95. **(B)** Standardizing procedures makes it possible for more workers being able to perform them. The other possible answers are not accurate statements. Routine assignments should last as long as they have to. It is not necessary to check routine duties. Procedural changes may or may not affect routine operations.

96. **(A)** Work flow and the sequence of operations is studied in order to determine the existing distribution of machinery, equipment and personnel, and the movement of same through the various operations needed to get the

job done. The other possible answers refer to problems or decisions that flow from the data collected about the existing distribution.

97. **(B)** The quotation merely states that a routine operation, by its very nature, won't adjust itself when conditions change. Of the answers presented the situation that best shows the truth of this is the one in which the method of filing papers needs to be changed because the bureau's functions have changed. New records have been created and records that were important, no longer are.

98. **(D)** To interpret the quotation, the key words to note are "self-expression" and "monotony". Without the first, the second is bound to follow. The other possible answers do not follow the logic of the quotation.

99. **(C)** The primary purpose of collecting, summarizing and analyzing data about unit operations is to discover the best and worst elements of the operation. This data is then used to correct inefficient elements, and adapt the most efficient elements to other parts of the operation.

100. **(A)** The most feasible way to increase typing output is to determine the typing skill needed for each piece of work, and assign a typist to the work commensurate with his or her skill. Typists are hired primarily to type, not be assigned to clerical work on a regular basis. It is not good practice to lower the degree of perfection needed for the unit's work just to increase output. Straight copy should be given to slow typists, and more difficult work should go to the more skilled typists.

101. **(D)** The quotation indicates that to use employees to the optimum effect, special skills must be conserved. In other words, proficient typists should be engaged in typing work, and not assigned to clerical tasks. It is a question of making use of what you have.

102. **(C)** Studies show that the fastest workers in a work unit generally decrease their production level toward the group norm, even though they are capable of producing more work. Peer pressure is one reason for this. Another is that no rewards are usually forthcoming for the faster completion of work, and there is no reason for the worker to exceed the norm. If anything, he or she is given more work, again without any tangible reward. Note that the fastest worker is not necessarily the most careful worker, or possesses the qualities needed to become the informal leader of the work unit.

103. **(D)** The work distribution chart does not generally show the sequence of performance of the various activities of the unit. It will show how long each activity takes, the different tasks of each worker, and help the supervisor determine whether the work is divided evenly among the staff.

104. **(B)** From the facts given, the usable space is $23' \times 13'$ = 299 square feet. Corner desks will each occupy $5'$ of the $23'$, which is the length of the room. Therefore, two more desks can be put between the two corner desks. The width taken up by each of the desks is $5'$ so that, given a total of $13'$ available in the total width of the room, there cannot be more than two desks in the width of the room. The total number of desks that can be placed in the room is 8 desks.

105. **(D)** Time and motion studies involve scrutiny of physical movements involved in work operations with an objective of eliminating, correcting, or shortening of those movements in order to promote increased efficiency.

106 **(C)** This chart depicts all physical movement involved in work operations and is usually utilized in time and motion studies.

107. **(C)** In order to install a work count system, the first thing to determine is what is to be counted, that is, you must first identify measurable items (e.g., number of forms completed, number of pages typed).

108. **(C)** Of the choices given this one should be selected because work operations are studied in time and motion studies.

109. **(B)** A decibel is a measurement of sound.

110. **(D)** An operation requiring public contact should be located on a floor where the office is most easily seen by and accessible to the public. This would generally be the street level of a building since it requires few steps or elevators to take, and an appropriate sign in the window makes the office seen by the public. Public contact work usually involves a large number of people coming in and out, and even if the elevators are in good working order, the volume of traffic will cause elevator delays for a good portion of the day. Note that traffic noises are usually heard far above street level.

PART TWO

Personnel

TRAINING

1. An administrator finds it necessary to work overtime correcting and revising records and reports prepared by his subordinates. Such a condition is probably due to
   (A) an insufficient number of assistants for the amount of work to be done
   (B) inadequately trained subordinates
   (C) standards required beyond the abilities of the subordinates
   (D) unnecessarily complicated methods of record keeping and reporting.

2. The staff conference, as a training method, can be used *least* effectively when
   (A) the backgrounds of the participants are diversified
   (B) there is wide difference of opinion concerning questions to be discussed
   (C) the participants are experienced in the problems to be discussed
   (D) the subjects discussed pose no problems.

3. An administrator was assigned the job of conducting a centralized training program for fifteen newly appointed supervisors, supplementing the individualized training by their immediate superiors. The administrator began the first session by asking the supervisors to suggest the subjects that they would want to have covered in the course. Of the following, the most likely result of such an approach is that
   (A) greater cooperation will be obtained from the course participants

   (B) leadership will tend to pass from the administrator to the more active course members
   (C) the most important problems of supervision will be covered
   (D) success or failure of the course will be the responsibility of the attending supervisors.

4. In a Fire Department the one of the following which is the main limitation of a policy of assigning limited service personnel as instructors is that
   (A) there may be excessive turnover among the instructors
   (B) the best instructors may not be obtained
   (C) the work may be too strenuous for some of the employees assigned
   (D) the instructors may have little interest in teaching.

5. The one of the following training methods likely to be most effective in developing a specific skill on the part of employees is
   (A) appropriate visual aids
   (B) selected readings
   (C) interesting demonstrations
   (D) repeated practice.

6. "Training prepares the organization member to reach satisfactory decisions himself without the need for the constant exercise of authority or advice by a superior." The aim of training expressed in this statement is
   (A) undesirable; the decision-making process should be completely centralized

(B) desirable; there should be no need to exercise authority

— (C) desirable; the decision making process should be as decentralized as possible

(D) undesirable; organization members even after training, cannot be expected to reach satisfactory decisions in many instances.

7. Assume that you have been assigned to train a group of supervisors on some new equipment. The one of the following criteria to which primary consideration should be given when planning your course of instruction is
(A) How much time will I have at my disposal?
(B) How much will this cost?
— (C) What should be learned in this course?
(D) What is the background of the trainers?

8. During a conference on the training program of a department it is suggested that a formal training course be initiated for administrators. This suggestion is best characterized as
(A) undesirable; concentrating on the training of lower level workers will bring optimum returns
(B) desirable; if administrators are trained there is less need to train men and junior officers
(C) undesirable; administrators may be held up to ridicule if such a training course is set up
— (D) desirable; training is a major part of an administrator's job and trained supervisors are needed to train subordinates.

9. Whenever a supervisor was asked a question by an employee the supervisor told the questioner to look up and report the answer to the department. This method of training is
— (A) undesirable; employees would be discouraged from asking questions
(B) desirable; employees would better remember information obtained through their own efforts
(C) undesirable; this would indicate that the supervisor doesn't know the answers
(D) desirable; the employee would become familiar with the Department's manuals and other reference books.

10. Of the following, the most important reason for evaluation of the outcomes of a training program by a supervisor is that
(A) more active participation may be obtained

from department members when such evaluations are shared
(B) the introduction of new or improved techniques is facilitated
— (C) shortcomings discovered can serve as the basis for further training
(D) success of the program is evidence of his qualities of leadership.

11. When an administrator finds that many of the supervisors under him make numerous mistakes on work which they should be able to do, the *most* probable cause for the mistakes is that the supervisors
(A) have poor aptitude for the work
— (B) have had insufficient training for the job
(C) are doing work that is too difficult
(D) have duties that are too varied.

12. The expenditures needed to maintain a training program for a large department are fully justified only if the
— (A) department's efficiency is noticeably improved or maintained at a high level
(B) instructors acquire knowledge over and above those required to do their routine work
(C) training closely parallels promotional examinations
(D) employees' knowledge is noticeably increased.

13. The best measures of the results of a formal training program are
(A) final test scores achieved by the trainees
(B) differences in performance between workers who took the training course and those who did not
(C) grades the workers trained make in their next promotion test
— (D) differences in performance of the workers trained, before and after training.

14. If all of the following methods of evaluating results of an employee training program are possible, which one is usually *most* valid
(A) reactions and opinions of the supervisory staff
(B) comparison of individual or group service ratings before and after the training period
(C) expressed reactions of the group being trained
— (D) comparison of performance of equal groups of employees who have been trained and those not trained.

15. In leading a training conference, it is usually best to make your introductory remarks, give the first question for discussion, and
   (A) call on a group member for response
   (B) ask for contributions or ideas from members in rotation around the table
   —(C) let the group members respond voluntarily
   (D) discuss the question and its problem at some length yourself.

16. A conscientious supervisor, in conducting on-the-job training, will normally find that _____ is the greatest challenge to his supervisory abilities. The above missing phrase is
   (A) relating the training to actual job requirements
   —(B) instilling a desire to learn in the employee
   (C) presenting the material to be learned
   (D) having the employee demonstrate that he has learned.

17. Suppose that as a supervisor you are instructing a group of workers in some aspect of the job. Of the following, the *least* valid principle for you to observe is that
   (A) referral to related experience should be emphasized wherever possible
   (B) emphasis should vary with the relative importance of each step in the technique
   —(C) absence of questions during the course indicates general understanding of the course
   (D) practice should be based on a real situation.

18. "The supervisor is expected to train his or her subordinates in all aspects of the job." Of the following, the best training principle for you to follow in order to secure broad application by the workers of the material taught to all possible types of situations is that
   (A) learning should be guided by the instructor
   —(B) insight should be developed into concepts and principles
   (C) there should be recurrent practice and review of learned units
   (D) review should repeat original presentation in identical form.

19. The modern concept of supervision is that it should be
   (A) dogmatic and authoritative
   (B) limited and non-critical

(C) concerned only with the needs of management
—(D) concerned with training and guidance.

20. Requiring supervisors to train their own subordinates may be especially advantageous to management, since this procedure facilitates
   —(A) placing the responsibility for a worker's substandard performance
   (B) discovering supervisors who have potentiality for further promotion
   (C) training employees in a variety of duties
   (D) measuring the supervisor's ability to cooperate with their subordinates.

21. The expenditures needed to maintain a training program for a large department are fully justified only if
   —(A) the department's efficiency is noticeably improved or maintained at a high level
   (B) the employees' knowledge of theories is noticeably increased
   (C) the training closely parallels promotional examinations
   (D) the employees' morale is improved.

22. A comment made by an employee about a training course was, "Oh, I suppose it's important for the job but it's a waste of time for me just to sit in that course and yawn while the instructor rambles on." The fundamental error in training methodology, to which this criticism points, is failure to provide
   (A) goals for the students
   (B) for individual differences
   (C) connecting links between new and old material
   —(D) for student participation.

23. The one of the following which is the chief reason for training supervisors is that
   (A) untrained supervisors find it difficult to train their subordinates
   (B) most persons do not start as supervisors and consequently are in need of supervisory training
   —(C) training permits a higher degree of decentralization of the decision-making process
   (D) training permits a higher degree of centralization of the decision-making process.

24. The head of a department assigned final responsibility for the training function to the personnel office. This assignment was
    (A) undesirable; this type of centralization prevents a staff organization from carrying out staff functions
    (B) undesirable; this responsibility must rest with the supervisor
    (C) undesirable; the personnel office usually does not have the technical "know how" to carry this responsibility
    (D) desirable; if training is left to the line officials, it never is accomplished.

25. A comment made by an employee about a training course was, "We never have any idea how we are getting along in that course." The fundamental error in training methods to which this criticism points is
    (A) no goals have been set for the students
    (B) failure to develop a feeling of need or active want for the material being presented
    (C) the training sessions may be too long
    (D) no attempt may have been made to connect the new material with what was already known.

26. Of the following training methods, the one that is generally most valuable in teaching employees new clerical skills is
    (A) organized group discussion
    (B) individual instruction on the job
    (C) use of visual aids, such as charts and pictures
    (D) supervised reading, research and inspection.

27. Of the following means that a bureau chief may utilize in training his understudy, the *least* acceptable one is for him to
    (A) give the understudy assignments which other employees find too difficult or unpleasant
    (B) discuss with the understudy the important problems that confront the bureau chief
    (C) rotate the assignments given the understudy
    (D) give the understudy an opportunity to attend some of the meetings of bureau chiefs.

28. Of the following, the most significant argument against making it compulsory for civil service employees to attend a training course is that
    (A) trainees must be receptive if training is to be successful

(B) most training requires additional time and expense on the part of the trainee
(C) training is highly desirable but not absolutely essential for adequate job performance
(D) incompetent work is generally reflected in poor service ratings.

29. "Any person thoroughly familiar with the specific steps in a particular class of work is well qualified to serve as a training course instructor in that work." This statement is erroneous chiefly because
    (A) the quantity of information possessed by an instructor does not bear a direct relationship to the quality of instruction
    (B) what is true of one class of work is not necessarily true of other types of work
    (C) a qualified instructor cannot be expected to have detailed information about many specific fields
    (D) the steps in any type of work are usually interrelated and not independent or unique.

30. The supervisor who has had much experience in the training of new employees knows that the most accurate of the following statements is that
    (A) generally, the stronger the incentive an employee has, the faster he will learn to perform the duties of his position
    (B) the average employee can accurately perform an operation after he has observed a skilled employee perform the operation
    (C) the chief difficulty in teaching an older employee a new method of performing an operation is usually that his mind functions more slowly than that of a younger person
    (D) it is easier for an employee to change his accustomed way of performing a clerical operation than to adopt a new way.

31. When training a new employee, you should not
    (A) correct errors as he makes them
    (B) give him too much material to absorb at one time
    (C) have him try the operation unless he can do it perfectly
    (D) avoid laying emphasis upon possibilities for mistakes.

32. Assume that you have been given the job of developing a procedure manual for your department

which will be used to train employees in the details of departmental procedures and which the employees can use for reference. During your preliminary planning period, it is *least* important that you

(A) determine the scope and level of the manual
(B) gather all the work flow charts available
(C) review other departmental procedure manuals
(D) determine the number of copies which will be needed.

33. Assume that new employees work at 70% efficiency for the first 100 working days of employment if there is no formal training program, and that when there is a formal training program, the 100 day period is reduced to 75 days. Further, assume a 250-day work year and an average salary of $12,000. The maximum amount which can economically be spent per employee on an orientation and indoctrination program on the basis of these data is most nearly

(A) $240
(B) $360
(C) $480
(D) $600.

34. The one of the following personnel administration techniques which when properly utilized will yield information concerning current training needs of an organization is the

(A) classification plan
(B) performance evaluation
(C) personnel register
(D) compensation plan.

35. "Many occupations are entirely or almost entirely limited to the public service." Of the following phases of administration, the one which is most justified by the above situation is increased activity in

(A) recruitment
(B) performance rating
(C) on-the-job training
(D) testing.

36. "Competent civil service personnel cannot come just from initial employment on a competitive basis and 'equal pay for equal work'." The one of the following additional factors which is of greatest importance in building up a body of competent civil service employees is

(A) analysis of work methods and introduction of streamlined procedures
(B) training for skill improvement and creating a sense of belonging
(C) rotation of employees from organization to organization in order to prevent stagnation
(D) treating personnel problems on a more impersonal basis in order to maintain an objective viewpoint.

37. Training programs, to be fully effective, should be concerned not only with the acquisition or improvement of skills but also with

(A) employee attitude and will to work
(B) the personality problems of the individual employees
(C) time and motion studies for the development of new procedures
(D) the recruitment of the best persons available to fill a given position.

38. Of the following, the most accurate statement of current theory concerning the ultimate responsibility for employee training is that

(A) each official should be ultimately responsible for the training of all employees under his or her direction
(B) ultimate responsibility for training should be in the hands of a training specialist in the central personnel agency
(C) a committee of employees selected from the trainees should be given ultimate responsibility for the training program
(D) a departmental training specialist should be assigned ultimate responsibility for employee training.

39. "A midwestern city which conducted an intensive training program for members of its police department, stressing the securing and presentation of evidence, has discovered that over a period of years the proportion of arrests followed by convictions has increased. It therefore concluded that the training program was effective." Of the following, the chief fallacy in this evaluation of the training program is that the

(A) experiment did not cover a sufficiently long period
(B) subject matter of the training course was too restricted to warrant generalization

(C) observed result may have been due to other causes

(D) number of arrests made would have been a better index of the value of the training course.

40. Of the following, the best evaluation of an in-service training course is the
    (A) extent to which the employees themselves feel that the course has been valuable
    (B) regularity of attendance at the course
    (C) extent to which the trainees employ knowledge derived from the course
    (D) difference in subsequent service ratings between those who took the course and those who did not.

41. "Training in civil service is the process of aiding employees to gain effectiveness in their present work through the development of appropriate habits of thought and action, skill, knowledge, and attitudes." Of the following, the chief limitation of this definition is that
    (A) attitudes are not frequently considered a proper field for civil service training
    (B) no consideration is given to training for promotability
    (C) insufficient meaning is given to what is implied by effectiveness in present work
    (D) formal education in institutions of higher learning is excluded.

42. In civil service training, the lecture method is generally accepted as most suitable for
    (A) enabling a group of experienced workers to profit by sharing their individual experiences
    (B) teaching solutions to difficult problems for which there are no generally accepted solutions
    (C) orienting a group in the objectives of the organization in which they are employed
    (D) leading a group to recognize a need for further training by the identification of pressing problems in their work which they are unable to solve for themselves.

43. "The increased competence of the employee should be reflected on the job, and the performance evaluation should measure competence in terms of job performance rather than in terms of courses completed." This statement is most accurately considered as an argument

(A) for compulsory rather than voluntary training
(B) against training designed specifically for job competence
(C) for basing promotion on ability to do a higher-job rather than service rating
(D) against credit for training courses in promotion tests.

44. Having supervised an in-service training course for subordinate clerical employees which has just been completed, it is your duty as a Principal Administrative Associate to apply the benefits of this training to the everyday task of your department. Of the following, the most effective means would be to
    (A) secure the active participation of the supervisors in fulfilling this program
    (B) devote your time to other matters since service ratings are sufficent incentives
    (C) send a form letter to each employee indicating that you expect an application of training to the job
    (D) award a prize to the three employees who, at the end of six months, realize your objective most completely.

45. Suppose that you have prepared a training course on the use of specialized new equipment for your office. Before actually beginning the course you should *first*
    (A) offer preferred assignments to those who successfully complete the course
    (B) explain the need and desirability of this training from the employees' viewpoint in order to get willing participation
    (C) issue an order to all employees to take the course since they may all be called upon to run the equipment
    (D) notify the workers that failure to cooperate with the Department in this program would be reflected in service ratings.

46. An orientation program for a group of new employees would *not* usually include
    (A) a description of the physical layout of the organization
    (B) a statement of the rules pertaining to leave, lateness, overtime, and so forth
    (C) detailed instruction on the job each employee is to perform
    (D) an explanation of the lines of promotion.

47. In teaching the job to a subordinate recently assigned to a unit, many teaching methods must be used. In general, however, the best way for the unit supervisor to train such a subordinate is by having him
    - (A) do the job under proper supervision
    - (B) listen to lectures
    - (C) observe the work of other subordinates
    - (D) study the written material.

48. Of the following the *least* desirable use of a new supervisor's probationary period by the administrator is to
    - (A) carefully check and evaluate performance of work assigned
    - (B) instruct the supervisor in the proper performance of assigned duties
    - (C) observe whether the supervisor is capable of performing the duties of the job efficiently
    - (D) train the supervisor for promotion to the next higher rank.

49. "The nature of the experience and education that are made a prerequisite to employment determines in large degree the training job to be done after employment begins." On the basis of this quotation, it is most accurate to state that
    - (A) the more comprehensive the experience and education required for employment the more extensive the training that is usually given after appointment
    - (B) the training that is given to employees depends upon the experience and education required of them before appointment
    - (C) employees who possess the experience and education required for employment should need little additional training after appointment
    - (D) the nature of the work that employees are expected to perform determines the training that they will need.

50. "Trained employees work most efficiently and with a minimum expenditure of time and energy. Suitable equipment and definite, well-developed procedures are effective only when employees know how to use the equipment and procedures." This quotation means most nearly that
    - (A) employees can be trained most efficiently when suitable equipment and definite procedures are used

(B) training of employees is a costly but worthwhile investment
    - (C) suitable equipment and definite procedures are of greatest value when employees have been properly trained to use them
    - (D) the cost of suitable equipment and definite procedures is negligible when the saving in time and energy that they bring is considered.

51. "A supervisor should always remember that the instruction or training of new employees is most effective if it is given when and where it is needed." On the basis of this quotation, it is most appropriate to conclude that
    - (A) the new employee should be trained to handle any aspect of his work at the time he starts his job
    - (B) the new employee should be given the training essential to get him started and additional training when he requires it
    - (C) an employee who has received excessive training will be just as ineffective as one who has received inadequate training
    - (D) a new employee is trained most effectively by his own supervisor.

52. It has been suggested that the in-service training of employees be continued from the time of their employment until the time of their leaving the department. Of the following, the chief justification for such a continuous program of in-service training is that
    - (A) a person's capacity for learning increases with age
    - (B) because of a natural tendency to forget what one has learned and not put into practice, training must be repeated at regular intervals
    - (C) employees usually are capable of further development on the job during the entire period of their employment
    - (D) for learning to be effective, successive stages in the learning process must be correlated and coordinated.

53. Of the following, the *first* step in instructing a new employee how to perform a specific task is to
    - (A) find out what the employee already knows about the task
    - (B) offer the employee incentive for improved performance of the task
    - (C) put the employee in the actual location for the work
    - (D) stress the key points of the task.

54. One of the factors that a supervisor is likely to overlook in training a new employee is that
    (A) most individuals learn better by observation than by performance
    (B) it is the employee that has to do the learning
    (C) the difficulty of performing a task is inversely proportional to the length of time necessary to comprehend the task that is to be performed
    (D) few people have both visual and auditory perceptions.

55. With the wholehearted support of top management, the training bureau of a public agency schedules a series of training conferences for all the supervisory and administrative employees in order to alter their approaches to the problems arising from the interaction of supervisors and subordinates. During the conferences, the participants discuss solutions to typical problems of this type and become conscious of the principles underlying these solutions. After the series of conferences is concluded, it is found that the first-line supervisors are not applying the principles to the problems they are encountering on the job. Of the following, the most likely reason why these supervisors are not putting the principles into practice is that
    (A) the training conferences have not changed the attitudes of these supervisors
    (B) these supervisors are reluctant to put into practice methods with which their subordinates are unfamiliar
    (C) the conference method is not suitable for human relations training
    (D) the principles which were covered in the conferences are not suitable for solving actual work problems.

56. Assume that you are the leader of a training conference dealing with supervisory techniques and problems. One of the problems being discussed is one with which you have had no experience, but two of the participants have had considerable experience with it. These two participants carry on an extended discussion of the problem in the light of their experiences and it is obvious from their discussion that they understand the problem thoroughly. It is also obvious that the other participants in the conference are very much interested in the discussion and are taking notes on the material presented. For you to permit the two participants to continue until the amount of time allowed for discussion of the problem has been exhausted would be
    (A) desirable chiefly because their discussion, which is based on actual work experience, may be more meaningful to the other participants than would a discussion which is not based on work experience
    (B) undesirable chiefly because they are discussing the material only in the light of their own experiences rather than in general terms
    (C) desirable chiefly because the introduction of the material by two of the participants themselves may put the other participants at ease
    (D) undesirable chiefly because the other participants are not joining in the discussion of the problem.

57. During a training session for new employees, an employee becomes upset because he is unable to solve a problem presented to him by the instructor. Of the following actions which the instructor could take, the one which would be most likely to dispel the employee's emotional state is to
    (A) give him a different type of problem which he may be able to solve
    (B) minimize the importance of finding a solution to the problem and proceed to the next topic
    (C) encourage the other participants to contribute to the solution
    (D) provide him with hints which would enable him to solve the problem.

58. Of the following aspects of a training program for supervisory personnel in a public agency, the aspect for which it is usually the most difficult to develop adequate information is the
    (A) determination of the training needs of the supervisory personnel in the agency
    (B) establishment of the objectives of the program
    (C) selection of suitable training methods for the program
    (D) evaluation of the effectiveness of the training program.

59. You are conducting a training conference for new supervisors on supervisory techniques and problems. When one of the participants in the conference proposes what you consider to be an unsatisfactory solution for the problem under discussion, none of the other participants questions the solution or offers an alternate solution. For you

to tell the group why the solution is unsatisfactory would be

(A) desirable chiefly because satisfactory rather than unsatisfactory solutions to the problems should be stressed in the conference

(B) undesirable chiefly because the participants themselves should be stimulated to present reasons why the proposed solution is unsatisfactory

(C) desirable chiefly because you, as the conference leader, should guide the participants in solving conference problems

(D) undesirable chiefly because the proposed unsatisfactory solution may be useful in illustrating the advantages of a satisfactory solution.

60. It is generally best that the greater part of in-service training for the operating employees of an agency in a public jurisdiction be given by

(A) a team of trainers from the central personnel agency of the jurisdiction

(B) training specialists on the staff of the personnel unit of the agency

(C) a team of teachers from the public school system of the jurisdiction

(D) members of the regular supervisory force of the agency.

61. You are responsible for training a number of your subordinates to handle some complicated procedures which your unit will adopt after the training has been completed. If approximately 30 hours of training are required, and you can arrange the training sessions during working hours as you see fit, learning would ordinarily be best effected if you scheduled the trainees to devote

(A) a half day each week to the training until it is completed

(B) one full day each week to the training until it is completed

(C) a half day every day to the training until it is completed

(D) full time to the training until it is completed.

62. "The control of clerical work in a public agency appears impossible if the clerical work is regarded merely as a series of duties unrelated to the functions of the agency. However, this control becomes feasible when it is realized that clerical work links and coordinates the functions of the

agency." On the basis of this quotation, the most accurate of the following statements is that the

(A) complexity of clerical work may not be fully understood by those assigned to control it

(B) clerical work can be readily controlled if it is coordinated by other work of the agency

(C) number of clerical tasks may be reduced by regarding coordination as the function of clerical work

(D) purposes of clerical work must be understood to make possible its proper control.

63. "A well-planned training program can assist new city employees to acquire the information they need to work effectively." Of the following, the information that a newly-appointed Clerk would need *least* in order to perform his work effectively is knowledge of the

(A) acceptable ways of taking and recording telephone messages

(B) techniques of evaluating the effectiveness of office forms used in the agency

(C) methods of filing papers used in his bureau

(D) proper manner of handling visitors to the agency.

64. "The employees' interest in the subject matter of a training course must be fully aroused if they are to derive the maximum benefits from the training." Of the following, the *least* effective method of arousing such interest is to

(A) state to the employees that the subject matter of the training course will be of interest to mature, responsible workers

(B) point out to the employees that the training course may help them to win promotion

(C) explain to the employees how the training course will help them to perform their work better

(D) relate the training course to the employee's interests and previous experiences.

65. In his first discussion with an employee newly appointed to the title of Clerk in a city agency, the *least* important of the following topics for a supervisor of a clerical unit to include is the

(A) duties the subordinate is expected to perform on the job

(B) functions of the unit

(C) methods of determining standards of clerical performance

(D) nature and duration of the training the subordinate will receive on the job.

66. The primary purpose of a probationary period for a new City employee is to
    (A) thoroughly train the new employee in his job duties
    (B) permit the new employee to become adjusted to his new duties
    (C) determine the fitness of the new employee for the job
    (D) acquaint the new employer fully with the objectives of his agency.

67. "A city employee should understand how his particular duties contribute to the achievement of the objectives of his department." This quotation means most nearly that
    (A) an employee who understands the functions of his department will perform his work efficiently
    (B) all employees contribute equally in carrying out the objectives of their department
    (C) an employee should realize the significance of his work in relation to the aims of his department
    (D) all employees should be able to assist in setting up the objectives of a department.

68. "Training promotes cooperation and teamwork, and results in lowered unit costs of operation." The one of the following which is the most valid implication of the above statement is that
    (A) training is of most value to new employees
    (B) training is a factor in increasing efficiency and morale
    (C) the actual cost of training employees may be small
    (D) training is unnecessary in offices where personnel costs cannot be reduced.

69. A supervisor administering on-the-job training to a new employee can make this training effective by correcting the errors that the employee makes in his work. To make the training effective, it would be most appropriate for the supervisor to correct the employee's errors
    (A) as soon as possible after the errors have become serious
    (B) after the employee has been given time to discover and correct his errors by himself
    (C) as soon as practicable after the errors have been discovered
    (D) in work review sessions scheduled at monthly intervals.

70. Of the following, the *least* acceptable procedure to follow in training new employees is to
    (A) reduce the job to be taught to its simpler units and start with the simple elements and gradually work up to the more complex elements
    (B) depart from the natural order in which a job is performed if the training process is facilitated by following a different order
    (C) impress upon the new employee that correctness in method of performing an operation must precede development of speed of performance
    (D) devote the same amount of time to the training of all new employees when preparing them for the same job assignments.

71. The experienced supervisor knows that the most acceptable of the following statements regarding the instruction and training of subordinates is that
    (A) if left alone, each employee develops a method of working which is best for his own individual ability and temperament
    (B) instruction manuals should describe both the correct and the incorrect methods of performing an operation
    (C) written instructions are particularly valuable for operations which are not performed frequently
    (D) the instructor should have the trainee perform an operation before showing the trainee the proper method of performing the operation.

72. Assume that you have been assigned as the leader of an employee training conference dealing with supervisory techniques and problems. At the sessions of the conference, one of the participants frequently asks you questions, the answers to which would require you to express your own opinion on the problem under discussion. Of the following, the *least* effective method to use in handling such a question is for you to
    (A) refer the question to the conference as a whole
    (B) request the participant asking the question to give his own opinion
    (C) direct the question to a participant who has had experience with such type of problem
    (D) answer the question directly with your own opinion and then ask the participants if they concur.

73. When training a new employee, you should not
    (A) correct errors as he makes them

(B) give him too much material to absorb at one time

(C) have him try the operation unless he can do it perfectly

(D) avoid laying emphasis upon possibilities for mistakes.

74. Of the following, the procedure which is *least* desirable in teaching a newly appointed clerk how to perform a complex clerical operation is for the instructor to

(A) perform each step of the clerical operation slowly so that the new appointee may see how each step is performed

(B) have the new appointee perform the clerical operation under the direct guidance of the instructor

(C) demonstrate the different incorrect methods of performing the work and explain clearly why each is incorrect

(D) describe the clerical operation which he is to perform and explain why and how it is to be performed.

75. "In assigning work to Miss Alden, her supervisor at first omitted only obvious details of the assignment. After Miss Alden had performed satisfactorily several jobs assigned in this manner, her supervisor then omitted less obvious details of the job to be performed. When Miss Alden demonstrated that she could handle such assignments satisfactorily, she was assigned work with only general instructions on the nature of the job to be done." The technique employed by Miss Alden's supervisor merits approval chiefly because it provides a method of

(A) developing employee initiative

(B) defining lines of authority

(C) eliminating overlapping functions

(D) establishing work standards.

76. "It is a long-standing policy of this agency to train its new employees by immediately assigning them regular production work under the direct supervision of an experienced worker who instructs and guides the new employee in the proper techniques of performing the work." Of the following assumptions that may be said to underlie the training policy of this agency, the *least* valid one is that

(A) on-the-job training is an effective training method

(B) experienced workers are qualified to train new employees

(C) formalized training programs are less practical than on-the-job training

(D) a trainee can become no more competent than his trainer.

77. A newly appointed clerk is assigned to a unit of a City agency at a time when the supervisor of the unit is very busy and has little time to devote to instructing the new employee in the work he is to perform. Of the following, the most appropriate method of training this employee is for the supervisor to

(A) instruct the new employee to observe several experienced clerks at work and question them regarding any aspect of the work he does not understand

(B) delegate the job of training this employee to an employee in the unit who is qualified to instruct him

(C) assign the new employee a simple task and inform him that more complex and varied duties will be given him when the supervisor is less busy

(D) have the employee spend his time reading the agency's annual reports and the laws, rules, and regulations governing its work.

78. "It is not possible to draw a hard and fast line between training courses for promotion and training courses for greater efficiency on the present job." This quotation means most nearly that

(A) to be worth while, a training course should prepare the employee for promotion as well as for greater efficiency on the present job

(B) training courses should be designated only to increase employee efficiency on the present job

(C) training courses should be given only to employees who are competing for promotion

(D) by attending a training course for promotion, employees may become more efficient in their present work.

79. Both praise and censure may be employed by the supervisor as motivating influences in training subordinates; however, for best results

(A) censure should be used when immediate improvement is sought, while praise should be emphasized when future improvement is desired

(B) censure should be utilized with regularity in order to keep employees on their toes

(C) censure should be used more often with inferior employees, while praise should be used more often with superior employees

(D) praise should be used more often than censure regardless of whether immediate or future improvement is the objective.

80. The type of training which is most suitable when it is desirable to give the maximum amount of information to the greatest number of people at one time is
(A) supervised practice
(B) the demonstration
(C) the lecture
(D) the seminar.

81. The type of training which is most suitable when it is desirable to check ability to do a job is
(A) study and testing
(B) supervised practice
(C) the case study method
(D) the conference.

82. In training, the application of theory to a practical situation is the distinguishing characteristics of the
(A) case study method
(B) conference
(C) instructional motion picture
(D) lecture.

83. Pooling the knowledge and experience of a group of trainees for their mutual benefit is most feasible when the training method used is
(A) study and testing
(B) supervised practice
(C) the conference
(D) the demonstration.

84. "It may be assumed that if all departments had qualified personnel officers, not all departments would be lacking adequate training programs. However, the most cursory examination of the situation will show that some departments do not have adequate training programs. Thus we must conclude that some of them lack qualified personnel officers." The argument presented in the report is
(A) correct; but the conclusion is false as the hypothesis is not true
(B) not correct; what can be concluded is that no department has a qualified personnel officer
(C) not correct; no conclusion with respect to the presence of personnel officers in departments can be drawn from the information
(D) not correct; what can be concluded is that the absence of an adequate training program in a department implies the absence of a personnel officer.

ANSWER KEY

1. B	18. B	35. C	52. C	69. C
2. D	19. D	36. B	53. A	70. D
3. A	20. A	37. A	54. B	71. C
4. B	21. A	38. A	55. A	72. C
5. D	22. D	39. C	56. D	73. B
6. C	23. C	40. C	57. D	74. C
7. C	24. B	41. B	58. D	75. A
8. D	25. A	42. C	59. B	76. D
9. A	26. B	43. D	60. D	77. B
10. C	27. A	44. A	61. C	78. D
11. B	28. A	45. B	62. D	79. D
12. A	29. A	46. C	63. B	80. C
13. D	30. A	47. A	64. A	81. B
14. D	31. B	48. D	65. C	82. A
15. C	32. D	49. B	66. C	83. C
16. B	33. B	50. C	67. C	84. C
17. C	34. B	51. B	68. B	

EXPLANATORY ANSWERS

1. **(B)** If an administrator must continually correct and revise records and reports prepared by subordinates, they have not been trained properly. Nothing in the question indicates that any of the other possible answers are correct.

2. **(D)** In this instance the staff conference method of training should not be used. The subject matter is straightforward and requires the trainees be given facts for which no differences of opinion need be aired in a group situation, as all the trainees have the same general background knowledge.

3. **(A)** In this situation the new supervisors are already experienced employees and will receive individual training in their specific duties by their own supervisors. Finding out what the group wishes to cover in the group training course insures the active participation, interest and cooperation of the trainees, since they are likely to feel that the course will be geared to their needs and desires, and will not duplicate material they have learned previously or which is being covered by their immediate supervisors.

4. **(B)** It takes specific qualities to be an effective instructor. These qualities are quite possibly not possessed by the limited service officers. Therefore, the training would be ineffective.

5. **(D)** The best way to develop a specific skill in an individual is to teach the worker the basics of the skill and then have him do it again and again until the correct way is instilled in the worker. The other possible answers do not appreciably help train for a particular skill.

6. **(C)** The training method expressed in the quotation leads to the very desirable ability of staff to make their own decisions without the need for constant advice and guidance, and the awareness of when higher-level advice is needed and/or authority must be obtained.

7. **(C)** In planning any training course, the administrator must first and foremost consider what should be learned. The other possible answers contain points that should be considered, but deal with the *means* to carry out this primary consideration.

8. **(D)** A very important part of the job of administrator is the training of subordinates. Therefore, training in an organization begins at the top. The administrator is usually trained first so that he or she is able to train immediate subordinates. This process works itself down until the immediate supervisors of the workers performing the line operations have undergone the training necessary to train the rank and file workers.

9. **(A)** The supervisor who never answers a question asked by a worker and always tells him or her to look it up and inform the staff will soon find that workers stop asking questions and often guess the answers and act accordingly, even if they are wrong. Or they will look up an answer but not tell the rest of the staff what they have learned. To train a worker to find the answer and report to staff works as *part* of a formal course, and may help answer a question, but should not constitute a continuous practice.

10. **(C)** Of the possible answers given, the evaluation of the outcome of a training program is needed primarily to discover what was right or wrong in the program so that subsequent courses can be improved.

11. **(B)** When supervisors, given their titles, qualifications and previous experience, are making more mistakes than they should, the need for specific training is indicated.

12. **(A)** Training programs cost time and money. The expense is only justixied if noticeable and continued improvement in performance results. Increased knowledge does not benefit the agency unless continued improvement in the work is evident and is a direct result of training.

13. **(D)** The results of a training program are best measured by comparing the performance of workers before and after completing the course. Other factors may have possibly caused improved performance, but the course of study must be accepted as mainly responsible. The other two possible answers do not prove that the training course improves job performance.

14. **(D)** Of the possible answers, the best way to evaluate a training program's results is to assess the performance of two groups of workers with equal job skills prior to training. Give the course to only one, and afterwards compare the performance of the two groups. The other possible answers are much less satisfactory indications of a training program's success.

15. **(C)** A training conference is not a formal class where the instructor dispenses information utilizing the lecture approach. Its success as a training technique depends on interaction between conference members and on group participation. Participants tend to be embarrassed when asked directly what they think the answer to a particular question is. The best way to begin is to throw out a question to be discussed by voluntary contributions from the conference members.

16. **(B)** The greatest challenge when training staff is instilling in the worker trainee the desire to learn. All of the other possible wnswers are challenges which a knowledgeable supervisor can learn to do, but the ability to motivate a worker with the desire to absorb and utilize the material being presented is the most difficult and requires the greatest skill.

17. **(C)** When trainees ask no questions, this very often means that they are not listening or absorbing the material being taught. It might indicate a lack of interest even though they may understand the subject matter. Questions show they are listening and trying to learn. The other possible answers are good training principles.

18. **(B)** The best training is the kind that helps the student or trainee handle other problems by relating the principles or concepts taught to solving new problems. A worker cannot be taught the answers to every problem, but if he or she knows the basic principles and concepts, he or she should be able to relate them to new situations. The other three possible answers will not necessarily enable a worker to do this.

19. **(D)** Currently supervision is based primarily on training and guiding a worker rather than taking the approaches given in the other possible answers.

20. **(A)** Supervisors who are not responsible for training their subordinates frequently find themselves blamed not only by management for the poor performance by these workers, but also by staff who state they cannot be blamed for mistakes in operation that the trainers did not cover. When a supervisor trains subordinates he or she is fully responsible for their performance. The other possible answers are not facilitated by requiring supervisors to train their own subordinates.

21. **(A)** Monies expended for training are justified only if efficiency and production are noticeably improved and maintained. The other possible answers only partly justify the expenditures or are not reasons why public monies should be spent to train employees.

22. **(D)** If a worker considers training a bore and a waste of time, the reason for this is that the training does not include sufficient participation by the workers. The way to maintain interest and to insure learning is to provide for active discussion and interplay of students with each other and with the instructor. The other possible answers are important pointers, but are not related to maintaining interest.

23. **(C)** Decision-making responsibility at the lowest practical level of the organization is a basic principle of good administration and therefore, training supervisors to assume this responsibility is highly important. Answers A and B are probably true for many supervisors, but their training in supervision is less important than the correct answer.

24. **(B)** In the final analysis, the responsibility for training must rest with the immediate supervisors because only they can truly teach each worker how to cope with the assigned duties and responsibilities. The personnel office may be responsible for coordinating training courses to prevent duplication of courses, and even to conduct courses in subjects common to many units of the agency,

but the training of a specific worker to do a specific job is the responsibility of the immediate supervisor.

25. **(A)** The criticism in this question points to the lack of goals set for the student. It is important the student know what he or she is expected to learn from the course, and be given indication whether progress is being made toward that goal.

26. **(B)** To teach new skills, especially in the clerical field, on-the-job instruction on an individual basis is the best method to use. Group discussion is not appropriate because there is little need for an interchange of opinions, questions among staff, and between staff and trainer. The use of visual aids is a training device or technique. Supervised reading, research and inspection are not appropriate teaching methods for a purely clerical function.

27. **(A)** An understudy should not be burdened with difficult or unpleasant jobs. He or she should be taught the duties of the chief so that he or she can take over in the chief's absence. The other possible answers are appropriate techniques for training, and therefore not correct.

28. **(A)** The reason for not ordering civil servants to attend a training course is that no one can learn very much unless he or she wants to learn, and taxpayers' money is wasted on a worker who will not benefit from a course in which he or she has no desire to attend.

29. **(A)** Good trainers are not just good productive workers, they are also good teachers. Teaching is an art that few possess without first being instructed how to teach, or even after such training. Many efficient workers will still lack the personal qualities and skills that are needed to be a successful trainer. The other possible answers are not appropriate to the question posed.

30. **(A)** Experienced trainers know, as a general rule, that the more one desires to learn, the more one will learn. This is especially true in a work situation. The other possible answers are false statements.

31. **(B)** A basic training maxim says: Do not overload the student with too much material at one time. We all absorb new material at different rates of speed, so the trainer must gauge his or her students' ability to absorb material when devising the training plan. The other possible answers are incorrect general training practices.

32. **(D)** The number of copies that will be needed for a procedural manual does not have to be determined during the planning stage because the number will not greatly affect what material should go in. The other possible answers are important material to be gathered in the preliminary stages of developing the manual.

33. **(B)** From the facts given in the question, one knows that based on a 250 day work year and an annual salary of $12,000, the salary for one work day is $48.00. Without training, the employee per annum works 150 days at 100% efficiency and 100 days at 70% efficiency (70 days useful work or 220 days of work). Thus, he is being paid an annual salary of $12,000 for 220 days work. With training, in a year the employee per annum works 175 days at 100% efficiency and 75 days at 70% efficiency (52.50 useful days work). Thus, he is being paid a $12,000 annual salary for 227.50 days work. Therefore, 7.5 days more useful work are produced annually with training than without. On a daily salary of $48.00, training is worth $360.00. The agency could economically spend that amount per employee on training.

34. **(B)** Of the possible answers, the study of employee evaluations is the best technique to discover what areas of the agency's work need to be included in training courses. For instance, if evaluations show deficiencies in the ability to file, a training course in that task is warranted. The other personnel administration techniques will not directly help discover current staff training needs.

35. **(C)** Since public service contains jobs not found in private industry, on-the-job training is usually more necessary in these fields. New workers will not have had the benefit of prior experience unless they previously worked in another governmental jurisdiction. Relatively few schools teach appropriate courses for government service.

36. **(B)** To build a competent civil service from persons hired on a competitive basis, there must be training both to improve the basic skills the individual brings to the job, and to help the new employee understand and appreciate the importance of group effort and teamwork in an agency whose aim is the public welfare and not personal profit. The other possible answers are of either incidental importance or of doubtful value in building a competent civil service.

37. **(A)** A major concern of training programs is improving worker attitudes towards both the agency and their work, and encouraging workers to do their best on the job. The other possible answers do not deal with problems which directly concern training programs.

38. **(A)** According to current theory, a supervisor is responsible for training immediate subordinates. Moreover, with the organizational structure each official must be ultimately responsible for correctly training all employees under his or her jurisdiction. Training specialists referred to in the other possible answers may give guidance, advice or coordinate programs, but the official under whom both the trainers (supervisors) and the trainees (staff) work, bears the responsibility for the success or failure of the training program.

39. **(C)** The chief problem with the conclusion drawn is that the increase in the proportion of arrests followed by

convictions might be caused by many factors other than the training course, e.g., less lenient judges and or juries, good or bad lawyers, more clear-cut crime situations, etc. The other possible answers given are false.

40. **(C)** The most effective way to evaluate a training course is to determine what use the trainees made of the material taught in the course. The other possible answers do not prove the success or failure of the course.

41. **(B)** In the civil service, training usually encompasses, in addition to effectiveness in a given position, a degree of preparation for assuming higher level responsibilities. The other possible answers are incorrect.

42. **(C)** The lecture method of civil service training is generally most acceptable and economical in orientation sessions where new employees learn personnel rules, regulations, and general structure of the organization, etc. Such data is factual in nature and the lecture method is most suitable for giving facts to a relatively large number of persons at one time. The lecture method would be a less suitable one for the situations described in the other possible answers because all of them require a give-and-take discussion between trainer and workers and among workers to be most effective.

43. **(D)** In essence, the quotation states that merely completing a training course does not entitle a worker to a better performance evaluation, but that the evaluation should be based on improved performance on the job. Based on this statement, it follows that credit for taking a training course should not be given in promotion tests. None of the other possible answers follow from the quotation.

44. **(A)** In order to apply the benefits of an in-service training course, supervisors of the workers just trained must fully support the course, and ensure that the knowledge gained is utilized in their daily activities and responsibilities. Without the supervisors' cooperation the in-service training program is useless. Other possible answers are either unwise or impractical ways to put the knowledge gained from the course to good use.

45. **(B)** Training in the use of new equipment should generally be done on a voluntary basis unless the new equipment will totally replace existing equipment. Unless a worker wants to learn how to use the new equipment, it is very difficult to make them learn. The trainer should ''sell'' the training by showing workers how it will help them do a better job, do it more quickly, and make the worker more promotable, etc. Note that the question is phrased so that you, as a trainer, are not in a position to offer the worker better assignments if they take the course, as in answer A.

46. **(C)** Orientation lectures serve to acquaint new employees, regardless of title, about matters of importance for all employees (wrong answers A, B and D). Detailed instructions to each employee about their specific duties comes from each worker's supervisor when he or she starts work.

47. **(A)** Although a new worker in the course of his or her training either learns from watching others or may have to read pertinent instruction manuals and procedures, the best way to teach him or her is to have them do the job itself under close supervision. Reading about it or watching others is not going to teach them as well as hands-on experience.

48. **(D)** The training of a supervisor still on probation in his or her new title should not focus on training him or her for promotion to the next level. That type of training comes later, when he or she is a permanent supervisor and is secure in the knowledge of the present job. Other possible answers are good practice for an administrator to use during the probationary period.

49. **(B)** In effect, the quotation says that the qualification requirements to get the job determine in large measure the kind of training that will be needed after employment. The correct answer follows logically from the quotation; the others do not.

50. **(C)** The correct answer paraphrases the quotation: Workers must be trained in order to use suitable equipment and definite procedures most effectively. The other possible answers do not follow from the quotation.

51. **(B)** The quotation says training new employees is most effective when and where it is needed. Of the possible answers the only one which refers to the need to give a new worker enough training to get him or her started, plus more training as needed, is B.

52. **(C)** A continuous program of in-service training is chiefly justified because workers are usually capable of learning more and developing their skills through the period of their employment. The other possible answers are either not necessarily true or are not related to the point raised in the question.

53. **(A)** Before instructing a new worker how to do a specific job, the trainer must first discover how much the worker already knows, so that training will not be repetitive. Unnecessary training is costly and should be avoided. The other possible answers are training devices which can be used after this first discovery.

54. **(B)** A supervisor, especially one who has not had considerable experience training others, most often forgets or overlooks the fact that each worker comes to training with his or her own experience, education, and ability to learn or remember. The supervisor instead superimposes his or her own knowledge and experience in teaching new material, and thus overlooks the fact that what to the trainer seems obvious may completely mystify the worker. The other possible answers are generally untrue statements.

55. **(A)** To alter supervisory practices used to solve problems of supervisor/worker relationships, a change in the attitude of the supervisors is needed. From the information given the only conclusion which can be reached is that the training conferences, while appearing to be carefully prepared and executed, failed to change the basic attitudes of the supervisors on this subject. And so, they are not utilizing the principles which the training sessions attempted to instill in them. The other possible answers are not justified from the information given.

56. **(D)** A leader of a training conference must keep control of the conference, and not allow it to be dominated by one or two people, even though the material these people are presenting is of general interest. A conference, to be successful, must include active participation by all attendees. Only by taking part in the discussion does an individual truly learn and contribute to the learning of his or her fellow trainees. Although the two participants in the situation presented appear very knowledgeable, others may have additional or different useful points to make. Their participation is vital for the conference to succeed and for you, as conference leader, to remain in control of the session.

57. **(D)** This is the point when the instructor should step in to assist the individual in extricating himself or herself from an embarrassing situation. The worker is new, has become flustered and there is no reason not to lend assistance at this point. Not to do so might have an adverse effect on the individual's future.

58. **(D)** To determine the effectiveness of a training program for supervisors is most difficult. There are many intangible aspects of the supervisor's job which cannot be accurately measured, and there are other aspects where increased effectiveness cannot be directly attributed solely to the completed training course. This is especially true with respect to evaluating degrees of attitudinal change. Information about the problems presented in the other possible answers is relatively easy to obtain.

59. **(B)** A conference leader may have to guide the participants in solving problems, but, as the question is posed, he or she should not tell the group why the solution presented is unsatisfactory. The leader's role is to stimulate the conference participants to see for themselves the problems involved with proposed solutions. The three other possible answers are not relevant.

60. **(D)** Immediate supervisors who are the most knowledgeable about the actual agency operations are the best persons to train operating subordinates in the daily operations. Outside specialists are not as well equipped to teach the practical daily work of the agency and operating staff.

61. **(C)** Experience and studies have shown that teaching complicated procedures should be done as expeditiously as possible. The mind then retains what is taught in one session, and relates it to the next session. To spend a full day at training staff in a complex procedure is not preferred because of the fatigue factor which may hinder learning. Therefore, in this question, a half day each day for approximately two weeks is best for learning and retaining the procedures.

62. **(D)** In effect, the quotation states clerical work in an organization may be controlled only if its purpose is understood in relation to the achievement of agency goals. The correct answer states this fact. The other choices can not be deduced from the quotation.

63. **(B)** The duties of a newly appointed clerk do not require him or her to evaluate the effectiveness of office forms. The other possible answers refer to information the clerk needs to know to do the job.

64. **(A)** Interest in the subject matter of a training course is not aroused by telling people it will interest them if they are "mature and responsible." It will be around if the workers learn the advantages they may derive from taking the course, and if the course is related to what workers have experienced.

65. **(C)** In the first discussion with a new employee it is not good supervisory or training technique to dwell on how standards of performance are determined. The new worker should be told the functions of the unit, the specific duties his or her title involves in that unit, and the type and duration of training he or she will receive.

66. **(C)** The probationary period is part of the examination for the job. It should primarily be used to determine whether the selection procedure has resulted in the appointment of a person who can successfully perform the job. The other possible answers contain useful activities that should be carried out during the first months of employment, but they are not the purpose for a probationary period.

67. **(C)** The quotation is paraphrased in the correct answer, while the other answers contain statements which may be true but are not related to the question.

68. **(B)** Training promotes efficiency in many ways. Efficient operations result in workers having self-pride. Cooperation and teamwork are also created throughout the organization.

69. **(C)** The best way to train an employee is to correct all errors as soon as they are discovered. This way the worker will best retain the reasons why the work was wrong, how it should be corrected, and the importance of not repeating the error in the future. Allowing any error to go uncorrected or undiscovered and corrected at a later date will diminish the worker's ability and willingness to find and correct his or her own mistakes, as well as diminish the importance of producing correct work.

70. **(D)** New workers differ in the knowledge they bring to the job and in their degree of and ability to learn something new. Therefore, training of new workers may take different lengths of time, even though they are learning the same job. The other possible answers are acceptable procedures to follow in training new employees.

71. **(C)** Written instructions are useful for those activities which the worker does infrequently because the instructions can be referred to as needed. Daily activities often do not need written instructions. The other possible answers are not acceptable statements concerning the instruction and training of subordinates.

72. **(C)** The conference leader must avoid giving his or her opinion on a matter because it might inhibit the participants from speaking freely. It would be better for another member of the conference to respond to this type of question.

73. **(B)** All of us remember the traumas of the first days on a new job and how difficult it was to remember the almost overwhelming amount of new information and material. The basic maxim of training is to give the worker only a certain amount of new material which he or she can absorb. Giving too much will only result in a diminishing of ability to absorb new material. The other possible answers are not good training techniques.

74. **(C)** It is not good training technique to teach a complex clerical operation by showing the worker the incorrect method of doing the work, it can only have harmful results. The proper way is contained in the data given in the other possible answers. Showing a worker the wrong way to do the job only confuses him or her, and explaining why the wrong method is wrong just adds unnecessary burdens to the already difficult process of learning the operation.

75. **(A)** The training method described in the question is a good technique to use in developing the worker's ability to find her answers to questions about the job, and to utilize her knowledge and initiative to solve problems and to complete assigned work. The other possible answers would not result from the training technique described.

76. **(D)** Very often the pupil is able to surpass the ability of the teacher in all endeavors. If this type of training was considered limiting in this area it would not be as widely used as it is.

77. **(B)** It is an acceptable and appropriate training policy in this situation to have an experienced worker instruct a new employee in the basic work of the unit. Mere observation of several workers at work is not good training procedure because not only should one person be responsible for guiding the new worker and giving him or her consistent answers to questions, but also this method may interfere with workers doing their assigned tasks in a timely manner. Assigning one simple task to the worker would be appropriate only if the supervisor expected to assume the training function shortly. The same result would be likely if the employee was left for any considerable period of time to read laws, procedures, etc.

78. **(D)** In effect the quotation says: It is hard to tell where training courses for efficiency in the present job end and training for promotion begins. The correct answer says much the same thing. The quotation does not state that to be a worthwhile training course it should both prepare for promotion and also for improvement on the present job, nor does it make any judgment whether a training course should be designed for only improving efficiency or only for purposes of promotion.

79. **(D)** A good supervisor uses both praise and censure for many reasons, but for training purposes it is better to use praise. It will increase the worker's self-confidence, and enable him or her to become a positive member of the work unit.

80. **(C)** The lecture method of training is an ideal way of dispensing information when student participation is not being sought. It is economical because a large number can be lectured to at the same time. The shortcoming of this training method is a lack of ability to comprehend how the training material is being absorbed by the students.

81. **(B)** The trainer demonstrates the proper way to perform the job, and the trainee is then permitted to perform the job under supervision where errors can be corrected immediately. It is an expensive training method but it is thorough.

82. **(A)** Book learning is applied to real life occurrences in this type of training. It is the time for practical application of the theories one has learned.

83. **(C)** The conference method of training is used mainly to encourage interchange of knowledge and experience among trainees.

84. **(C)** The quotation ends with an erroneous conclusion. In fact, a lack of adequate training programs in some departments does not mean that they lack qualified training officers.

EMPLOYEE EVALUATION

DIRECTIONS FOR ANSWERING QUESTIONS

Each question has four suggested answers, lettered A, B, C, and D. Decide which one is the best answer and on the sample answer sheet (all answer sheets are at the front of the book) find the question number and darken the area, with a soft pencil, which corresponds to the answer that you have selected.

1. Of the following, the *least* important objective of a modern employee evaluation system which is applied to civil service positions is to
   (A) validate selection procedures
   (B) improve the quality of supervision
   (C) furnish a basis for the construction of a position classification plan
   (D) foster the development of good employee performance.

2. "The problem of developing tests for the selection or evaluation of personnel is enormously complicated by the paucity of our information as to what we are trying to measure." In other words, it is difficult to find adequate
   (A) criteria
   (B) samples
   (C) test reliability
   (D) experimental methods.

3. The validity of employee performance ratings or merit ratings by supervisors is such that they are generally best regarded as a measure of an employee's
   (A) general value to the organization, either present or future
   (B) aptitude for his job
   (C) relationship with his supervisor
   (D) relationship with other employees.

4. The one most important thing in obtaining valid evaluation ratings is

   (A) training the raters
   (B) avoiding "halo effect"
   (C) proper selection of the factors to be rated
   (D) selection of an adequate number of factors.

5. Periodic evaluation of the performance of employees may most effectively advance their competence if
   (A) used to help the employees to become aware of their own capacities and the directions in which they might improve
   (B) some persons other than the immediate superior is given responsibility for the preparation of the evaluation
   (C) used only at the time of change of status or dismissal
   (D) the ratings are based entirely on factors which can be objectively measured.

6. Psychologists generally consider that most human traits are distributed among groups of individuals in accord with the normal curve. That is, most people possess an average amount or degree of a trait but a few individuals will possess very large or very small amounts of the trait. Bearing this concept in mind, a supervisor in giving service (efficiency) ratings on a three-point scale (above average, average, below average) to a group of ten employees should give average ratings to
   (A) six employees
   (B) not less than five nor more than seven employees

(C) employees who give normal satisfactory performance

(D) all employees.

7. The main goal of any employee evaluation program should be, the
   (A) recognition of good employee performance
   (B) recognition of poor employee performance
   (C) improvement of employee performance
   (D) providing a means of comparison of employee performance.

8. If an employee under your supervision disagrees with your evaluation of his or her work, the most desirable way for you to handle the situation would be to
   (A) suggest that he take the case to a higher authority
   (B) explain that you are in a better position than he to know whether or not his work is up to standard
   (C) suspend him for ten days
   (D) discuss specific details with him, showing where improvement is necessary.

9. In judging traits such as the initiative or cooperation, an administrator making an efficiency rating is not likely to be misled by his
   (A) fear of initiative on the part of the employee rated
   (B) tendency to rate employees slightly higher than is warranted
   (C) impression of the individual's personality as a whole
   (D) desire to give each employee a different rating.

10. The Probst system is best described as a method of
    (A) job analysis
    (B) employee evaluation
    (C) evaluating experience requirements
    (D) adjusting wages to cost of living.

11. The one of the following which is the *least* valid feature of a sound employee evaluation system is that
    (A) employees should be rated on real and concrete traits
    (B) employees should be informed promptly of ratings assigned to them by their supervisors
    (C) employees should be rated on different traits simultaneously to achieve objectives

(D) provision should be made for employee's appeals from supervisors' ratings.

12. After you have submitted your annual evaluations of the work of your subordinates, one of them whose work has not been satisfactory complains to you that your evaluation was unjustified. For you to avoid discussing the evaluation but to point out two or three specific instances where the employee's work was below standard is
    (A) desirable; an employee should be told what aspects of his work are unsatisfactory
    (B) undesirable; once the evaluation has been submitted there is no point in reconsidering it
    (C) desirable; once the evaluation has been submitted there is no point in reconsidering it but a discussion of the employee's weaknesses may help
    (D) undesirable; it would have been better to explain how you arrived at your evaluation.

13. Assume that you are conferring with a supervisor who has assigned to his subordinates efficiency ratings which you believe to be generally too low. The supervisor argues that his ratings are generally low because his subordinates are generally inferior. Of the following, the evidence most relevant to the point at issue can be secured by comparing efficiency ratings assigned by this supervisor
    (A) with ratings assigned by other supervisors in the same agency
    (B) this year with ratings assigned by him in previous years
    (C) to employees recently transferred to his unit with ratings previously earned by these employees
    (D) with the relative order of merit of his employees as determined independently by promotion test marks.

14. The one of the following which should be considered the least important objective of a jurisdiction's annual service rating system is
    (A) rate the employees on the basis of their potential abilities
    (B) establish a basis for assigning employees to special types of work
    (C) provide a means for recognizing superior work performance
    (D) reveal the need for training as well as the effectiveness of a training program.

15. If you were required to give employee evaluations to employees under your supervision, you should consider as most important during the current period
    (A) the volume of work performed and the salary and grade of an employee
    (B) the length of service and the volume of work performed by an employee
    (C) the previous service rating given him
    (D) the personal characteristics and the quality of work of an employee.

16. An employee evaluation system provides for penalizing an employee who is often late. Of the following, the assumption not implicit in this practice is that
    (A) punctuality is conducive to efficiency
    (B) the amount of time spent at work is indicative of the amount of work done
    (C) there are individual differences in the optimum hours of work
    (D) punctuality is desirable for the maintenance of discipline.

17. The supervisors of five units in a department all of which do the same work rated the work performance of their subordinates as follows

Unit	Superior	Satis-factory	Unsatis-factory
A	0	6	0
B	5	5	1
C	0	4	4
D	2	6	1
E	7	2	0

Upon receiving these reports, the administrative officer should
    (A) compare each employee's rating with the rating he received the previous year and if there is a marked difference average the ratings
    (B) throw out those ratings which seem unreasonable such as those for Units A and E and ask the supervisors to submit new ratings
    (C) confer with the five supervisors, review the standards in use and point out the necessity for uniform action, leaving final decision with the supervisor
    (D) do nothing; the ratings while somewhat unusual are not markedly so.

18. The basic objectives of a plan for evaluating the performance of employees of a large public or-

ganization fall into several categories. Of the following, the one which is *least* likely to be such an objective is to
    (A) provide a norm for acceptable performance
    (B) make the application of personnel policies as objective as possible
    (C) improve quality of personnel already employed
    (D) improve the quality of personnel seeking employment.

19. In the course of study on the causes for employee separation, it is decided to have supervisors rate each employee who has left the organization on a number of traits. For the information obtained from the supervisors to be of maximum value, the traits selected should be
    (A) objectively measurable
    (B) carefully defined
    (C) the ones each supervisor believes to be most important
    (D) related to each other.

20. The one of the following which is the most common flaw in the administration of an employee performance rating system is
    (A) the failure to explain the objectives of the system to employees
    (B) the lack of safeguards to prevent supervisors from rating employees down for personal reasons
    (C) the tendency for rating supervisors to rate their employees much too leniently
    (D) the fact that employees are aware of the existence of the system.

21. The performance rating standards in a city department have been criticized by its employees as unfair. The one of the following procedures which would probably be most effective in reducing this criticism is to
    (A) publish a detailed statement showing how the standards were arrived at
    (B) provide for participation by employee representatives in a possible revision of the standards
    (C) allow individual employees to submit written statements about the standards employed
    (D) arrange for periodic meetings of the entire staff at which the standards are discussed.

22. The recommendation has been made that explicit information be made available to all public em-

ployees of a jurisdiction concerning the procedure to be followed when appealing from a performance rating. To put this recommendation into effect would be

(A) desirable primarily because employees would tend to have greater confidence in the performance rating system

(B) undesirable primarily because a greater number of employees would submit appeals with no merit

(C) desirable primarily because the additional publicity would spotlight the performance rating system

(D) undesirable primarily because all appeals should be treated as confidential matters and all efforts to make them public should be defeated.

23. The best of the following ways to reduce the errors in supervisors' ratings of employee performance caused by variations in the application of the rating standards is to

(A) construct a method for translating each rating into a standard score

(B) inform each supervisor of the distribution of ratings expected in his unit

(C) review and change any rating which does not seem justified by the data presented by the rating supervisor

(D) arrange for practice sessions for supervisors at which rating standards will be applied and discussed.

24. The least essential factor in the successful application of an employee evaluation system is

(A) careful training of reporting officers

(B) provision for self-rating

(C) statistical analysis to check reliability

(D) utilization of objective standards of performance.

25. Of the following, the one which is not an aim of employee evaluation plans is

(A) establishment of a fair method of measuring employee value to the employer

(B) application of a uniform measurement to employees of the same class and grade however different their assignments may be

(C) application of a uniform measurement to employees of the same class and grade performing similar functions

(D) establishment of a scientific duties plan.

26. Employee evaluation may with least justification be employed by the administrative officer as a means of aiding him to

(A) determine the type of training and development needed to increase the worth of individual employees

(B) increase efficiency by establishing an incentive and stimulus for good work

(C) acquire a more systematic and objective view of the merits of individual employees

(D) discourage relatively less competent employees from trying for advancement.

27. Assume that an employee under your supervision complains to you that your evaluation of his work is too low. The most appropriate action for you to take *first* is to

(A) explain how you arrived at the evaluation of his work

(B) encourage him to improve the quality of his work by pointing out specifically how he can do so

(C) suggest that he appeal to an impartial higher authority if he disagrees with your evaluation

(D) point out to him specific instances in which his work has been unsatisfactory.

28. "A new employee's performance should be evaluated quarterly during the probationary period, and at least once a year after the probationary period." Of the following, the chief justification for the less frequent formal evaluation of employee performance after the probationary period is that

(A) over-supervision of experienced employees is unnecessary and undesirable and may create resentment on the part of the employee

(B) the employee has already proven himself satisfactory by passing his probationary period

(C) the older employee reacts more quickly and responsively to supervision

(D) the supervisor has already achieved a considerable degree of familiarity with the employee's capabilities, performance and need for further training.

29. Assume that you are preparing a report evaluating the work of a clerk who was transferred to your unit from another unit in the agency about a year ago. Of the following, the method that would

probably be most helpful to you in making this evaluation is to
(A) consult the evaluations this employee received from his former supervisors
(B) observe this employee at his work for a week shortly before you prepare the report
(C) examine the employee's production records and compare them with the standards set for the position
(D) obtain tactfully from his fellow employees their frank opinions of his work.

30. When asked to comment upon the efficiency of Miss Smith, a stenographer, her supervisor said, "Since she rarely makes an error, I consider her very efficient." Of the following, the most valid assumption underlying this supervisor's comment is that
(A) speed and accuracy should be considered separately in evaluating a stenographer's efficiency
(B) the most accurate stenographers are not necessarily the most efficient
(C) accuracy and competency are directly related
(D) accuracy is largely dependent upon the intelligence of a stenographer.

31. In a public agency, standards of work performance may be established more easily for some types of work than for others. Of the following types of work, the one which would lend itself most readily to the establishment of standards of performance is that done by
(A) a clerk who is assigned to give information to visitors to the agency
(B) a stenographer to a bureau chief who performs all his secretarial work
(C) a clerk assigned to compute employee withholding tax deductions
(D) an accountant who is assigned to examine the records of private firms doing business with the agency.

32. "A primary objective of an office supervisor is to obtain at least standard performance from all the employees in his unit, that is, performance comparable to that which would be expected from a satisfactory, competent employee." When the supervisor of a large stenographic unit notices that one of his subordinates consistently exceeds the performance standards set for the unit, it is most logical for the supervisor first to

(A) commend this subordinate for her work achievements
(B) examine the performance standards set for the unit to determine whether they should be changed
(C) encourage this subordinate by giving her more varied assignments
(D) have this subordinate show other employees of the unit how to increase their production.

33. Of the following, the one which is *not* considered to be an important purpose of the service rating systems most commonly used
(A) supplement the written examination in selecting qualified employees for promotion
(B) are useful in the improvement of work performance of employees
(C) permit employees to present their grievances to their superiors at periodic intervals
(D) are useful indicating training needs of employees.

34. "To determine the productivity of the office worker, one must look beyond the particular piece of work done and consider the result that is accomplished. If there is no useful result, there is no product, and in such a case the employee is to be considered a non-producer." On the basis of this quotation, it is most accurate to conclude that
(A) where two employees are performing similar types of work, one may be unproductive and the other productive
(B) an employee who performs a given task efficiently must necessarily be considered a productive worker
(C) the product of a typist is the typewritten material she has prepared
(D) office workers are usually less productive than factory workers.

35. Suppose that you are required to prepare a report evaluating the services of the stenographers you supervise. Of the following, the stenographer who should be considered *least* capable is the one who
(A) stated that she could not work overtime when requested on several occasions to do so
(B) was dissatisfied with the nature of the work assigned to her
(C) attempted on several occasions to procure a transfer to another department
(D) was unable to follow instructions in the performance of routine duties.

36. Assume that you are attending a departmental conference on efficiency ratings at which it is proposed that a man-to-man rating scale be introduced. You should point out that, of the following, the chief weakness of the man-to-man rating scale is that
    (A) standards for comparison will vary from judge to judge
    (B) judges are unable to select their own standards for comparison
    (C) the standard for comparison shifts from man to man for each person rated
    (D) not every person rated is given the opportunity to serve as a standard for comparison.

37. The report of the head of Unit Y to his bureau chief on the performance of a new clerical employee indicates that the performance is not up to the expected standard. After reading the report, the bureau chief transferred the employee to Unit X. This action on the part of the bureau chief was
    (A) in line with good personnel practice; an employee who does poorly in one place may do better in another
    (B) premature; an attempt to discover the cause of the poor performance should be made first
    (C) was in the best interests of the organization; whenever a supervisor cannot get along with a subordinate for whatever reason, it is desirable to transfer the subordinate
    (D) undesirable; unsatisfactory employees should be dismissed and not transferred from unit to unit.

38. A new employee who has shown that she is capable of performing superior work during the first month of her employment falls far below this standard after the first month. For the supervisor to wait until the end of the probationary period and then recommend that she be discharged if her work is still unsatisfactory is
    (A) undesirable; she should have been discharged when her work became unsatisfactory
    (B) desirable; there is no place in the civil service for unsatisfactory employees
    (C) undesirable; he should immediately attempt to determine the cause of the poor performance

    (D) desirable; the employee is entitled to prove herself.

39. A performance standard refers to
    (A) a description of duties
    (B) the characteristics of a given job
    (C) the goals to be achieved by an individual
    (D) the personal qualities necessary for a given job.

40. Assume that as a Principal Administrative Associate you conduct, from time to time, work performance studies in various sections of your agency. The units of measurement used in any study depend on the particular study and may be number of letters typed, number of papers filed, or other suitable units. It is most important that the units of measurement to be used in a study conform to the units used in similar past studies when the
    (A) units of measurement to be used in the study cannot be defined sharply
    (B) units of measurement used in past studies were satisfactory
    (C) results of the study are to be compared with those of past studies
    (D) results of the study are to be used for the same purpose as were those of past studies.

41. Suppose you are the administrator in charge of a large unit in which all of the clerical staff perform similar tasks. In evaluating the relative accuracy of the clerks, the clerk who should be considered to be the *least* accurate is the one
    (A) whose errors result in the greatest financial loss
    (B) whose errors cost the most to locate
    (C) who makes the greatest percentage of errors in his work
    (D) who makes the greatest number of errors in the unit.

42. Reports on work performance are likely to be most reliable when they can be based upon
    (A) qualitative evaluation
    (B) quantitative data
    (C) self-evaluation
    (D) supervisor's estimates.

ANSWER KEY

1. C	10. B	19. B	28. D	37. B
2. A	11. C	20. C	29. C	38. C
3. C	12. D	21. B	30. C	39. C
4. A	13. C	22. A	31. C	40. C
5. A	14. A	23. D	32. A	41. C
6. C	15. D	24. B	33. C	42. B
7. C	16. C	25. D	34. A	
8. D	17. C	26. D	35. D	
9. C	18. D	27. A	36. A	

EXPLANATORY ANSWERS

1. **(C)** Employee evaluation is based on the worker's performance in assignments attached to the title and position in which he or she is employed. The position classification plan, on the other hand, is based on and constructed from the duties and responsibilities assigned to a position, not on the employee's performance of them.

2. **(A)** You are asked to interpret what the quotation says, which is that the primary problem in developing tests to evaluate personnel performance is in the difficulty of finding adequate criteria. What is lacking is an absolute science in the selection of tests that will accurately predict just how well an individual will perform on the job.

3. **(C)** Studies have shown that the principal problem in obtaining fair evaluations of workers is the tendency of many supervisors who, because they are not given or do not successfully use objective standards against which to measure employee effectiveness, tend to rate their subordinates primarily on the basis of their relationships with the supervisor.

4. **(A)** Well-trained raters will produce effective performance evaluations. Most supervisors are mainly concerned with fulfilling their responsibilities, and regard the process of evaluating their subordinates as a necessary, but by and large unproductive task. A proper training course which encompasses what is expected to be accomplished through evaluating performance of subordinates should convince supervisors of its worth. The training course also goes a long way towards eliminating differences assigned by various raters. A serious shortcoming of this process is that the ratings of a strict and lenient rater are given the same consideration.

5. **(A)** Periodic evaluations are most useful if the worker learns what he or she is doing correctly, and where his or her errors lie and how to correct them. The most objective performance evaluation will not help the worker achieve competency if the evaluation is not used by the supervisor to help the worker gain such competency.

6. **(C)** In this question you are told that most employees' performance level falls in the average range of competency for any given performance factor, that is, employees who give normal satisfactory performance.

7. **(C)** An employee evaluation system should primarily be used as a supervisory tool to point out a worker's problems and strengthen his or her good points. The results of an evaluation can also be used to reward good performance or bring to light poor ones, but the evaluations should be used primarily as a training device.

8. **(D)** For an employee evaluation system to be most effective, a supervisor must convince the worker that the evaluation of each performance factor is objective, and explain in what ways the worker did not meet objective standards of good performance and how improvement is possible. Only after this attempt is unsuccessful can other remedies be considered.

9. **(C)** Initiative and cooperation characteristics of a worker are well defined and an administrator is not likely to be influenced by an individual's personality as a whole. On the other hand, the rating of an administrator in these two areas is likely to be influenced by a desire to give each of the workers a different rating, or a tendency to assign ratings slightly higher than warranted for a fear of the repercussions by a worker following the rating process. These last three instances as depicted in choices A, B, and D are likely to produce ratings which are not entirely valid.

10. **(B)** The Probst system of performance evaluations is a system which sets standards, and then compares employee performance to these standards.

11. **(C)** The best rating system provides for each factor or trait to be rated separately in order to achieve as much objectivity as possible. For example, a secretary is rated on his or her transcribing ability separately from his or her receptionist skill, and so on.

12. **(D)** After a supervisor has prepared an evaluation the overall rating should be discussed in detail with the worker, and the rating for each measurable factor explained. Note that it is not good policy to base an overall evaluation on two or three specific instances of superior or inferior work. Most instances of unusual performance should be considered and evaluated in the context of the worker's entire performance.

13. **(C)** A disparity in ratings would indicate something amiss and should be investigated. The present supervisor could be too harsh in the assignment of ratings or it could be that a strained relationship between supervisor and subordinates has resulted in inferior work performance.

14. **(A)** An annual employee evaluation system does not rate employees on potential ability because overall ratings are based on current performance.

15. **(D)** This choice and the preamble of, the question defines the process of employee evaluation. The supervisor assigns ratings to subordinates based on work performance and personal characteristics as they pertain to the duties of the position.

16. **(C)** The provision for penalizing an employee for frequent lateness does not imply that individuals have different optimum hours of work, but rather that timely completion of an agency's work and determination of individual salaries are based on all employees performing similar duties to meet standards of production.

17. **(C)** Because of the disparity in ratings, a conference should be called to ensure that the five supervisors fully understand the rating factors. During this conference it would also be prudent to make an attempt to equate the differences between the raters. Following this, if the ratings still stand, appropriate measures should be taken, e.g., perhaps the workers in units A, C, and D need additional training.

18. **(D)** An employee evaluation plan might help clarify the characteristics, knowledge, skills, and abilities needed for success on the job, but this relates to the testing of applicants for employment, not to improving the quality of those seeking employment.

19. **(B)** It is most important that everyone define the traits of separated workers in the same way, and the degree to which each ex-employee possessed the trait being presented in a consistent manner. For example, regarding the trait of carelessness, what one supervisor believes to be careless may be insignificant to another. Traits to be measured should be those which are most common to all workers and to the needs of the jobs held, and then carefully applied by each supervisor to fit a departed worker.

20. **(C)** Innumerable studies regarding the administration of an employee rating system have shown the most common flaw to be overly lenient ratings. The best evaluation system possible to compensate for this is therefore the one with the most objective measurements. Thus, if objective standard of 80 words a minute typing equals normal performance, then 60 wpm typing would be poor and would cut down on the supervisor's tendency to be lenient.

21. **(B)** Workers would be more prone to accepting standards that their representatives had a part in setting. Since acceptance of standards by workers is difficult under any circumstances, this would make it somewhat easier.

22. **(A)** A procedure that allows employees to file grievances against performance evaluations gives workers confidence in the rating system and an opportunity to disagree with their supervisor's evaluations. Since the best devised standards are only as objective as the supervisor's use of them, the system must provide for redress of a worker's real or imagined grievances.

23. **(D)** As far as possible, supervisors should know and understand evaluation standards, and apply them in as consistent and fair a manner as possible. The best way to do this is to have private training sessions for supervisors where they practice together rating different workers under different situations. They can also discuss differences of opinions, and arrive at common understandings.

24. **(B)** An employee evaluation system generally does not provide for self-evaluation. This process calls for supervisors to evaluate subordinates with the objective of improving work performance.

25. **(D)** An employee evaluation plan is not concerned with establishing a scientific statement of a duties plan. The employee rating plan emphasizes what the employees are supposed to be doing in the titles they hold.

26. **(D)** Employee evaluation plans should not be used to discourage employees from trying to advance under the civil service system. The evaluation plan is primarily designed to help the employee do better at his or her present job. Note that this does not mean that a worker who has been evaluated as less than competent in his or her present job must be promoted if he or she is reached on a civil service list.

27. **(A)** This is the first course of action to take. It may clear the situation up immediately. If not, the supervisor must then resort to production records, etc.

28. **(D)** An employee evaluation is a tool to help the supervisor improve an employee's job performance. Since he or she cannot be as familiar with an employee's capabilities or need for further training during the probationary period, more frequent evaluations are necessary.

29. **(C)** A worker should be evaluated on the basis of the standards for the work and the title to which he or she has been assigned under your supervision. Prior evaluations for work done under another supervisor and possibly different in work content and requirements should not be involved in the current evaluation.

30. **(C)** The supervisor is evidently equating competency (efficiency) with accuracy, and not considering speed as part of the definition of efficiency.

31. **(C)** It is easier to establish work standards for assignments when the activities can be most readily measured and standardized. The other possible options involve variables not easily measured.

32. **(A)** It is good supervisory practice to acknowledge outstanding performance at the time it is noticed. Nothing in the information given justifies the need to re-examine existing performance standards, or have the stenographer show others how to increase their production. Giving the superior stenographer more varied assignments is a possible step to consider taking, but not the first one.

33. **(C)** An employee evaluation system should allow employees to submit formal grievances against their annual ratings during a given period following assignment of final ratings only.

34. **(A)** This question tests your ability to read and understand a quotation that states productivity is equated only with the accomplishment of useful work. It is possible that if two employees are given the same type of work, one will do complete, useful, and competent work, therefore being productive while the other will not.

35. **(D)** The least capable stenographer is the one who does not accomplish the routine work he or she has been assigned. The other possible answers are problems a supervisor must deal with, but are not indications of his or her capability.

36. **(A)** The chief weakness of a man-to-man rating scale is that the standards one supervisor will use in making judgments will not always be the same as those used by another, so that agency-wide evaluations will be unequal.

37. **(B)** From the data given, you must assume that the report gave no indication why the performance was substandard. No indication is given that the supervisor tried to improve the worker's performance, nor that the matter was discussed with the worker acknowledging that the employee did not belong in the unit. Without such knowledge the bureau chief's action must be deemed premature.

38. **(C)** A good supervisor should note any marked decrease in performance, and should attempt to find its causes and correct the situation as soon as possible. No new employee should be discharged before an attempt has been made to find the cause, especially in the case presented, since the worker is known to be capable of performing superior work.

39. **(C)** A performance standard is the amount of work an individual adequately trained should be able to perform during a given period. It is the goal to be achieved by an individual assigned to work where a standard has been determined.

40. **(C)** In order to make it possible for the results of two studies of work performance to be compared, the same units of work standards must be utilized. If it is not, an objective comparison of two studies will be impossible. If a function is changed or discontinued and its replacement is to be compared with the previous function, some formula must be devised for comparison purposes. However, if an operation has not changed drastically the same work standards should be used in both studies if they are to be compared.

41. **(C)** Accuracy, by its very definition, has nothing to do with the results of errors made (loss of time, money, etc.). The clerk who makes the greatest number of errors is not necessarily the least accurate because he or she may complete more units of work than other clerks whose number of errors are lower because they do less work. Accuracy means the number of errors compared with the work completed.

42. **(B)** The most reliable reports on work performance contain as much quantitative data as possible since such data can be verified by actual count. We can count the number of letters written, but cannot as reliably verify qualitative evaluations, self-evaluations, or superior's estimates.

DELEGATION OF AUTHORITY

DIRECTIONS FOR ANSWERING QUESTIONS

Each question has four suggested answers, lettered A, B, C, and D. Decide which one is the best answer and on the sample answer sheet (all answer sheets are at the front of the book) find the question number and darken the area, with a soft pencil, which corresponds to the answer that you have selected.

1. Of the following, the information that is generally considered most essential in a departmental organization survey chart is
   (A) detailed operation of the department
   (B) lines of authority
   (C) relations of the department to other departments
   (D) the department's responsibility to the Mayor.

2. Of the following, the most important principle in respect to delegation of authority that should guide you in your work if you are in charge of a bureau is that you should
   (A) delegate as much authority as you effectively can
   (B) have all decisions confirmed by you
   (C) discourage the practice of consulting you on matters of basic policy
   (D) keep all authority centralized in yourself.

3. The one of the following which is *least* valid as a guiding principle for you, in your work in building spirit and teamwork in your bureau is that you should attempt to
   (A) convince the personnel of the bureau that public administration is a worthwhile endeavor
   (B) lead every employee to visualize the integration of his own individual function with the program of the whole bureau
   (C) develop a favorable public attitude toward the work of the bureau
   (D) maintain impartiality by convenient delegation of authority in controversial matters.

4. Two of the bureau heads under your jurisdiction are in constant conflict in respect to the authority of one of the unit heads to consult certain records in the office of the other. Of the following, the most helpful action which may be taken immediately to eliminate this friction is to
   (A) call both unit heads into conference with yourself to explain the necessity for cooperation
   (B) ask each unit head separately to be more cooperative with the other
   (C) transfer the disputed records to a third unit head and center authority in the hands of this third person
   (D) define the authority of each unit head.

5. Your bureau is assigned an important task. Of the following, the function that you, as an administrative officer, can least reasonably be expected to perform under those circumstances is
   (A) division of the large job into individual tasks
   (B) establishment of "production lines" within the bureau
   (C) performance personally of a substantial share of all the work
   (D) preparation of a report to your superior on the general outcome of the work.

6. In public administration functional allocation involves
   (A) integration and the assignment of administrative power
   (B) the assignment of a single power to a single administrative level

(C) the distribution of a number of subsidiary responsibilities among all levels of government

(D) decentralization of administrative responsibilities.

7. If the supervisor cannot readily check all the work done in his unit, he should

(A) hold up the work until the supervisor can personally check it

(B) work overtime until the supervisor can personally finish it all

(C) ask the superior to check the work

(D) delegate part of his work to a qualified subordinate.

8. Bureau X is composed of several clerical units, each supervised by a unit head accountable to the bureau chief. Assume that the bureau chief has a special task for an employee of one of the clerical units and wishes to issue instructions directly to the employee regarding this task. The *least* appropriate of the following procedures for the bureau chief to follow is to

(A) issue the instructions to the employee without notifying the employee's unit head

(B) give the instructions to the employee in the presence of the unit head

(C) ask the unit head to send the employee to him for instructions on this special task

(D) tell the employee to inform his unit head of the bureau chief's instructions.

9. Of the following factors, the one which is of *least* importance in determining the number of subordinates that an individual should be assigned to supervise is the

(A) nature of the work being supervised

(B) qualifications of the individual as a supervisor

(C) capabilities of the subordinates

(D) lines of promotion for the subordinates.

10. The administrator should know that in managing his division he or she should avoid

(A) assigning definite responsibilities to his or her immediate subordinates

(B) delegating necessary authority wherever responsibility has been assigned

(C) making a subordinate responsible to more than one supervisor

(D) keeping employees currently informed about actions taken, new developments, and other matters affecting their work.

11. As division chief, you find that one of your new unit heads is constantly bogged down with detail work. This was not the case with his predecessors. The work load of the unit has remained unchanged. Of the following the most likely reason that this unit head is so overloaded with work is that

(A) he or she assigns too much important work to his subordinates

(B) he or she has failed to delegate some of the work to other members of this staff

(C) your division has too many unit supervisors

(D) this unit has too much detail work assigned to it.

12. Written instructions to a subordinate are of value because they

(A) can be kept up to date

(B) encourage initiative

(C) make a job seem easier

(D) are an aid in training.

13. The one of the following functions of a supervisor which can be most successfully delegated is

(A) responsibility for accomplishing the unit's mission

(B) handling discipline

(C) checking completed work

(D) reporting to the bureau chief.

14. A study of the supervision of employees in an agency reveals that the bureau chiefs are reluctant to delegate responsibility and authority to their assistants. This study is most likely to reveal, in addition, that

(A) the organizational structure of this agency should be centralized

(B) the bureau chiefs tend to spend too much of their time on minor aspects of their work

(C) the number of employees supervised by the bureau chiefs is excessive

(D) significant deviations from planned performance are not called to the attention of the bureau chiefs.

15. The delegation of responsibility and authority to subordinates by their superior generally does *not*

(A) facilitate a division of labor or the development of specialization

(B) permit the superior to carry out programs of work that exceed his immediate personal limits of physical energy and knowledge

(C) result in a downward transfer of work, both mental and manual

(D) involve a transfer of ultimate responsibility from superior to subordinate.

16. Of the following, a recognized procedure for avoiding conflicts in the delegation of authority is to
    (A) delegate authority so as to preserve control by top management
    (B) provide for a workable span of control
    (C) review all assignments periodically
    (D) assign all related work to the same control.

17. The chief of a central files bureau which has 50 employees, customarily spends a considerable portion of time in spot-checking the files, reviewing material being transferred from active to inactive files and similar activities. From the viewpoint of the department top management, the most pertinent evaluation which can be made on the basis of this information is that the
    (A) bureau may need additional staff
    (B) supervisor has not made a sufficient delegation of authority and responsibility
    (C) bureau needs an in-service training course as the work of its employees requires an abnormal amount of review
    (D) filing system employed may be inadequate.

18. ''Much of the current criticism of the administration of large organizations is basically a criticism of our failure to place the same emphasis on accountability that we do on authority and responsibility.'' The one of the following acts which is most likely to insure accountability for the discharge of responsibilities inherent in the delegation of authority is the
    (A) establishment of appropriate reports and controls
    (B) delegation of authority so made as to support functional or homogeneous activities
    (C) delegation of authority so made as to preserve unity of command
    (D) decentralization of responsibility and authority.

19. A commanding officer best exemplifies leadership ability by
    (A) setting aside time for self-development and study in order to improve administrative techniques

(B) delegating authority to subordinates so as to have time to plan office activity on a long-term basis

(C) devoting the major portion of his time to supervising subordinates so as to stimulate continuous improvement

(D) formulating a time schedule covering routine duties so as to conserve time for proper performance of his professional duties.

20. A principle which must be recognized by officials of superior rank is that the most constructive aspects of leadership are those which are exercised ''face-to-face.'' The superior official who recognizes this principle will
    (A) avoid situations which will require direct control of the actions of subordinates several ranks below him
    (B) emphasize coordination of the work of subordinates rather than assume direct long-distance control
    (C) insist that communications from his office to members of his command be as short and direct as possible
    (D) place major responsibility for the execution of duties on the immediate superior of the workers involved.

21. A supervisor of a unit may safely delegate certain of his functions to subordinates. Of the following, the function which can most safely be delegated is the
    (A) settlement of employee grievances
    (B) planning and scheduling of the production of the unit
    (C) improvement of production methods of the unit
    (D) maintenance of records of the work output of the unit.

22. ''To delegate work is one of the main functions of the supervisor. In delegating work, the supervisor should remember that even though an assignment is delegated to a subordinate, the supervisor ultimately is responsible for seeing that the work is done.'' The most valid implication of this quotation for a supervisor is that he should
    (A) delegate as few difficult tasks as possible so as to minimize the consequences of inadequate performance by his subordinates
    (B) delegate to his subordinates those tasks which he considers most difficult

(C) check the progress of delegated assignments periodically to make certain that the work is being done properly

(D) assign work to a subordinate without holding him directly accountable for carrying it out.

23. A recently developed practice in administration favors reducing the number of levels of authority in an organization, increasing the number of subordinates reporting to a superior, and also increasing the authority delegated to the subordinates. This practice would most likely result in

(A) an increase in the span of control exercised by superiors

(B) an increase in detailed information that flows to a superior from each subordinate

(C) a decrease in the responsibility exercised by the subordinates

(D) a decrease in the number of functions performed by the organization.

ANSWER KEY

1. B	6. C	11. B	16. D	21. D
2. A	7. D	12. D	17. B	22. C
3. D	8. A	13. C	18. A	23. A
4. D	9. D	14. B	19. C	
5. C	10. C	15. D	20. D	

EXPLANATORY ANSWERS

1. **(B)** An agency organization chart shows the various units, divisions and bureaus within the agency. It should clearly indicate to whom each unit directly reports and is directly responsible, moving up the hierarchical ladder to the head of the agency. This will indicate the lines of authority throughout the agency.

2. **(A)** Authority is a means of getting work done, not an end in itself. It includes finding and utilizing the best way to do a job, and the right and duty of the person to make decisions which will not ordinarily be countermanded by superiors. A good administrator delegates authority to the lowest possible level of supervision. This does not mean persons in lower levels should make policy, or make decisions where they do not fully understand the agency's policy.

3. **(D)** A good administrator should not, in order to appear impartial, "conveniently" delegate authority in controversial matters. This action does not build team spirit or even maintain impartiality. It merely foists onto others the authority and responsibility for actions which rightly should have remained with the administrator.

4. **(D)** The problem posed is that of unclear delineation of respective authority between two unit heads. The best procedure for the administrator to follow is to define their respective authority. The administrator who merely stresses that the two unit heads should cooperate, or who seeks to solve the problem by giving the authority to a third person, is not solving the problem at all.

5. **(C)** The administrator would not be expected to personally do most of the work. An administrator does, however, divide the job into workable components, assigns a worker or team of workers to each component part, establishes a production line or other method to move the work along, and prepares final reports to the superior.

6. **(C)** The responsibilities for some functions should be centralized, others would work more efficiently if they

were decentralized. A good example of a centralized function would be the purchasing of supplies and equipment. Mass purchasing would probably be more economical. On the other hand, certain functions would be more efficient if they were decentralized. A good example of this is public relations. Because of peculiarities in the operation of an agency, no one would be able to promote good and proper public relations better than the agency itself.

7. **(D)** In many instances a supervisor cannot personally check the accuracy of work done by subordinates. The best way to handle this fact of administrative life is to delegate part of the responsibility to a qualified subordinate.

8. **(A)** For the head of the unit not to be informed by the bureau chief regarding an employee is an incorrect procedure. The direct supervisor should always be informed in this type of situation so that he or she can plan the unit work accordingly. It is also considered a common courtesy to do so.

9. **(D)** From an administrative point of view, lines of promotion are of no real importance in determining how many persons should be reporting to a supervisor. What is important is the nature of the work being done and the degree of need for supervision. The qualifications of the individual supervisor must also be considered.

10. **(C)** A basic principle of good administrative organization is to provide that no worker be made responsible to more than one supervisor at any given time for the completion of regularly assigned duties.

11. **(B)** If the work load has remained constant, the reason probably is that the new supervisor has not delegated detail work to subordinates.

12. **(D)** Written procedures can be of great help when a supervisor is teaching a new or changed procedure to the

staff. It helps the supervisor to remember all points being taught. It gives the worker something to refer to after the training is finished, and will help to settle controversial points when the worker is doing the job.

13. **(C)** A supervisor is personally responsible for getting the work of the unit done, for maintaining discipline, and for reporting on the unit's functioning to superiors. The supervisor can and should delegate much of the review of completed work, especially routine work, to a qualified subordinate.

14. **(B)** The most likely result of this is bureau chiefs who spend too much time on minor matters such as checking on work or keeping records. The study may show any or all of the other answers to be true, but these cannot be surmised from the information given.

15. **(D)** Ultimate responsibility for the performance of a function remains with the superior who delegated the authority to the supervisor. In the end the superior will have to answer if anything goes wrong. On the other hand the superior will hold the supervisor accountable.

16. **(D)** It is an excellent procedure, if possible, to assign responsibility for the performance of work, which is related, to the same individual. The only restriction would be a limitation of any one individual to do so. If work which is related is split for the purpose of delegation of authority, conflicts are likely to arise such as who should have performed a given part of the work.

17. **(B)** The chief's role is to plan, coordinate and evaluate work, not to do detailed review of staff activities. Note that there is nothing in the information given to indicate that the work has been unsatisfactory so that the supervisor feels he or she has to personally spot-check it.

18. **(A)** Proper delegation of authority and responsibility demands that there be a method to ensure that the au-thorized person is doing the job correctly. The best way to ensure accountability is to have an adequate, meaningful reporting and control system.

19. **(C)** Leadership ability requires that a supervisor work directly with subordinates in stimulating their interest in, and enthusiasm for, the work. Note that all other possible answers are techniques that a supervisor can properly adopt to get the unit's work done properly, but they do not relate to the leadership quality.

20. **(D)** Immediate supervisors rely on direct oral orders to instruct their subordinates. These oral orders are usually more readily acceptable to workers because they are not impersonal and they can be "tailored" to suit an individual's needs. No one is more suited to communicate with a worker than the immediate supervisor.

21. **(D)** The responsibility for the correct maintenance of records which indicate a unit's work output can reasonably be delegated to a subordinate. Handling employee grievances, planning and scheduling production, and improving production methods are supervisory functions which should ordinarily be reserved for the supervisor, whose actions are likely to be accepted by the staff.

22. **(C)** The supervisor will ultimately have to answer to his or her superiors if anything goes wrong. Therefore, the supervisor should check the work for proper progress and can hold the subordinate accountable, but in the end the supervisor retains ultimate responsibility for all functions within his or her jurisdiction.

23. **(A)** The question refers to the practice of utilizing relatively few hierarchical levels and therefore increasing the number of employees reporting to each supervisor, and also to increasing subordinate authority. This practice naturally results in an increase in the span of control of the supervisor.

POSITION CLASSIFICATION AND PERSONNEL ADMINISTRATION

DIRECTIONS FOR ANSWERING QUESTIONS

Each question has four suggested answers, lettered A, B, C, and D. Decide which one is the best answer and on the sample answer sheet (all answer sheets are at the front of the book) find the question number and darken the area, with a soft pencil, which corresponds to the answer that you have selected.

1. Assume that a salary standardization program has been instituted in a large city. Of the following, the aspect of a standardized salary scale likely to be most effective from the viewpoint of establishing a wage incentive is
   (A) a narrow salary range for each job
   (B) provision for regular salary increments for each job
   (C) a definite minimum salary for each job
   (D) a definite maximum salary for each job.

2. The one of the following which is least valid as a criterion for evaluating a duties statement in a class specification is
   (A) Does it define the level of the work performed?
   (B) Does it provide for doing related work as required?
   (C) Does it show interrelationships with other jobs?
   (D) Does it define the scope of the work performed?

3. The "classified service" refers most accurately to that part of the civil service
   (A) over which the chief executive has the nominal appointing power
   (B) classified into a graded service
   (C) under the jurisdiction of the Department of Personnel

   (D) for which definite salary ranges have been established by law.

4. In accordance with best public personnel practice, the one of the following who is least appropriately classified as an exempt employee is
   (A) a confidential secretary to the head of a New York City department or agency
   (B) a deputy to the head of a New York City department or agency with power to formulate decisions in the absence of the department head
   (C) an administrator in a New York City department or agency with power to make important administrative decisions and regulations
   (D) an employee appointed by the chief executive to assist in the formulation of policy and in carrying out the mandate of the electorate.

5. In public administration, horizontal movement of personnel refers most directly to
   (A) transfer from a position in one department to a position in another department
   (B) cross-promotion from one type of work to another type of work of higher calibre
   (C) equivalent rates of appointment and resignation at the entrance levels
   (D) vestibule training for development of greater skill in the job.

6. Of the following, the item of information on an experience record sheet which is likely to indicate most accurately the quality of the experience offered by a candidate for an administrative position would be
   (A) the exact title of the candidate in his present job and the title of the most nearly equivalent job in the City Service
   (B) the total number of employees in the firm in which the candidate is employed and the number of employees directly supervised by him
   (C) an organization chart of the firm in which the candidate is employed and an indication of the candidate's position in the hierarchy
   (D) an accurate list of the precise types of administrative tasks performed by the candidate during an average day.

7. The one of the following which is least frequently included in a class specification is
   (A) typical tasks
   (B) number of vacancies
   (C) minimum qualifications
   (D) line of promotion.

8. In classification surveys, a desk audit most accurately refers to
   (A) interviewing of employees while they are on the job
   (B) preliminary sorting of questionnaires by organizational units
   (C) charting and analyzing of positions in an organizational unit
   (D) careful logical analysis of the duties and responsibilities of the employee by the classifier.

9. Of the following, the chief distinction between a "position" and a "class" in public personnel administration is that
   (A) a position, unlike a class, is a specific set of duties
   (B) the chief duties of a class, unlike a position, vary according to assignment
   (C) a position is divided into several classes according to salary
   (D) a class includes positions at various levels.

10. Suppose that a classification survey is under way in a large City department. Each employee has been requested to describe his or her duties on a questionnaire form. Of the following, the least significant criticism of this procedure as a method of classification analysis is that
   (A) analysis of a large number of questionnaires is likely to be expensive and time-consuming
   (B) employees are likely to report their jobs inaccurately
   (C) the terminology employed in the questionnaires is not likely to be standard
   (D) each employee is likely to present his or her own viewpoint of what his or her job entails.

11. In public administration, the essence of classification is described most accurately as determining
   (A) whether a particular job assignment is most appropriate in terms of the total organization
   (B) whether a particular rate of pay is appropriate for the level of the job and its customary duties
   (C) whether two positions are sufficiently similar to be grouped together
   (D) which of two titles better suits a job assignment.

12. Work flow charts are used in an organization primarily because they
   (A) indicate present and future objectives clearly
   (B) are frequently used records
   (C) clearly indicate when each operation will be performed
   (D) summarize the work procedures of the organization.

13. The one of the following pieces of information which is of *least* importance in setting up the schedule for a given job is the time
   (A) which is required to perform each component of the job
   (B) when the source material will be available
   (C) the job will take under adverse conditions
   (D) by which the job must be completed.

14. "A classification analyst sorts jobs horizontally and vertically." Of the following, the *least* important job factor to be considered with respect to vertical placement is
   (A) independence of action and decision
   (B) determination of policy
   (C) kind and character of work performed
   (D) degree of supervision received.

Questions 15 and 16 are based on the following paragraph:

"People must be selected to do the tasks involved and must be placed on a payroll in jobs fairly priced. Each of these people must be assigned those tasks which he or she can perform best; the work of each must be appraised, and good and poor work singled out appropriately. Skill in performing assigned tasks must be developed, and the total work situation must be conducive to sustained high performance. Finally, employees must be separated from the work force either voluntarily or involuntarily because of inefficient or unsatisfactory performance or because of curtailment of organizational activities.''

15. A personnel function which is not included in the above description is
    (A) classification
    (B) training
    (C) placement
    (D) severance.

16. The underlying implied purpose of the policy enunciated in the above paragraph is
    (A) to plan for the curtailment of the organizational program when it becomes necessary
    (B) to single out appropriate skill in performing assigned tasks
    (C) to develop and maintain a high level of performance by employees
    (D) that training employees in relation to the total work situation is essential if good and poor work are to be singled out.

17. "When, in the process of developing a classification plan, it has been decided that certain positions all have distinguishing characteristics sufficiently similar to justify treating them alike in the process of selecting appointees and establishing pay rates or scales, then the kind of employment represented by such positions will be called a 'class'." According to this paragraph, a group of positions is called a class if they
    (A) have distinguishing characteristics
    (B) represent a kind of employment
    (C) can be treated in the same manner for some functions
    (D) all have the same pay rates.

18. The one of the following which is *not* among the most common of the compensable factors used in wage evaluation studies is
    (A) presence of avoidable hazards
    (B) physical demand

(C) responsibility for the safety of others
(D) working conditions.

19. Assume that you have been assigned to prepare a plan for conducting a large scale job classification survey. Of the following, the best suggestion for reducing the number of appeals from the final allocations likely to be received after the classification study has been completed is to
    (A) have supervisors check statements of employees on classification questionnaires
    (B) allocate present positions to proposed classes according to jurisdictional assignments
    (C) adjust salary to present level of work performed by employees
    (D) allow employee participation throughout the classification process.

20. There are four basic systems of job evaluation which have been extensively used by government and industry. The one of the following which is *not* one of these is the
    (A) Benchmark system
    (B) Factor Comparison system
    (C) Point system
    (D) Job Classification system.

21. Of the following, the chief justification for a periodic classification audit is that
    (A) salaries should be readjusted at frequent intervals
    (B) some degree of personnel turnover should always be expected
    (C) a career service requires regular promotion opportunities
    (D) positions frequently change over a period of time.

22. Suppose that a competitive civil service examination has been ordered to fill a certain position in an intermediate grade in your department. This position is at present being filled by a provisional employee. You have been assigned to work in cooperation with a representative of the Department of Personnel in determining the qualifications which will be required of applicants for this position. The one of the following which should merit *least* consideration in setting up the necessary qualifications is the
    (A) duties of the position
    (B) duties of the position which is next in line of promotion

(C) amount of on-the-job training that will be given to the person appointed from the list

(D) educational background of the present incumbent.

23. "The job analyst should be a master of the scientific method, since his work and the effects of his work will be evaluated or criticized according to the rules of scientific procedure." According to the above statement, the job analyst should be
   (A) able to apply scientific techniques to his work
   (B) trained in the sciences
   (C) specifically trained in job analysis
   (D) willing to have his work criticised.

24. "Classification may most properly be viewed as the building of a structure." The fundamental unit in the classification structure is the
   (A) assignment
   (B) position
   (C) service
   (D) rank.

25. The use of the probationary period in the public service has become an approved practice especially where the state tenure laws guarantee long-term continuous employment. Of the following, the most important use of the probationary period is that it
   (A) reveals aspects of performance and attitude toward the job not adequately measured by formal examination
   (B) supplies confirming evidence of academic and cultural fitness not measurable in formal test procedures
   (C) introduces the new employee to the office and the work situation which conditions future performance
   (D) provides the new employee with a sound basis for self-improvement.

26. The one of the following situations which is most likely to result from a too highly specified assignment or definition of responsibility is that
   (A) there will be no standard against which to measure the efficiency of the organization
   (B) duplication and overlapping of functions will be encouraged
   (C) sufficient channels to collect and coordinate all performances may not be provided
   (D) essential tasks which have not been explicitly mentioned in the assignment may not get done.

27. Temporary assignment of an employee to the duties of the higher position is a device sometimes used to determine promotability. The use of this procedure, especially for top positions, is
   (A) desirable; no test or series of tests can measure fitness to the same extent as actual trial on the job
   (B) undesirable; the organization will not have a responsible head during the trial period
   (C) desirable; employees who are on trial tend to operate with greater efficiency
   (D) undesirable; the organization would tend to deteriorate if no one of the candidates for the position was satisfactory.

28. Frequently, when accumulating data for a salary standardization study, the salaries for certain basic positions are compared with the salaries paid in other agencies, public and private. The one of the following which would most usually be considered one of these basic positions is
   (A) Office Manager
   (B) Administrative Assistant
   (C) Chief Engineer
   (D) Junior Typist.

29. "The process of classification is also instrumental in revealing organizational defects and inadequacies in the flow of work and thus is an important means for improving operating management." According to the above passage
   (A) the purpose of classification is to reveal organizational defects
   (B) operating management cannot be improved without proper classification
   (C) the operational set-up of an organization can benefit from classification
   (D) inadequacies in the flow of work constitute the most important organizational defect.

30. "It is theoretically conceivable that some single work unit exists which can be used to measure the workload of an entire city department. If this work unit really existed and were known, and if the sole purpose of the work measurement program were to evaluate the performance of a department on an overall basis, two figures would be required to measure work efficiency." These are the total number of such work units and
   (A) the total man-hours used
   (B) the number of employees engaged
   (C) the scheduled number of work units
   (D) a measure of the work-load efficiency.

31. The one of the following which is not usually included in a class specification is
    (A) a definition of the duties and responsibilities covered
    (B) the statement of minimum qualifications necessary to perform the work
    (C) a description of the recruitment method to be used
    (D) a statement of typical tasks performed.

Make use of the following paragraph in answering Questions 32 and 33:

"In evaluating education for a particular position, education, in and of itself, is of no value except to the degree in which it contributes to knowledge, skills, and abilities needed in the particular job. On its face, such a statement would seem to contend that general educational development is not to be considered in evaluating education and training. Much to the contrary, such a proposition favors the consideration of any and all training but only as it pertains to the position for which the applicant applies."

32. On the basis of the above paragraph, in evaluating education for a particular position
    (A) general education should be given as much weight as specialized education
    (B) only specialized education should be considered
    (C) both general and specialized education should be considered
    (D) specialized education is of no value unless it is supplemented by general education.

33. In evaluating training in accordance with the criteria set up in the above paragraph, high school education is
    (A) of no value for a position requiring specialized training
    (B) essential in all occupations involving work other than manual labor
    (C) desirable in any occupation
    (D) of value to the degree to which it is needed in the particular position.

34. The first prerequisite to the formulation of any compensation plan for a public agency is the collection and analysis of certain basic data. Data are not usually collected for this purpose in regard to
    (A) working conditions in the agency
    (B) the wage paid in the agency at present
    (C) labor turnover in the agency
    (D) the age and sex distribution of the employees.

Make use of the following paragraph in answering Questions 35 and 36.

"A duties classification is not the same thing as a pay plan. Duties classification may be a vital element upon which a compensation structure is based and administered. But compensation must also be governed by other factors, such as quality of performance and length of service as well as by basic economic and social considerations. Further, classification serves many uses other than governing pay."

35. According to the above paragraph
    (A) a duties classification cannot be set up without an accompanying pay plan
    (B) a pay plan is not related to a duties classification
    (C) a duties classification cannot function without a pay plan
    (D) a duties classification is of importance in the formulation of a pay plan.

36. According to the above paragraph, a change in the value of the dollar would be most likely to affect
    (A) only the duties classification
    (B) only the pay plan
    (C) both the duties classification and the pay plan
    (D) neither the duties classification nor the pay plan.

37. "In a large organization, proper recruitment is not possible without the existence of an effective position classification system." One of the following best explains why this is the case because otherwise, effective means of determining the capabilities and characteristics of prospective employees are of little value
    (A) unless these are related to the salary scale and current economic conditions
    (B) without a knowledge of the essential character of the work to be performed in each position
    (C) where no attempt to classify the different recruitment approaches has been made in advance
    (D) if there has been no attempt made to obtain the cooperation of the employees involved.

38. The one of the following which is usually not considered part of a classification survey is
    (A) grouping positions on the basis of similarities
    (B) preparing job specifications

(C) analyzing and recording specific job duties

(D) adjusting job duties to employee qualifications.

39. "The pay plan is a vital aspect of a duties classification. In fact, in most areas of administration pay plan and classification are synonymous." This statement is
   (A) correct in general; while the two are not, in general, synonymous, the pay plan is such a vital aspect that without it the classification plan is meaningless and useless
   (B) not correct; while the pay plan is a vital aspect of a classification plan it is not the only one
   (C) correct in general; pay plan and duties classification are simply two different aspects of the same problem—"equal pay for equal work."
   (D) not correct; although classification is usually a vital element of a pay plan, a pay plan is not essential to the preparation of a duties classification.

40. As a result of a study of the operations of the Federal Government, a recommendation was made that for purposes of reduction in force, employees be ranked from the standpoint of their over-all usefulness to the agency in question. The one of the following which is a major disadvantage of this proposal is that it would probably result in
   (A) efficient employees becoming indifferent to the social problems posed
   (B) a sense of insecurity on the part of employees which might tend to lower efficiency
   (C) the retention of employees who are at or just past their peak performance
   (D) the retention of generalists rather than specialists.

41. In general, the one of the following which is the first step in the construction of a test for the selection of personnel is to
   (A) determine what the duties of the position to be filled are
   (B) investigate the relationships among abilities and capacities required for success in the position to be filled
   (C) study examinations which have been given in the past for similar positions
   (D) evaluate existing examining instruments to determine their adequacy for making the desired selection.

42. "The employee who has been 15 years in the same job is less fit for promotion than the employee who has been 5 years in the job." A system of seniority credits toward promotion based upon this philosophy would most probably
   (A) add a positive but decreasingly large seniority increment for each additional year of service
   (B) give zero seniority credit after 15 years of service
   (C) assign a negative but increasingly larger increment for each year of service
   (D) deduct seniority credit for each year of service beyond a critical year less than 15.

43. "Labor turnover in any organization should be about 10–12 per cent." Of the following, the best justification for this statement is that
   (A) positions at the lower levels in an organization should be rotated at fairly frequent intervals
   (B) absence of any dismissals at all may result in loss of employee initiative
   (C) opportunity should be available for advancement of competent personnel
   (D) no employee should be kept too long on any one job.

44. In making a position analysis for a duties classification, the one of the following factors which must be considered is the
   (A) capabilities of the incumbent
   (B) qualifications of the incumbent
   (C) efficiency attained by the incumbent
   (D) responsibility assigned to the incumbent.

45. Assume that a proposed class specification has been submitted to you for criticism. Of the following, the least valid criterion for evaluating the merits of this specification is:
   (A) Is the title appropriate for all the duties normally performed by persons to be assigned this title?
   (B) Do all the persons who are to be assigned this title now possess titles which are at least reasonably similar?
   (C) Should all the persons who are to be assigned this title receive approximately the same compensation?
   (D) Could a single examination be used to select all persons to be appointed under this title?

46. Of the following devices used in personnel administration, the most basic is

(A) classification
(B) performance rating
(C) appeals
(D) in-service training.

47. The "determination of essential factors in a specific kind of work and of qualifications of a worker necessary for its competent performance" is most accurately defined as
    (A) job analysis
    (B) micro-motion study
    (C) cost analysis
    (D) production control.

48. "Time studies" examine and measure
    (A) past performance
    (B) present performance
    (C) long-run effect
    (D) influence of change.

49. The administrative officer of a department is considering the problem of whether an increase in the regular staff is required to perform efficiently the work of the department. Of the following questions, the one whose answer would be most diagnostic of whether such increase is needed is
    (A) Are temporary employees hired for short peak load periods?
    (B) Does the present regular staff keep the work of the department up to date?
    (C) Are the regular employees dissatisfied with their present working conditions?
    (D) Are there cases of irregular hours of work due to occasional overtime matched by equivalent time off?

50. A general practice is to require satisfactory completion of the probationary period before an employee is eligible for promotion. The one of the following which is not an assumption underlying this procedure is that
    (A) it is desirable that an employee show at least a certain minimum ability on a job before he is promoted to a higher job
    (B) ability on one job is correlated in some degree with ability on the next higher job
    (C) outstanding success on one job is predictive of success on higher jobs
    (D) long service on a job is not necessary for success on a higher job.

51. It has been maintained by some authorities that there is an increasing need for adequate evaluation of administrative management by means of measuring devices. Of the following, the least valid criterion that may be applied to determine the adequacy of a proposed measuring technique is that it must
    (A) avoid the fallacy of breaking down the administrative function into component elements
    (B) take into consideration the practical conditions under which the administrative officer operates
    (C) eliminate the element of personal opinion in application
    (D) not only be a valid device in fact but must be sound, clear and convincing in appearance.

52. The one of the following which is not a valid principle that may be employed to guide you in executive planning is that
    (A) the executive planner analyzes the job to be sure of the objective and then divides the job into individual tasks
    (B) executive planning is a preliminary function, ceasing once the organization is in operation
    (C) the executive planner must have available constant knowledge of the work load of each unit so that he may make assignments which will be carried out on time
    (D) organization should be planned to suit the job to be done, rather than the converse.

53. Of the following, the one which is not a proper function of an accounting system is to
    (A) document the necessity for the expenditure of certain funds
    (B) reveal the financial condition
    (C) facilitate necessary adjustments in rate of expenditure
    (D) aid in the making of an audit.

54. "Some organizations now question the effectiveness of extreme job specialization. It is felt that in some instances it may be more advantageous to enlarge the scope of individual jobs, thus providing the employee with a greater variety of tasks." Of the following, the one which is *least* likely to be a result of enlarging the scope of jobs is
    (A) an increase in the employee's job responsibilities
    (B) a decrease in the number of job titles in the organization

(C) an increase in the number of tasks performed by an employee

— (D) a decrease in employee flexibility.

55. In the administration of a selection program, the standardization of qualifications is important primarily because it
    (A) eliminates the need for comparing candidates with each other
    (B) enables examiners to eliminate subjective judgment as a factor in the selection process
    — (C) makes the task of comparing candidates easier and more reliable
    (D) provides a basis for the development of sound programs.

56. In position classification, the one of the following factors which is of *least* importance in classifying a clerical position is the
    (A) degree of supervision under which the work of the position is performed
    (B) amount of supervision exercised over other positions
    — (C) training and experience of the incumbent of the position
    (D) extent to which independent judgment must be exercised in performing the duties of the position.

57. The position classifying bureau of the central personnel agency in a public jurisdiction is normally *not* responsible for
    (A) allocating individual positions to classes
    (B) assigning titles to classes of positions
    (C) establishing minimum qualifications for positions
    — (D) determining which positions are necessary.

58. The one of the following which is generally considered to be an essential element in the process of classifying a position in a civil service system is the
    — (A) comparison of the position with similar and related positions
    (B) evaluation of the skill with which the duties of the position are being performed
    (C) number of positions similar to the position being classified
    (D) determination of the salary being paid for the position.

59. Position classifications can *not* be utilized to establish
    (A) appropriate assignment of employees
    (B) effective training programs
    — (C) equitable time and leave regulations
    (D) good organization and supervision.

ANSWER KEY

1. B	13. C	25. A	37. B	49. B
2. C	14. C	26. D	38. D	50. C
3. C	15. A	27. A	39. D	51. A
4. C	16. C	28. D	40 .B	52. B
5. A	17. C	29. C	41. A	53. A
6. C	18. A	30. A	42. D	54. D
7. B	19. D	31. C	43. C	55. C
8. A	20. A	32. C	44. D	56. C
9. A	21. D	33. D	45. B	57. D
10. D	22. D	34. D	46. A	58. A
11. C	23. A	35. D	47. A	59. C
12. C	24. B	36. B	48. B	

EXPLANATORY ANSWERS

1. **(B)** A standardized salary scale is most effective in establishing wage incentive if it provides for regular salary increments after definite periods of time, and if the employee performs satisfactorily during that period. The other possible answers are actually hindrances to establishing wage incentive.

2. **(C)** In evaluating a duties statement in a class specification, the inter-relationships between jobs covered by the class specification and jobs covered by other class specifications is generally not included. Emphasis in the duties statement is on the work of the people covered in the class specification. If the specific duties of the positions are based on an inter-relationship with other titles, this information would be included. Thus, for example, the specification for the Secretary to the Assistant Commissioner would include, as part of the duties statement, the fact that the incumbent of the position serves as secretary to the Assistant Commissioner, but would not list the duties of the Assistant Commissioner. The other possible answers show criteria which are involved in evaluating all duties statements.

3. **(C)** In New York City, the Classified Service refers to all classes of positions which are under the jurisdiction of the New York City Department of Personnel, including those in the Competitive, Non-Competitive and Exempt classes.

4. **(C)** A position is put into the Exempt Class because it has been determined that for one reason or another, such as

confidentiality, it is not deemed practical to hire on a competitive basis. There are no stated qualifications that an individual must meet to acquire this type of position. Appointments to administrative positions with considerable policy making discretion is usually not considered a candidate for an exempt position.

5. **(A)** This type of move does not involve a promotion, and usually involves the performance of duties at the same level of responsibility.

6. **(C)** In order to best understand the quality of experience offered by a candidate for an administrative position, the organization chart of the agency where the candidate was or is working should be studied. The degree of independence from higher level supervision can be seen from the chart as well as the relative supervisory/administrative functions assigned to the candidate of the position he or she holds or held. Titles are not good indicators of the administrative nature of the job since they are not standardized throughout public and private industry. The number of persons supervised will not tell anything about either the level or kind of supervision exercised or the level or quality of the work being supervised. Listing the types of administrative work done daily does not tell how much of the time is spent on these tasks or the quality of the administrative task being performed.

7. **(B)** A class specification does not tell the number of vacancies existing in that class of positions. That number will, of course, vary throughout the year, and has no

relevance to the class specification which concerns the duties and responsibilities, qualification requirements, and lines of promotion for that particular class of positions.

8. **(A)** In classification studies a desk audit is just what the term implies—an audit or interview with the individual while he or she is on-the-job. The other possible answers refer to other actions in the classification process.

9. **(A)** The difference between a position and a class is that a position refers to one job with its specific duties and responsibilities whereas a class (or class of positions) refers to all positions which are sufficiently similar in nature and in qualification requirements to warrant use of the same title and pay range.

10. **(D)** Any classification study involves determining exactly what the duties of each position are, and the person who best knows those duties is the one actually doing the job. This is true whether the study is done by desk audits, questionnaires, or some other method. The other possible answers are criticisms of the questionnaire method.

11. **(C)** Classification refers to the grouping of positions into the same title (class) based on similarities of duties, responsibilities and qualifications needed to do the work.

12. **(C)** Work flow charts are most useful in presenting a clearer picture of how a particular job is being done. This helps to spot problem areas, note duplications of effort, discover more efficient, and cheaper ways to do the job, etc. Work flow charts do not usually refer to future objectives unrelated to the work currently being undertaken, and do not usually summarize the work procedures of the agency.

13. **(C)** To most usefully help a unit accomplish its tasks, a schedule for completing a job should include due dates for all the major components involved, as well as the expected date of final completion. These individual dates may include leeway for emergencies, but once the dates are firm, they should be adhered to, if at all possible. It is not generally useful to know how long it will take to get the job done if certain conditions become adverse, and the inclusion of this type of information as a separate part of a schedule only lessens the positive nature of the schedule.

14. **(C)** The determination of vertical placement of a position is based primarily on the degree of responsibility one assumes while performing it. Therefore, an individual performing a complex job may be placed in a low position vertically because the work performed will be subject to direct supervision, and the individual will not be afforded much of an opportunity for independent action.

15. **(A)** The quotation refers to many different personnel functions, but does not include the classification function.

16. **(C)** The quotation indicates most of the main functions carried out in personnel work, and how these functions are related to the task of producing the best level of performance possible from each employee. None of the other possible answers are implied in the quotation.

17. **(C)** The quotation defines a class as a number of positions whose distinguishing characteristics are similar enough to justify selecting people to fill them in the same way and pay them in the same pay range. The other possible answers give only partial indications of what the quotation says.

18. **(A)** Compensation assigned to a job is dependent on many factors which include responsibility assumed, type of work, special skills required, etc. The presence of avoidable hazards is not a factor, because they simply should be avoided. If they were unavoidable, it might be a factor in determining salary.

19. **(D)** Experience has shown that if employees have actively participated throughout the classification process, they are less likely to appeal the final allocations of their positions. Participation assures the worker that allocations are unbiased, are based on statements of the duties involved which were derived after discussion with each worker, etc. Having the supervisor check on employee statements in classification questionnaires will result in more accurate allocations, but will not necessarily result in fewer appeals (answer A). The two other possible answers are not related to the question.

20. **(A)** The Benchmark system has not been used as an evaluation of job performance because essentially it is a factor in measuring work performed against previously determined standards. Usually the only determination made as a result of it is whether or not minimum requirements set for a job are being met. There really is no opportunity in this system to measure by how much standards were exceeded.

21. **(D)** Jobs change over a period of time as new methods, new equipment, new procedures and new employees are put in the jobs. A periodic classification audit will discover those jobs whose duties and responsibilities have changed to such a degree that a new or different job title is now appropriate. The other possible answers are not germane to the question.

22. **(D)** Of the factors given the choice which warrants the least consideration is the educational background of the incumbent, simply because the incumbent for one reason or other could be over-qualified for the position he or she is presently holding. What would be important is the determination of the minimum educational background for an individual being considered for appointment to the position, but this is an entirely different matter.

23. **(A)** You are being tested for close reading of the question. The use of scientific techniques forms an essential part of a system ruled by scientific procedure.

24. **(B)** A position is a set of related duties that can be performed by one individual within a given time frame. A study of the position in an organization is the first step in the classification process.

25. **(A)** Probation is considered part of the examination or selection process. It tests qualities needed for the job which a formal examination may not be able to adequately test, such as cooperativeness, willingness to learn, etc. All of the other possible answers are less important uses of the probationary period or simply not correct answers.

26. **(D)** There must be some latitude for independent action in any work assignment. In its absence, workers will stagnate and become bored easily. The alternative is to have directions for every step in the process, and this is impractical in most work situations. Workers would never develop in this type of operation.

27. **(A)** Temporary assignment to the duties of higher positions enables management to determine if the individual could hold that position on a permanent basis. No test or series of tests measures certain characteristics required of top leadership as well as temporary assignment. The other possible answers either do not get to the heart of the issue, or are directed at problems with this procedure which are of little concern.

28. **(D)** Of the possible answers, the only basic title which can be used to compare salaries paid with similar titles used in private industry is Junior Typist. The duties assigned to all other titles are of a higher level and vary within different private industries and between private industry and the government service.

29. **(C)** The classification process emphasizes a close study of individual jobs. This study is bound to bring to light existing inefficiencies in the organization's operation.

30. **(A)** The total amount of work done and the time it takes to perform the work, add up to an excellent means of evaluation of what is being accomplished for the money expended in the performance of the work.

31. **(C)** The method to recruit individuals does not properly belong in a class specification, which is a formal description of the duties, responsibilities, and qualification requirements of the particular class of positions. Methods of recruitment to fill positions will vary depending on the needs of the agency, availability of potential candidates, etc.

32. **(C)** The quotation says any education should be evaluated in terms of its appropriateness to the particular position being filled. On this basis the only appropriate answer is the one that includes both general and special education. Other answers cannot be implied from the quotation.

33. **(D)** Again, the quotation says education is valuable to the degree that it contributes to the knowledge, skills and abilities needed to do the job. A high school education is valuable insofar as it is needed to fill a particular position. The other possible answers do not follow from the quotation.

34. **(D)** Essentially a compensation plan is primarily based on work performed. The value of the work to the organization basically determines the amount of compensation to be paid. Just who is performing the work is an unimportant and secondary matter in a compensation plan.

35. **(D)** The paragraph states, in essence, that a pay plan must take into consideration the duties of the positions involved, which is what the correct answer states. The other possible answers cannot be implied from the quotation.

36. **(B)** Duties classification may be an important part of a pay plan, but the latter takes into consideration economic factors as well. Nothing in the paragraph states a change in dollar value would have any effect on the duties classification.

37. **(B)** The quotation says proper recruitment requires an effective position classification system. The classification system describes and classifies positions according to their duties and responsibilities. Therefore, the reason the quotation is correct is that without such a description of the job duties there is no effective way to determine what capabilities and characteristics to look for in recruiting prospective employees.

38. **(D)** A classification survey is based on the jobs actually being done, and includes analyzing actual duties, grouping positions with similar duties, and preparing job specifications. A classification survey does not change job duties, but examines only what is actually done by each worker.

39. **(D)** A classification plan can exist with or without the existence of a pay plan, since it merely classifies jobs actually being done. On the contrary, a pay plan, based on the principle of equal pay for equal work, cannot exist without a classification plan to show which jobs are identical or very similar to other jobs.

40. **(B)** This type of retention plan would tend to establish a sense of insecurity in the minds of employees. The so called permanent tenure inherent in civil service appointments would be diminished to the point that any individual could be dismissed just by declaring the job he or she was doing was not "important."

41. **(A)** A proper test for selection of employees to fill particular positions must be based on the knowledge, skills and abilities needed to do those jobs. Therefore, the first step in the construction of the test is to determine what are the actual duties of the positions. The other possible answers are steps which come later.

42. **(D)** A principle of personnel administration states that in the normal course of events a worker should achieve

promotion to higher positions more or less on a regular basis. A worker who has remained at the same job for a period of fifteen years implies a lack of ability. On the surface, it does not seem fair when a worker who has stayed on the same job for a period of years is regarded less for promotion. The fact that he or she has not achieved advancement for a long period will, however, be held against him or her.

43. **(C)** Labor turnover at about 10–12% is advisable primarily because it provides for promotional opportunities for competent, career-minded employees. Answers A and D are inappropriate, and answer B cannot be assumed from the information given in the question.

44. **(D)** The study of a position in order to classify it into the existing classification scheme involves the examination of the duties and responsibilities assigned to the position and not the factors given in the other possible answers.

45. **(B)** When evaluating the merits of a proposed class specification you should concern yourself only with the duties presently assigned to the incumbent or prospective title holders. Whether they are reasonably similar titles now is of no importance. The specification should have a title which is appropriate to the duties of the positions, and the duties should be sufficiently similar so that the same pay is appropriate and the same test can be given to cover the duties encompassed in the specification.

46. **(A)** The classification plan is basic to the personnel activities given in the other possible answers. Without a classification of duties and responsibilities into appropriate titles, appeals against possibly wrong allocations of titles, performance rating, and in-service training programs cannot function effectively.

47. **(A)** The preamble in the question defines the function of job analysis. Micro-motion studies emphasize physical movement of operations, cost analysis, and production control. This assures that qualitative and quantitative standards are being met.

48. **(B)** Time studies always involve work operations presently in use. Their purpose is to possibly shorten the time spent in work performance without the lessening of work efficiency.

49. **(B)** The primary consideration is whether the present regular staff is sufficiently large enough to complete the usually assigned work in a timely manner. Although it is proper, efficient, and economical to hire temporary staff for short peak load periods, and to delegate overtime to handle such situations, the capability of regular staff to keep relatively up-to-date over the long term is the controlling factor.

50. **(C)** The assumption that cannot be made from this general practice is that an outstanding performance on the lower job is a good indicator of success upon promotion. The completion of probation can only predict a degree of positive correlation with ability to do the work at the next level. Answers A, B, and D cannot be assumed from the data given.

51. **(A)** In order to evaluate administrative management, the component elements must be broken down and evaluated separately, e.g., ability to plan, ability to coordinate different functions, etc. Unless the various components are broken down and measured separately, the result will be a vague, meaningless, unscientific, and in many instances indefensible, total figure which will be useless in helping the administrator to improve his or her performance. The other possible answers may be construed as valid.

52. **(B)** Executive planning is a primary, basic, on-going function of an administrator. An executive must plan every activity for which he or she has been given responsibility. The other possible answers are valid principles to guide an executive in planning the agency's activities.

53. **(A)** An accounting system does not involve justifying or documenting the expenditure of funds, but merely accounts for how those funds are being or have been spent. The other possible answers are proper functions of an accounting system.

54. **(D)** The enlargement of the scope of individual jobs will increase the flexibility of each employee because it will enable each worker to do many more tasks than if he or she specialized in one particular task. The other possible answers will very likely result from enlarging the scope of a job.

55. **(C)** Standardization of qualifications makes it easier to establish classes of positions, which make the entire classification process easier to administer. It also enhances the flexibility of the staff.

56. **(C)** To classify a clerical, or any position, the training and experience of the present incumbent need not be considered. In position classification, the position, with its duties, responsibilities and the qualification requirements, is classified, not the person in the position. The other possible answers contain factors which must be considered in classifying the position.

57. **(D)** The classification bureau normally plays no part in determining what positions are necessary in the agency. Classification is concerned only with positions which have been or are being established and budgeted by top management in order to accomplish specified duties. The classification bureau is concerned with the duties described in the other possible answers.

58. **(A)** The most essential element in classifying a position is comparing the duties and responsibilities assigned to that position with the duties and responsibilities of simi-

lar and related positions, and determining whether it is sufficiently similar to use the same title, qualification requirements and the same test to fill both positions. Classification is not concerned with how well duties are performed or salaries.

59. **(C)** Position classification has no relation to the establishment of time and leave regulations, but can be used to help assign workers to the position for which they are qualified. It also can be an aid to training workers to do the assigned work appropriate to the positions they hold. Further, a good position classification system, where every person is in the correct title and doing the work indicated in the class specification for his or her specific title, can aid in the establishment of good organization and supervision.

COMMUNICATIONS, RECORDS, AND REPORTS

DIRECTIONS FOR ANSWERING QUESTIONS

Each question has four suggested answers, lettered A, B, C, and D. Decide which one is the best answer and on the sample answer sheet (all answer sheets are at the front of the book) find the question number and darken the area, with a soft pencil, which corresponds to the answer that you have selected.

1. From the viewpoint of administration of a division, reports serve a chief administrator primarily to
   - (A) help the administrator exercise control
   - (B) improve the quality of planning, both current and future
   - (C) determine disciplinary needs
   - (D) evaluate personnel effectiveness in each of the operations.

2. Of the following, the most effective method for keeping the relationship of ideas understandable in a report is to use
   - (A) adequate footnotes and references
   - (B) qualifying statements
   - (C) appropriate related material
   - (D) carefully defined terms.

3. Assume that the Chief Administrator asks you to conduct a study for him of a particular situation within the Department and to recommend necessary changes. After your study you submit a fairly long although informal report. The one of the following sections which should come first in this report is a
   - (A) description of how you went about making the study
   - (B) summary of the conclusions that you reached
   - (C) discussion of possible objections to the recommendations and their refutation

   - (D) complete statement of the benefits to be derived from following your recommendations.

4. The chief purpose in preparing an outline for a report is usually
   - (A) to insure that the report will be of the desired length
   - (B) to insure that every point will be given equal emphasis
   - (C) to insure that principal and secondary points will be properly related to the framework of the whole
   - (D) to insure that the language of the report will be appropriate to its content and that technical terms will be clearly explained.

5. The basic reason for including an index in a report is to
   - (A) obviate the need for a table of contents
   - (B) give proper credit to contributors
   - (C) list related reports
   - (D) facilitate reference to specific subjects.

6. Which of the following may be considered the most direct result of the use of well-planned forms?
   - (A) uniform interpretation of departmental policies
   - (B) establishment of procedures that are practical in relation to the capacities of the staff

(C) simplification of clerical procedures and increased speed of office processes

(D) constructive supervision of personnel.

7. The appendix of a report should contain
   (A) minority opinions
   (B) all tabular presentations and footnotes
   (C) controversial material which might bring about complications if included in the body of the report
   (D) material which, although not essential to the understanding of the text, is necessary as supporting evidence.

8. In preparing a report aimed at giving information concerning a complex and extensive matter, which of the following devices will in general do the most to provide clarity and ease of reading?
   (A) personalized style
   (B) short sentences
   (C) repetition and paraphrasing
   (D) one idea to a paragraph.

9. Reports are valuable in the determination of the policies and plans of an organization chiefly because
   (A) they take the place of many individual communications
   (B) they help to reveal existing trends and to predict future problems
   (C) they can be read by all persons who help in the formation of policies
   (D) they serve to acquaint the employees with decisions as soon as they are made.

10. One of the best methods of presenting a recommendation in a report is to do so in such a manner that
    (A) it comes as a surprise to the reader
    (B) the evidence is presented in such a way that the recommendation is suggested to the reader before it is definitely disclosed to him
    (C) it magnifies the aspect of the problem the researcher finds most interesting
    (D) it appears to urge the reader to change his opinions.

11. Which one of the following is considered good practice in formulating a questionnaire?
    (A) frame the question to elicit replies in averages or percentages
    (B) ask only that which has a direct bearing on the problem to be solved

(C) as a general rule, frame questions to secure opinions rather than factual data
(D) increase the reliability of answers to the questionnaire by making the questions personal.

12. In an office where a large amount of correspondence deals with recurring problems, one of the following techniques that may best be employed to lessen the time required for answering letters is to
    (A) group incoming correspondence by subject matter and handle different subjects on different days of the week
    (B) prepare pertinent form letters and form paragraphs that can be inserted in letters
    (C) issue monthly bulletins containing examples of satisfactory replies concerning problems of a recurrent nature
    (D) set aside a certain portion of each day for answering letters.

13. In the preparation of a recommendation report, the administrator should take all but which one of these steps before he begins to write:
    (A) consider the problem demanding solution
    (B) determine the standards governing the selection or the decision
    (C) make a comparison of several possible methods and types of solutions
    (D) prepare an index.

14. When writing reports the simplest and most direct way of focusing the reader's attention upon the topic under discussion is to
    (A) put the topic idea in the first sentence of the paragraph
    (B) place all important points in italics
    (C) begin the report in a humorous vein
    (D) use simple language.

15. The principal value of prompt, accurate, and complete reports is that such reports
    (A) impress superior officers with the necessity for action
    (B) mark the efficient person
    (C) provide excellent reference material
    (D) expedite official business.

16. When writing a special report, which of the following would be most useful?
    (A) a sample idea of a former report
    (B) a tonic idea

(C) an index

— (D) an outline.

17. What is the purpose of the closing section of reports?

— (A) pointing out the whole report and making its final meaning clear

(B) making the report more interesting to the reader

(C) clearly stating the exact subject of the report and its over-all purpose

· (D) to show the writer's purpose and his viewpoints toward the subject.

Questions 18, 19, and 20 are based on the following:

Prior to revising its child care program, the Department of Health feels that it is necessary to get some information from the mothers served by the existing program in order to determine where changes are required. A questionnaire is to be constructed to obtain this information.

18. Of the following points which can be taken into consideration in the construction of the questionnaire, the one which is of LEAST importance is

— (A) setting up a control group so that answers received can be compared to a standard

(B) the aspects of the program which seem to be in need of change

(C) the type of person who will fill out the questionnaire

(D) testing the questionnaire for ambiguity in advance of general distribution.

19. To discuss this questionnaire with all mothers who have been asked to answer it, before they actually fill it out is

(A) desirable; the mothers may be able to offer valuable suggestions for changes in the form of the questionnaire

(B) undesirable; it is of some value but consumes too much valuable time

— (C) desirable; cooperation and uniform interpretation will tend to be achieved

(D) undesirable; it may cause the answers to be biased.

20. Of the following items included in the questionnaire, the one which will be of LEAST assistance for comparing attitudes toward the program among different kinds of persons, is

— (A) name

(B) address

(C) age

(D) education.

21. While setting up a reporting system to help the department planning section, an administrator proposed the policy that no overlap or duplication be permitted even if it meant that some minor areas were left uncovered. This policy is

— (A) undesirable; duplication is preferable to leaving any area uncovered

(B) desirable; the presence of overlap and duplication indicates defective planning

(C) undesirable; setting up general policy in advance of the specific reporting system may lead to inflexibility

(D) desirable; it is not necessary to get complete coverage in order to be able to plan operations.

22. "In order to make the collection of data in a study purposeful, a working hypothesis is necessary." An inference that is *least* in accord with this statement is

(A) in the absence of a working hypothesis, the collection of data may be diffuse

— (B) a working hypothesis widens the area of investigation and the variety of data to be collected

(C) a working hypothesis concentrates attention on particular aspects of the study which are considered significant

(D) the use of a working hypothesis will eliminate collection of useless or meaningless data.

23. During a conference of administrative staff personnel, the department head discussing the letters prepared for his signature stated, "Use no more words than are necessary to express your meaning." Following this rule in letter writing is, in general

— (A) desirable; the use of more words than are necessary is likely to obscure the meaning and tire the reader

(B) undesirable; it is frequently necessary to elaborate on an explanation in order to make certain that the reader will understand

(C) desirable; terse statements give government letters a business-like air which impresses readers favorably

(D) undesirable; terse statements are generally cold and formal and produce an unfavorable reaction in the reader.

24. With respect to a report prepared by a computer installation, the one of the following changes which is LEAST likely to cause a change in the procedure for preparing the report is a change in the
    (A) volume of work
    (B) source documents
    (C) time allowed for the preparation of the report
    (D) employees assigned.

25. A subordinate submits a proposed draft of a form which is being revised to facilitate filling in the form on a typewriter. The draft shows that the captions for each space will be printed below the space to be filled in. This proposal is
    (A) undesirable; it decreases visibility
    (B) desirable; it makes the form easy to understand
    (C) undesirable; it makes the form more difficult to understand
    (D) desirable; it increases visibility.

26. "Forms control only accomplishes the elimination, consolidation and simplification of forms. It contributes little to the elimination, consolidation and simplification of procedures." This statement is
    (A) correct; the form is static while the procedure is dynamic; consequently control of one does not necessarily result in control of the other
    (B) not correct; forms frequently dictate the way work is laid out; consequently control of one frequently results in control of the other
    (C) correct; the procedure is primary and the form secondary; consequently control of procedure will also control form
    (D) not correct; the form and procedure are identical from the viewpoint of work control; consequently control of one means control of the other.

27. "Reports submitted to the department head should be complete to the last detail. As far as possible, summaries should be avoided." This statement is, in general,
    (A) correct; only on the basis of complete information can a proper decision be reached
    (B) not correct; if all reports submitted were of this character a department head would never complete his or her work
    (C) correct; the decision as to what is important

and what is not can only be made by the person who is responsible for the action
    (D) not correct; preliminary reports, obviously, cannot be complete to the last detail.

28. "The adoption of a single consolidated form will mean that most of the form will not be used in any one operation. This would create waste and confusion." This conclusion is based upon the unstated hypothesis that
    (A) if waste and confusion are to be avoided a single consolidated form should be used
    (B) if a single consolidated form is constructed, most of it can be used in each operation
    (C) if waste and confusion are to be avoided, most of the form employed should be used
    (D) most of a single consolidated form is not used.

29. Assume that you are in charge of a unit with 40 employees. The department head requests immediate preparation of a special and rather complicated report which will take about a day to complete if everyone in your unit works on it. After breaking the job into single components and assigning each component to an employee, should more than one person be instructed on the procedure to be followed on each component?
    (A) No; the procedure would be a waste of time in this instance
    (B) Yes; it is always desirable to have a replacement available in the event of illness or any other emergency
    (C) No; in general, as long as an employee's job performance is satisfactory, there is no need to train an alternate
    (D) Yes; the presence of more than one person in a unit who can perform a given task tends to prevent the formation of a bottleneck.

30. Assume that you are the head of a major staff unit and that a line unit has requested from your unit a special report to be complete in one day. After reviewing the request you decide that much time would be saved if two items which you know are superfluous are omitted from the report. You discuss the matter with the head of the other unit and he still insists that the two items are essential for his purposes. The one of the following actions which you should take at this stage is to
    (A) plan to complete the report, including the items, as expeditiously as possible

(B) write a memorandum to the department head giving both opinions fairly and asking for a decision

(C) plan to complete the report without the two items, as expeditiously as possible

(D) devise a plan for preparing the report without the two items which will permit you to add them later if they prove necessary although some time may be lost.

31. A supervisor is frequently required to prepare various types of written reports. The one of the following features which is *least* desirable in a lengthy report is that

(A) the style of writing should be readable, interesting, and impersonal; it should not be too scholarly, nor make use of involved sentence structure

(B) recommendations and conclusions resulting from the facts incorporated in the body of the report must appear only at the end of the report so that readers can follow the writer's line of reasoning

(C) in determining the extent of technical detail and terminology to be used in the presentation of supporting data, such as charts, tables, graphs, case examples, etc., the technical knowledge of the prospective reader or readers should be kept in mind

(D) the body of the report should mention all the pertinent facts and develop the writer's ideas in such a way that the recommendations will be a logical outgrowth of the arguments presented.

32. The *least* accurate of the following statements concerning the construction of an organization chart is that

(A) the relative positions of the boxes representing subdivisions in a line type organization should be determined by the hierarchical relationship of the subdivisions

(B) the main functions of subdivisions may be designated on the chart

(C) if the organization is complex, there may be a master chart and subsidiary charts

(D) the sizes of the boxes representing subdivisions of the organization should vary with the relative number of employees in the subdivisions.

33. Suppose that a large number of semi-literate residents of this city have been requesting the assis-

tance of your department. You are asked to prepare a form which these applicants will be required to fill out before their requests will be considered. In view of these facts, the one of the following factors to which you should give the greatest amount of consideration in preparing this form is the

(A) size of the form

(B) sequence of the information asked for on the form

(C) level of difficulty of the language used in the form

(D) number of times which the form will have to be reviewed.

34. Your department plans to install a suggestion box into which its employees may place their suggestions for improving departmental policies and procedures. As a reward for submitting a practical suggestion, additional vacation allowance will be granted to the author of each suggestion. The amount of additional vacation allowed will depend upon the value of the suggestion, as determined by a panel of judges. To institute a procedure whereby the identity of the author will be concealed from the judges by the secretary of the department until the value of the suggestion has been determined would be

(A) undesirable; many employees will refrain from making suggestions if they know that the suggestion will be judged anonymously

(B) desirable; many employees will be encouraged to be frank and outspoken in their criticism, such straightforward criticism is of more value to a department than suggestions for improvement

(C) undesirable; if a suggestion is not clearly presented, the judges will be unable to obtain clarifying information from the author

(D) desirable; it provides for strict impartiality in judging the worth of an idea and may thus encourage employee participation in the plan.

35. A research study is scientific when its data are subjected to logical analysis resulting in the development of a generalization and when the data are secured by

(A) experiment

(B) statistics

(C) probability measures

(D) chance.

36. As a result of a preliminary study the statement was made, ''The probability is 80% that a New Yorker uses some means of public transportation to go to work.'' This statement
    (A) expresses a meaningful relationship between workers in New York and public transportation
    (B) is meaningless; it should read ''The probability is 80% that a randomly selected New Yorker uses . . .''
    (C) expresses a meaningful relationship between New Yorkers who use some means of public transportation to go to work and those who do not
    (D) is meaningless; it should read, ''A randomly selected probability that a New Yorker. . . .''

37. ''Sampling'' is the name given to devices for learning about large masses by observing a few individuals. The one of the following which is a basic assumption of all sampling theory is that the sample is
    (A) representative of the population
    (B) a random selection
    (C) stratified by dominant characteristics
    (D) chosen in an arbitrary manner.

38. In order to decide if a sample is adequate, the most practical empirical method is to
    (A) compare the selected sample with several others of the same size
    (B) determine the probable error of the sample
    (C) compare the sample with the population from which it was drawn
    (D) determine the extent of bias that existed in selection of the sample.

39. The type of survey among the following which requires least questioning of people is one relating to
    (A) land use
    (B) income level in various areas
    (C) recreational needs
    (D) housing facilities.

40. Before beginning a field study, it is desirable as a first step to
    (A) set up schedules or other observation recording devices prior to planning the actual operational steps
    (B) check documentary sources and records to review the work of others in the same field

    (C) establish the conditions in the proposed field study which will emphasize the objective viewpoint
    (D) decide if the study is to be based on a sample or the complete population.

41. The questionnaire as a method of securing information from a large number of persons has the distinct advantage of economy over the personal interview. It also has the advantage of
    (A) usually resulting in a representative sample
    (B) avoiding antagonism often encountered in personal interviews
    (C) having practically no limitations in range
    (D) requiring less care in preparation than the personal interview method.

42. A distinct limitation of a sample survey by questionnaire as a tool in research is
    (A) it is difficult to determine whether or not the responses are representative of the total group
    (B) it is generally too brief to be satisfactory in producing relevant data
    (C) it is impersonal and anonymous in nature, with consequent loss of personal contact validity
    (D) it is of proven value only when directed to a homogeneous group.

43. A consideration which is of *least* importance in constructing a schedule for use in surveys or field studies is
    (A) avoid items or questions which, although of value, might arouse the antagonism of the informant
    (B) avoid questions or terms that can be answered by a simple ''yes'' or ''no''
    (C) prepare a dummy table in advance to make certain that the schedule will call for pertinent data
    (D) arrange schedule items so that tabulation of data is facilitated.

44. ''If you use a concrete word when you might use an abstract one you are handicapping yourself in your task of preparing comprehensive and understandable reports.'' This advice is
    (A) good; the use of concrete words prevents effective generalization
    (B) bad; it is easier to prepare a report whose meaning is clear if the concrete is preferred to the abstract

(C) good; it is easier to prepare a report whose meaning is clear if the abstract is preferred to the concrete

(D) bad; the use of abstract words prevents any effective generalization.

45. The most acceptable of the following guides in preparing the specifications for a form is that
    (A) when forms are to be printed on colored paper, the dark shades of colored paper should be used
    (B) "tumble" or "head-to-foot" design should be used if forms printed on both sides of the sheet are to be placed in binders with side binding
    (C) provision for ballot-type entries should be made if items requiring "yes" or "no" entries are to appear on the form
    (D) all-rag ledger paper rather than all-wood pulp bond paper should be used for forms which will receive little handling and will be kept for a short time.

46. You find it advisable to prepare a series of three printed forms. In actual practice, all three forms will be filled out simultaneously by typists and then placed in separate files for future reference. Of the following the least valid principle which you should consider in designing the forms is that
    (A) all three forms should be of the same size, preferably a size fitting standard filing cabinets
    (B) the space between successive headings specifying the type of information to be included should be a multiple of the standard type-writing space
    (C) provision should be made for placing on the reverse side of each form a symbol giving the principal subdivision under which that form is to be filed
    (D) duplicated items should be placed in the same position on each form.

47. In making your periodic report to your superior, you should keep in mind that the chief importance of the report lies in the fact that it
    (A) constitutes a document to which there will be frequent reference
    (B) is a means of checking on your efficiency
    (C) is the basis of information handed on to the highest executive officers of your government

(D) allows your superior more effectively to exercise his function of direction, supervision and control.

48. Department X maintains district offices in each of the five boroughs of the City. Data gathered by the district offices are submitted monthly to the main office on a standard set of forms which are somewhat complicated. Of the following methods of issuing detailed instructions for filling out the forms properly, the one generally considered most acceptable is
    (A) incorporating the instructions in the department's procedure manual
    (B) including an instruction sheet with each package of blank forms sent to a district office
    (C) printing the instructions on the back of each form
    (D) conducting periodic staff conferences devoted exclusively to discussions of the proper method of filling out the forms.

49. Of the following systems of designating the pages in a looseleaf manual subject to constant revision and addition, the most practicable one is to use
    (A) decimals for main divisions and integers for subdivisions
    (B) integers for main divisions and letters for subdivisions
    (C) integers for main divisions and decimals for subdivisions
    (D) letters for main divisions and integers for subdivisions.

50. It is commonly accepted as a desirable practice in public administration to prepare and distribute employee handbooks. The one of the following which is not an assumption underlying this practice is that it will
    (A) assist in training probationary employees
    (B) increase employee feeling of security by clarifying the department's policies
    (C) enable the administrative staff to solve more quickly problems relating to the assignment of personnel
    (D) ultimately result in sufficient savings to make up the cost of publication.

51. It has been suggested that in preparing a procedure manual each subdivision, no matter how short, be printed on a separate page. The one of

the following estimates of this suggestion which would influence most the decision as to its usability is that it is

(A) good; readability will be increased

(B) poor; it will make for a bulkier, harder-to-handle manual

(C) of little consequence; the advantages and disadvantages of the proposed procedure are all minor

(D) poor; ease of reference will be decreased.

52. Assume that you are in charge of preparing a procedure manual of about 100 pages for a large clerical unit. After you have decided to use a looseleaf format, one of your subordinates proposes that only one side of the page be printed. This proposal is

(A) good; replacement of obsolete pages is made easier

(B) poor; cost is increased

(C) good; provision is automatically made for employee's notes

(D) poor; it will increase the size of the manual, making it more difficult to use.

53. While you are designing the layout for a departmental procedure manual, it is suggested that you carefully arrange your reading material so that there will be a minimum amount of blank space on the page. Of the following judgments of this suggestion, the one which is the most valid basis for action is that it is

(A) bad; readability and ease of reference will be decreased

(B) good; the cost of production can be increased considerably without any great disadvantage

(C) of little or no importance, more or less blank space on the page will not affect the value of the manual

(D) good; it will make for a smaller, easier to handle book.

54. After the planning of an employee's procedure manual had been completed, the suggestion was made that the manual should be prepared and arranged so that changes could be made readily. Of the following decisions with respect to this suggestion, the one which is most desirable from the viewpoint of good administration is that the suggestions should

(A) not be considered as it is generally impossible to prepare a satisfactory manual which will take everything into consideration

(B) be followed only if it does not conflict with the planned layout

(C) be used even if it is somewhat more costly than the planned layout

(D) be noted and acted upon at the next revision of the manual.

Assume that a committee has been established in a hypothetical city department to prepare manuals for procedure for clerks in the various grades in the Clerical Service in that department. You have been appointed to the committee and have been assigned to prepare the manual of procedure for Clerks, Grade 2. (This is now the lowest grade in the Clerical Service.) The scope of this manual is to be limited to information and instructions which will be of assistance to Clerks, Grade 2 in carrying out the duties that should normally be assigned to them. Questions 55 to 61 consist of sets of four possible topics which might be included in this manual. Assume that all four topics in each question pertain to the work of the department. You are to select from each set of four topics the one topic which is **LEAST PERTINENT** for inclusion in the manual you are preparing. For each question, indicate as your answer the capital letter preceding the topic which you consider **LEAST PERTINENT** for your manual.

55. (A) charging out material withdrawn from files

(B) handling incoming letters containing enclosures

(C) estimating costs of clerical operations

(D) index of office form numbers.

56. (A) the tickler file

(B) standards for evaluating clerical efficiency

(C) techniques in inserting material in envelopes

(D) glossary of special terms used in the department.

57. (A) formulating mailing and filing policies

(B) operating numbering and dating machines

(C) techniques in sorting and alphabetizing

(D) procedure for transferring material to inactive files.

58. (A) collecting outgoing mail

(B) value of inservice training program

(C) securing office supplies from the stock room

(D) rules for alphabetic indexing.

59. (A) advantages of centralized filing
    (B) preparing papers for filing
    (C) cross indexing
    (D) taking telephone messages.

60. (A) routing incoming correspondence
    (B) arranging guide cards in file drawers
    (C) adjusting disagreements among fellow employees
    (D) issuing information to callers.

61. (A) securing documents from inactive files
    (B) proper postage for letters and packages
    (C) designing effective office forms
    (D) classifying and coding material for filing.

62. "The personnel survey is a systematic and reasonable exhaustive analysis and statement of the facts and forces in an organization which affects the relations between employees and management, and between employees and their work, followed by recommendations as to ways of developing better personnel policies and procedures." On the basis of this quotation, it is *least* accurate to state that one of the purposes served by a personnel survey is to
    (A) appraise operating efficiency through an objective study of methods of production and a statistical interpretation of the facts
    (B) set forth items and causes of poor morale in an inclusive way and in their proper perspective
    (C) secure the facts to determine whether there is need of a more progressive personnel policy in an organization where personnel work is as yet undeveloped
    (D) evaluate the effectiveness of a personnel policy where a progressive policy is already in operation.

63. From the viewpoint of administration of a division, reports serve a chief administrator primarily to
    (A) help the administrator exercise control of his or her responsibilities
    (B) improve the quality of planning, both current and future
    (C) determine disciplinary needs
    (D) evaluate personnel effectiveness in each of the varied operations.

64. "A manual that is essentially designed to present detailed procedures and policies is not neces-

sarily a good training medium, nor is a manual designed for high-level administrators likely to be satisfactory for use at lower levels." The most valid implication of this quotation is that
    (A) a manual to be effective should be flexible enough to apply to any working level in an organization
    (B) the uses to which a manual will be put and the people who will use it should be carefully determined before it is prepared
    (C) the more detailed procedures a manual contains, the more effective it will be for the use of administrators
    (D) the degree of difficulty encountered in the preparation of a manual varies with the purpose for which it is designed and the people for whom it is written.

65. "A procedure manual of a public agency is potentially more usable than are files of individual messages or bulletins, but usability and usefulness are not routine by-products of the manual form." The most valid implication of this quotation is that
    (A) the purpose of a manual should not be confined to an explanation of routine procedures
    (B) a manual may prove to be unsuitable for some of its anticipated uses
    (C) individual messages or bulletins are more likely to be of use than are manuals
    (D) a manual suffers from certain limitations that are not found in individual messages or bulletins.

66. "Constant study should be made of the information contained in reports to isolate those elements of experience which are static, those which are variable and repetitive, and those which are variable and due to chance." Knowledge of those elements of experience in his organization which are static or constant will enable the operating official to
    (A) fix responsibility for their supervision at a lower level
    (B) revise the procedure in order to make the elements variable
    (C) arrange for follow-up and periodic adjustment
    (D) bring related data together.

The following sections appeared in a report on the work production of two bureaus of a department. Base your answers to questions 67 to 71 on this information. Throughout the report, assume that each month has 4 weeks.

"Each of the two bureaus maintains a chronological file. In Bureau A, every 9 months on the average, this material fills a standard legal size file cabinet sufficient for 12,000 work units. In Bureau B, the same type of cabinet is filled in 18 months. Each bureau maintains three complete years of information plus a current file. When the current file cabinet is filled, the cabinet containing the oldest material is emptied, the contents disposed of and the cabinet used for current material. The similarity of these operations makes it possible to consolidate these files with little effort.

"Study of the practice of using typists as filing clerks for periods when there is no typing work showed:

(1) Bureau A has for the past 6 months completed a total of 1500 filing work units a week using on the average 100 man-hours of trained file clerk time and 20 man-hours of typist time.

(2) Bureau B has in the same period completed a total of 2000 filing work units a week using on the average 125 man-hours of trained file clerk time and 60 hours of typist time.

This includes all work in chronological files. Assuming that all clerks work at the same speed and that all typists work at the same speed, this indicates that work other than filing should be found for typists or that they should be given some training in the filing procedures used. It should be noted that Bureau A has not been producing the 1,600 units of technical (not filing) work per 30 day period required by Schedule K, but is at present 200 units behind. The Bureau should be allowed 3 working days to get on schedule."

67. What percentage of the total number of filing work units completed in both units consist of the work involved in the maintenance of the chronological files? (approximate answer)
    (A) 5%
    (B) 10%
    (C) 15%
    (D) 20%.

68. If the two chronological files are consolidated, the number of months which should be allowed for filling a cabinet is

(A) 2
(B) 4
(C) 6
(D) 8.

69. The maximum number of file cabinets which can be released for other uses as a result of the consolidation recommended is
    (A) 0
    (B) 1
    (C) 2
    (D) 3.

70. If all the filing work for both units is consolidated without any diminution in the amount to be done and all filing work is done by trained file clerks, the number of clerks required (35 hour work week) is
    (A) 4
    (B) 5
    (C) 6
    (D) 7.

71. In order to comply with the recommendation with respect to Schedule K, the present work production of Bureau A must be increased by
    (A) 50%
    (B) 100%
    (C) 150%
    (D) an amount which is not determinable on the basis of the data given.

72. Of the following, the one which is the most direct result of a well planned report form is that it
    (A) establishes procedures that are practical in relation to the ability of the staff
    (B) gives the appearance of efficiency which sets up good public relations
    (C) provides a means of supervising subordinate as well as supervisory personnel
    (D) simplifies the use of the report for the desired objectives.

73. In determining the type and number of records to be kept, the governing principle should be that records are primarily
    (A) sources of verification of actions taken, should verification be required
    (B) raw material for statistical analysis and therefore invaluable
    (C) aids in attaining the objectives of the department rather than objectives in themselves

(D) tangible evidence of the types of activities in which the department is engaged.

74. The most difficult aspect of making an administrative management survey is
    (A) following through
    (B) the analysis of the problem
    (C) the identification of the problem
    (D) writing a report of the survey.

75. In a management survey, check lists are used principally
    (A) as a guide to areas that require coverage
    (B) as a guide to recommended methods and systems
    (C) to insure standardization of techniques
    (D) to insure that the unit being surveyed has all the material available for analysis.

76. The one of the following which is *not* an essential characteristic of good management reporting is that it
    (A) be a straightforward statement of facts
    (B) be written in terms understandable to the recipient
    (C) have many charts and graphs
    (D) have specific and sufficient detail.

77. The principal advantage of oral reports as compared to written reports is that they
    (A) are likely to be more complete
    (B) are likely to be more truthful
    (C) may be interrupted for clarification or elaboration
    (D) include information which cannot be put into written reports.

78. A summary of a lengthy narrative report submitted to a top staff member should usually be provided
    (A) as part of the report
    (B) before the report is submitted
    (C) immediately following submission of the report
    (D) only when specifically requested.

79. Aside from requirements imposed by authority, the frequency with which reports are submitted or the length of the interval which they cover should depend principally on the
    (A) availability of the data to be included in the reports

(B) amount of time required to prepare the reports
(C) extent of the variations in the data with the passage of time
(D) degree of comprehensiveness required in the reports.

80. In collecting objective data for the evaluation of procedures which are used in his agency, an administrator should, in every case, be careful
    (A) to take an equal number of measurements from each source of information
    (B) not to allow his beliefs about the values of the procedures to influence the choice of data
    (C) to apply statistical methods continuously to the data as they are gathered to assure maximum accuracy
    (D) not to accept data which are inconsistent with the general trend established by verified data.

81. The source data for a system of statistical control are based primarily on the needs of the
    (A) methods analysts
    (B) statisticians
    (C) top staff
    (D) unit level.

82. The one of the following which would be the best reason for an agency to eliminate a procedure for obtaining and recording certain information is that
    (A) it is no longer legally required to obtain the information
    (B) there is no advantage in obtaining the information
    (C) the information could be compiled on the basis of other information available
    (D) the information obtained is sometimes incorrect.

83. In an office with 20,000 pieces of diversified incoming or outgoing correspondence each month, the most efficient of the following ways of managing and maintaining centralized files of correspondence would usually be to group the correspondence
    (A) alphabetically according to sender or recipient
    (B) alphabetically by subject in a separate folder for each month

(C) chronologically according to sender or recipient

(D) chronologically within subject areas.

84. Work reports should usually be initially directed to the
   (A) central office
   (B) highest staff member
   (C) next supervisory level
   (D) statistical unit.

85. "Guide letters" may be defined as
   (A) letters used to mark off any specified number of other letters
   (B) memoranda to employees on proper procedure
   (C) printed letters to be sent out in a single mailing after addition of salutations
   (D) sample letters upon which actual letters may be based to meet specific situations.

86. Division of work is best analyzed by means of a
   (A) flow chart
   (B) flow process chart
   (C) work count
   (D) work distribution chart.

87. In carrying out a work simplification program, it is desirable for the methods analyst to
   (A) avoid contacts with employees involved in the work
   (B) encourage participation of employees involved in the work
   (C) assume limited supervision of the employees involved in the work
   (D) disregard recommendations of supervisors of employees engaged in the work.

88. In the process of work simplification, the most desirable of the following approaches to use *first* is usually to
   (A) analyze forms
   (B) ascertain problem areas
   (C) chart all processes and procedures
   (D) survey equipment.

89. In the box design of office forms, the spaces in which information is to be entered are arranged in boxes containing captions. Of the following, the one which is generally *not* considered to be an acceptable rule in employing box design is that
   (A) space should be allowed for the lengthiest anticipated entry in a box
   (B) the caption should be located in the upper left corner of the box
   (C) the boxes on a form should be of the same size and shape
   (D) boxes should be aligned vertically whenever possible.

90. Assume that a new unit is to be established in a city agency. The unit is to compile and tabulate data so that it will be of the greatest usefulness to the high-level administrators in the agency in making administrative decisions. In planning the organization of this unit, the question that should be answered *first* is
   (A) What interpretations are likely to be made of the data by the high-level administrators in making decisions?
   (B) At what point in the decision-making process will it be most useful to inject the data?
   (C) What types of data will be required by high-level administrators in making decisions?
   (D) What criteria will the high-level administrators use to evaluate the decisions they make?

91. Of the following, the *first* step that should be taken in a forms simplification program is to make a
   (A) detailed analysis of the items found on current forms
   (B) study of the amount of use made of existing forms
   (C) survey of the amount of each kind of form on hand
   (D) survey of the characteristics of the more effective forms in use.

92. Of the following, the type of subject matter which would be *least* suitable for a form letter instead of an individually prepared letter is a notice of
   (A) receipt of a request for information
   (B) resignation from a staff member
   (C) the date to appear for an interview
   (D) the period during which applications will be accepted.

93. Binding correspondence and other documents together with fasteners or other devices is most clearly acceptable when the material involved
   (A) cannot be replaced
   (B) is similar in form and content

(C) pertains to similar general subjects

(D) relates to a particular person, project, or transaction.

94. Files of active records should contain all records
    - (A) likely to be needed for the conduct of current business
    (B) obtained within the last 12 months
    (C) obtained within the last 5 years
    (D) which may be referred to in the future.

95. Assume that you have been assigned to assist in the revision and improvement of office forms used by the employees in your agency. Of the following, the most important principle for you to follow in this assignment is that
    (A) use of the forms should be confined to as few employees as possible
    (B) enough information should be recorded on the forms to make reference to other office records unnecessary
    (C) a standard procedure should be set up to insure that the revised forms contain the same titles and form numbers as the forms they replace
    (D) the recording of information on the forms and the handling of the forms should be simplified as much as possible.

96. Assume that you are the head of a central stenographic unit that serves a large number of clerks who answer routine inquiries from the public. You notice that many of the letters of reply dictated by these clerks are almost identical. Of the following, the most efficient course of action for you to take in connection with this matter is to
    (A) assign one of your subordinates to specialize in typing these letters
    (B) reduce the monotony of the work by dividing it evenly among the stenographers in the unit
    (C) suggest to your stenographers that these letters be typed at one time after a sufficient number have been accumulated
    (D) recommend the preparation of a form letter to be used in answering this correspondence.

97. The most effective method for a public agency to use to prevent the retention of unused, obsolete forms is to
    (A) limit the number of different forms that are authorized for use at one time

(B) destroy the oldest forms at regular intervals

(C) introduce revised forms only when the supply of forms they are to replace is exhausted

(D) examine the forms in use at periodic intervals to determine their usefulness.

98. The use of well designed office forms in an agency contributes most directly to the
    (A) gradual increase in the number of forms used
    (B) simplification of clerical procedures and increased speed of office processes
    (C) uniform interpretation of agency policies
    (D) improvement of public relations because of public appreciation of efficient management.

99. Assume that you have been requested to design an office form which is to be duplicated by the mimeograph process. In planning the layout of the various items appearing on the form, it is *least* important for you to know the
    (A) amount of information which the form is to contain
    (B) purpose for which the form will be used
    (C) size of the form
    (D) number of copies of the form which are required.

100. "Many office managers have a tendency to overuse form letters and are prone to print form letters for every occasion, regardless of the number of copies of these letters which is needed." On the basis of this quotation, it is most logical to state that the determination of the need for a form letter should depend upon the
    (A) length of the period during which the form letter may be used
    (B) number of form letters presently being used in the office
    (C) frequency with which the form letter may be used
    (D) number of typists who may use the form letter.

101. Of the following, the best reason for using "form" letters is that they
    (A) enable an individual to transmit unpleasant or disappointing communications in a gentle and sympathetic manner
    (B) present the facts in a terse, business-like manner
    (C) save the time of both the dictator and the

typist in answering letters dealing with similar matters

(D) are flexible and can be easily changed to meet varying needs and complex situations.

102. The chief of the Application Bureau of a City agency is drawing up a new application form for the use of persons applying for services rendered by his agency. The bureau chief anticipates that several thousand of these forms will be filed monthly by applicants. These filed applications are to be kept by the agency for one year and then destroyed. From the point of view of practicality and economy, the bureau chief should specify that

(A) the size of the form be 5″×9″ rather than 5½″×8½″

(B) the type of paper used for the form be onionskin paper rather than bond paper

(C) a year's supply of the forms be ordered at once rather than a small quantity for use during a trial period

(D) in printing the form, different sizes of type be employed rather than different colors of ink to emphasize certain sections of the form.

103. The forms design section of a City agency recommended that the sizes of the forms used by the agency be limited to the sizes that can be cut with the least amount of waste from either 17″×22″ or 17″×28″ sheets. Of the following,

the size that does *not* comply with this recommendation is

(A) 4¼″×5½″

(B) 3¾″×4¼″

(C) 3½″×4¼″

(D) 4¼″×2¾″.

104. Suppose that you are assigned to prepare a form from which certain information will be posted in a ledger. It would be most helpful to the person posting the information in the ledger if, in designing the form, you were to

(A) use the same color paper for both the form and the ledger

(B) make the form the same size as the pages of the ledger

(C) have the information on the form in the same order as that used in the ledger

(D) include in the form a box which is to be initialed when the data on the form have been posted in the ledger.

105. The one of the following that is *not* generally considered to be an advantage of the use of printed form letters in replying to inquiries is that they

(A) are flexible and may be easily changed to meet varying situations

(B) save the time of the stenographer or typist by reducing the amount of typing required

(C) relieve the dictator of the task of dictating letters containing identical wording

(D) make possible prompter replies to inquiries.

ANSWER KEY

1. A	22. B	43. B	64. B	85. D
2. C	23. A	44. B	65. B	86. D
3. B	24. D	45. C	66. A	87. B
4. C	25. A	46. C	67. C	88. B
5. D	26. B	47. D	68. C	89. C
6. C	27. B	48. A	69. A	90. C
7. D	28. C	49. C	70. D	91. B
8. B	29. A	50. C	71. D	92. B
9. B	30. A	51. B	72. D	93. D
10. B	31. B	52. A	73. C	94. A
11. B	32. D	53. A	74. C	95. D
12. B	33. C	54. C	75. A	96. D
13. D	34. D	55. C	76. C	97. D
14. A	35. A	56. B	77. C	98. B
15. D	36. B	57. A	78. A	99. D
16. D	37. A	58. B	79. C	100. C
17. A	38. A	59. A	80. B	101. C
18. A	39. A	60. C	81. D	102. D
19. C	40. B	61. C	82. B	103. B
20. A	41. C	62. A	83. D	104. C
21. A	42. A	63. A	84. C	105. A

EXPLANATORY ANSWERS

1. (A) From an administrative point of view, reports are useful primarily to help control the administration of a unit. They help the administrator to know the progress and problems of operations throughout the unit. The other possible answers show the value of reports in other aspects of the job not directly concerned with administration.

2. (C) Any report is more readily understood if its content is related to facts and knowledge well known to its readers. The most difficult subject matter can be simplified by relating it to everyday happenings.

3. (B) Fairly long reports should begin with a summary of the conclusions because a supervisor wants to know what you have discovered, and may not have the time to read the whole report. Therefore the supervisor's interest must be gained quickly.

4. (C) An outline for a report is used primarily to ensure a proper relationship between important, secondary and/or supportive points covered in the report. An outline is not useful in the situations presented by the other answer choices.

5. (D) An index is needed, especially in a long and complex report, to help the reader easily find specific points he or she wishes to read without having to scan the entire report or entire portions. An index does not mean that the report should not contain a Table of Contents in order to supply the reader with the main sections. The other possible answers concern data which is not found in the index.

6. (C) Well-planned forms will assist, simplify, and speed up complex procedures considerably. The other possible answers contain results which may or may not be directly helped by the design of well-planned forms.

7. (D) The answer depicts and defines the use of an index in a report.

8. (B) Short sentences always make it easier for the reader to comprehend the thoughts and facts brought forth. Repetition does not generally make the material easier to

follow, although illustrations of a complex point can clarify an issue. All reports, regardless of complexity, should contain only one major thought per paragraph.

9. **(B)** Reports are most useful for an organization because they will show the reader what has occurred, whether these occurrences are random or show a trend, and whether predictions can be made based on these occurrences. The other possible answers may not necessarily be true of a particular report, and are of secondary importance. The staff may still have to submit individual communications, ask questions, and give informal information. Although the staff can learn about decisions made without using reports, policy-makers do not have to read reports in order to make decisions.

10. **(B)** Recommendations should be made in a report in such a fashion that the reader inevitably comes to the same conclusion as the writer of the report, based on the material submitted. The recommendation should be a logical outgrowth of the facts presented in the main body of the report.

11. **(B)** It is good practice to confine questions to those which directly relate to the purposes of the questionnaire. Inclusion of extraneous material only complicates tabulation of findings, accumulates useless data, and tends to annoy the respondent. Questionnaires should not elicit opinions unless that is its purpose, e.g., an opinion poll. Answers should be easily tabulated "yes" or "no." Averages or percentages which make the compilation of data difficult should be avoided. If percentages are necessary, the answers elicited should fall into categories which are easy for the respondent to follow and for one to tabulate. Personal questions do not increase reliability of responses. They often just annoy the respondent, and should be included only if the information is pertinent to the purposes of the questionnaire.

12. **(B)** Good administrative practices require the use of forms, form letters and form paragraphs to speed up the process of handling problems, and insure uniformity of response to similar situations. The other possible answers are clearly unsatisfactory ways to handle the problem presented.

13. **(D)** An index is prepared after the material has been written, and is based on the contents of the report. All the other possible answers are steps to be taken before writing the report.

14. **(A)** The best way to draw the attention of a reader quickly to the main topic of a report is to include a strong introductory sentence at the beginning of a paragraph. The other possible answers will not focus the reader's attention on the main point as well as answer A.

15. **(D)** The main purpose of reports is to help get the business of the agency done as expeditiously and accurately as possible. Some reports prove to be good reference material, others may be used to focus attention on

the need for action on the subject, but all reports should help expedite the agency's work. Reports are commonly used to compare work completed with work scheduled to be completed during a given period.

16. **(D)** It is most useful to outline the material in a special report to make sure that all pertinent material is included. This material is then arranged in a logical manner, and extraneous material is eliminated. The other possible answers are not as useful in the preparation of a special report.

17. **(A)** The closing section of a report should summarize the main points, and make the results, true meaning, and conclusions clear to the reader. The other possible answers are not appropriate when concluding a report.

18. **(A)** Based on the information given, when constructing a questionnaire there is no need to set up a control group. The questionnaire seeks information, and there are no standard answers against which responses can be compared. The other possible answers contain points which are necessary to consider when constructing a questionnaire.

19. **(C)** It would be a very worthwhile idea to discuss the questionnaire's purpose and information desired with the respondents, so that they know exactly what each question means, and are willing to respond to the entire questionnaire. This does not mean, however, that you tell them which answers you want, just the meaning of the questions. The time will be well spent if the result is willing respondents and meaningful responses to the questionnaire.

20. **(A)** Questionnaires asking for opinions or attitudes should not require respondents to give their names because many people will be reluctant to answer honestly if they are identified. In order to compare the attitudes of different kinds of people, their ages, education and backgrounds may be highly useful.

21. **(A)** All activities in an organization must be covered in a reporting system. Nothing can be left unreported. It is far more desirable to have duplication in the reporting of an activity than to permit any activity to go unreported.

22. **(B)** The purpose of a working hypothesis is to focus collected data. If it widens the area of investigation, it should be thrown out and a new working hypothesis selected.

23. **(A)** Letters written by other staff for the signature of the department head should generally be brief and to the point in order to avoid ambiguity and insure that the department's official position is clearly stated.

24. **(D)** The procedure for preparing reports will not change appreciably after a computer installation just because the employee preparing the report is changed. The same data will be used, and thus the same computer process

needed. The other possible answers may result in a change in the procedure because all of them may require the use of different machines, different format, etc.

25. **(A)** The basic principle in designing a form is to arrange the material so that the individual filling it out can easily "read and do." On a form designed for typewriter use, captions printed below the space are inefficient. The typist must first read the caption, and then move the carriage back to the blank space. The efficient way makes the caption immediately visible to the typist, who then proceeds to the blank space.

26. **(B)** Form-control does more than eliminate useless, duplicative or difficult to understand forms. It can also change procedures. Thus, if two forms are combined, the entire procedure for recording information may have to change. It should be noted that a change in procedure may also necessitate a change in the form.

27. **(B)** Department heads must know the "bottom line" of all agency activities, and are usually not directly concerned with the details of operation. In a report they should be given the essentials and the summary of conclusions, so that they do not have to waste valuable time in reading non-essential facts or details.

28. **(C)** The unstated hypothesis is, that a form should be used to avoid waste and confusion. There is no justification in the quotation for any of the other possible answers.

29. **(A)** Unnecessary training is costly and wasteful.

30. **(A)** A staff unit exists to help the line units do the primary work of the agency, and must accede to the ultimate decisions of the line official. The staff unit head may feel that certain items are superfluous, but he or she is not in the position to really know the full details, and does not bear the final responsibility for the nature of the material in the report.

31. **(B)** In a lengthy report it is not desirable to place conclusions and recommendations at the end. Busy executives should be able to immediately discover the results and conclusions of a report to see if they need to read all of it.

32. **(D)** Differences in the sizes of boxes on an organizational chart usually indicate the relative importance of sub-divisions within the hierarchy, not the number of persons in that sub-division. An organization chart is designed to show organizational relationships, and is not concerned with staffing. Its primary purpose is to show lines of authority.

33. **(C)** When preparing a form to be filled out by a semi-literate population, the most important factor to consider is language which can be easily understood by that population. If they do not understand the questions, the good form design considerations mentioned in the other possible answers are of no help.

34. **(D)** Any good suggestion program requires anonymity of suggestors until suggestions are evaluated. This should insure impartiality. Suggestors would have confidence in this type of program, and would be encouraged to submit suggestions.

35. **(A)** Research is scientific only when the data resulting from it is obtained from direct action and investigation. The data cannot have resulted from statistical studies, chance or probability measures.

36. **(B)** If it is determined that 80% of New Yorkers use public transportation to go to work, then there is an 80% chance that a New Yorker picked at random also does. If the selection is not made at random, that probability is lost because any other means of selection could alter the result. For instance, if you investigated this fact in an apartment house within walking distance of commercial enterprises, you are likely to encounter working people who are able to walk to work, and thus the 80% probability would no longer hold true.

37. **(A)** If a sample does not represent any given population, you cannot generalize from the information obtained. The information is true merely for those individuals interviewed, and therefore worthless. Random selection and stratification of dominant characteristics are sampling techniques, not basic assumptions.

38. **(A)** In statistical studies, experience will determine just how large a sampling should be. If one has determined from experience that a sampling of a certain number is large enough to establish a fact, when similar facts are to be determined, it would be prudent to use the same size sampling.

39. **(A)** A survey of land use requires little need to question individual people in detail when compared to the other possible answers.

40. **(B)** Of the possible answers, the first step to be taken in a field study would be to obtain background data such as previous documents, records and reports about the area under study. The other possible answers are steps to be taken later.

41. **(C)** A questionnaire can cover far more ground in terms of both the number and type of questions raised than would a personal interview since less time is required to obtain answers from a questionnaire than from an interview.

42. **(A)** The chief problem of a sample survey by questionnaire is that although the total sample group receiving questionnaires may be representative of the total population, the responses actually completed by respondents may not be.

43. **(B)** The correct answer is the choice which is not true. Questions with "yes" or "no" answers can indeed be

useful and if possible they should be used extensively. These answers require no interpretation.

44. **(B)** Since the use of abstract words in a report can result in misunderstandings and in a lack of comprehension by the reader, concrete terms are preferred. Generalizations can be made from material regardless of whether abstract or concrete words are used.

45. **(C)** If a simple "yes" or "no" is required when answering items of a form, ballot-type entries are the clearest and easiest way both for the respondent and tabulator. All other possible answers are not good form design guides.

46. **(C)** It makes no sense to include, on the reverse side of a form, provision for a symbol giving the principal subdivisions under which the form is to be filed. If the forms are to be filed in three separate places, they may each be of a different color to expedite filing. The other possible answers contain good ideas for design.

47. **(D)** A periodic report to a supervisor is used primarily to help the supervisor do his or her job of controlling, planning and supervising the work. All other possible answers are secondary or are only partial reasons which are encompassed in the primary reason.

48. **(A)** The key word is "detailed." Detailed instructions belong in a procedural manner where they can be referred to. It is possible that they will be too lengthy to include on the back of the form which will eventually be filed. Conferences seek input from participants, it is not a place to enunciate proper procedure.

49. **(C)** The standard way to designate pages in a loose-leaf manual which is subject to frequent changes is to use integers for main divisions and decimals for subdivisions, i.e., 1, 1.1, 1.2, 1.3, etc. Use of integers and letters is appropriate for report writing, but is generally impractical for manuals subject to frequent revision.

50. **(C)** Employee handbooks tell all workers, regardless of title, what they need to know about the whole organization, its major functions, rules and regulations applicable to all workers, etc. They do not give data which would help solve problems relating to assignment of personnel.

51. **(B)** A procedural manual should be easy to use. Making it bulkier by putting short subdivisions on separate pages will not make it easier to read or to find particular subdivisions when needed, but will make it harder to handle. Proper numbering of subdivisions and use of an index and table of contents would be better ideas.

52. **(A)** Using only one side of a page makes replacement of revised material easy and inexpensive. A manual of 100 pages is not too bulky or difficult to handle. Only those pages of material which have to be revised will have to be reproduced and replaced. If the front and back of each page were used, both sides would have to be reproduced even though only one page needed revision.

53. **(A)** Sufficient blank space in a procedural manual should be left between each division and subdivision to insure readability, and serve as an aid when referring to pertinent material. The manual's increased bulk caused by the additional blank space is minor in comparison with the positive benefits gained.

54. **(C)** An employee procedural manual should provide for ease in making changes. Stagnant organizations are ineffective. There should be a constant thrust for improvement. These changes in operation must be reflected in procedural manuals.

55. **(C)** The general principle to remember is that a procedural manual should tell the workers the correct procedures to follow in order to accomplish their assigned tasks. A manual of procedures for Clerks, Grade 2 need not contain any data regarding the estimate of costs for clerical operations, because this data has no pertinence to their work.

56. **(B)** Procedural manuals are considered a training device and, in time, workers have to refer to them less and less. Standards for evaluating work do not belong in them, and should be stated in an appropriate personnel bulletin.

57. **(A)** The procedure used to formulate policy generally does not belong in an operating manual. Such a manual may contain data given in other possible answers.

58. **(B)** Although procedural manuals might refer to the existence of in-service training programs which deal specifically with the work of Clerks, Grade 2, they do not generally refer to their value.

59. **(A)** Again, procedural manuals deal with actual steps to get specific work done. Therefore, arguments for or against centralized filing do not belong in an operating procedures manual.

60. **(C)** The method used to adjust disagreements among employees does not belong in a procedural manual. Issues shown in the other possible answers do belong in a manual of procedures.

61. **(C)** Data about designing effective office forms should not be included in a manual of procedures for Clerks, Grade 2, because such work is not ordinarily appropriate to persons in that title.

62. **(A)** The quotation deals solely with the meaning of a personnel survey, and as such, there is no way to relate a personnel survey to methods for appraising operating efficiency. The information described in the other possible answers can be obtained from a personnel survey.

63. **(A)** Reports are not an end in themselves. They are indicators of actions to be or not to be taken.

64. **(B)** Different manuals are prepared for different purposes and different levels of staff. Therefore, before a particular manual is prepared, its uses and the people who will use it are of primary importance.

65. **(B)** In effect, the quotation says that while a particular manual may be usable, it is not necessarily useful merely by being in a manual form. Of the possible answers, the correct one implies that a manual may not in fact be usable for some of the purposes originally thought.

66. **(A)** An operating official who knows which elements of experience are static or constant can develop a procedure or standard method to oversee that experience. Responsibility for the supervision of that experience can then be assigned at a lower level.

67. **(C)**
$$A - 12,000 \div 9 = 1,333 \qquad 1,500 \times 4 = 6,000$$
$$B - 12,000 \div 18 = \underline{667} \qquad 2,000 \times 4 = \underline{8,000}$$
$$ 2,000 \qquad\qquad\qquad 14,000$$

$$\frac{2,000}{14,000} = \frac{1}{7} = 14\frac{1}{3}\%$$

68. **(C)** Since Unit A completes 1,330 work units in a month, and Unit B completes 660 work units in a month, the two complete about 2,000 work units together. At this rate, it will take six months to fill a cabinet which holds 12,000 work units.

69. **(A)** Since the work load is not being reduced, the same amount of files will be necessary.

70. **(D)** First, lay out the relevant information given:

Work units per week	Clerk man-hours	Typist man-hours
A — 1,500	100 (+4)	20
B — 2,000	125 (+12)	60

Convert Typist man-hours to Clerk man-hours as indicated on first line, at 5 to 1: $20 \div 5 = 4$ and $60 \div 5 = 12$.
Add all man-hours: $100 + 4 + 125 + 12 = 241$ man-hours
Divide 241 by 35 (hours per week) $= 6\frac{31}{35}$.
Seven clerks will have to be assigned to complete the 3,500 weekly file operations.

71. **(D)** We are given no information about the nature of work to be done with respect to Schedule K, or who is to do the work (technical staff or clerks?). Without such information, there is no way to tell how much work production must be increased.

72. **(D)** If a report form is well-planned, it becomes much easier to use. A form does not establish a procedure, although changes in the procedures may result after a form has been developed. A form may be a supervisory tool regardless of how well it has been designed.

73. **(C)** Records are never an end in themselves. They are a means to an end. They are the source of determining whether actions should or should not be taken.

74. **(C)** A management survey is usually taken when there is a problem which warrants corrective measures to be taken. The identification of the cause of the problem is the most difficult aspect of a management survey.

75. **(A)** Check lists are useful tools to indicate which areas are needed to be covered in the management survey. They do not serve in any significant way the purposes listed in the other possible answers.

76. **(C)** The need for charts or graphs in a good management report depends on the purpose of the report, the nature of the data collected, the persons receiving the report, and other factors. Therefore, it is not essential to good management reporting.

77. **(C)** Oral reports allow the listener to interrupt whenever he or she wants clarification or additional information. In this way the listener is more certain he or she fully understands the report. Oral reports may or may not be more complete or truthful, and may or may not include information which the speaker cannot put into a written report.

78. **(A)** A lengthy narrative report should always include a written summary so that the busy executive can, if he or she chooses to read only the summary, still understand the basic tenets of the report.

79. **(C)** The purpose of a report is to help get the work of the agency done, and should be written as frequently as is needed. This frequency primarily depends on the kind and extent of changes that occur over time. If, for example, experience shows that with respect to a particular matter no essential change occurs in a month, but within two months meaningful changes are likely to occur, the reports may be needed on a bi-monthly basis. The other possible answers are also considered to help decide how often to submit reports, but are not as crucial as the correct answer.

80. **(B)** The administrator's most important need here is to ensure that the data will objectively evaluate the procedure. An administrator who knows in advance that his or her data will prove only his or her preconceived opinions about the procedure is not conducting an objective study, and the results obtained will not, in many instances, be a true picture of the procedure's worth.

81. **(D)** The unit supervisor is in the best possible position to identify the data that will best reflect the operation of his or her responsibilities.

82. **(B)** Information is obtained and recorded for many different reasons, including legal ones, but if study shows that there is no real reason to obtain the data, the agency should cease to do so.

83. **(D)** Good files are those where needed material can be most easily and accurately retrieved. With large volumes of diversified mail being constantly received, the best filing technique for ease of retrieval is filing by subject matter and then chronologically. The filing methods given in the other possible answers present difficulties for easy retrieval.

84. **(C)** A supervisor should critically review all reports of work done in his or her unit before they are sent to other units or to other people in the agency. The supervisor thus has the opportunity to approve, disapprove or correct the work report, and to take any actions he or she deems proper.

85. **(D)** The answer is self explanatory. However, it should be duly noted that "guide" letters are used only on a frequent basis. An example of this would be if an individual was confronted with a number of similar situations that would call for similar responses. They differ from "form" letters in that "form" letters are preprinted and need a minimum of information typed into the letter.

86. **(D)** Flow charts and flow process charts depict a process, the work count, and the amount of work being performed by each individual. The work distribution chart indicates the amount and types of work being performed by all of the members of the staff.

87. **(B)** Methods analysis work requires active consultation with the employees who do the work because they know best what is going wrong, and may have useful solutions. Furthermore, in order to institute new methods successfully, the active cooperation of workers is vital, and the best way to elicit cooperation is to have the workers involved in the analytic, proposal, and implementation stages.

88. **(B)** In trying to simplify work, the first thing to do is discover what problem areas exist, and to concentrate on these areas. The other possible answers are later steps in the analytic process.

89. **(C)** The size and shape of a box depends upon the expected length and the nature of the data to be contained in the box. Therefore, the size and shape of each box may differ sharply.

90. **(C)** The first thing to be determined is what data will be required by high-level administrators. Once this is known, the staffing of the unit can be determined, and further organizational steps taken. The other possible answers do not directly concern the initial organization of the unit.

91. **(B)** At the beginning of a forms simplification program the first thing that must be known is the number, type, and the amount of use made of each existing form, so that unnecessary and unused forms can be considered for elimination.

92. **(B)** Form letters should be used when needed to give the same impersonal and factual data to many individuals. A form letter can be used to acknowledge receipt of a request for information, the date to appear for an interview, dates of acceptance of applications, etc. A resignation from a staff member requires a personalized answer, both to maintain good personnel relations and to single out the specifics usually required to answer each resignee.

93. **(D)** The use of fasteners and similar devices should be confined to a relatively small number of pages, or the material will not stay bound. All material should be related to one person or activity for ease of retrieval and for use by the staff.

94. **(A)** Active files should be used just for that purpose, i.e., for holding items related to current uncompleted business.

95. **(D)** In general, the most important principle to bear in mind concerning good office forms is to keep the recording of information and the handling of the forms as simple as possible.

96. **(D)** Routine inquiries are best and most efficiently handled by use of form letters. The other possible answers are less appropriate and less efficient ways to handle the situation described.

97. **(D)** The best way to prevent retention of unused obsolete forms is to set up a standard procedure requiring examination, at specified intervals, of all forms for continued usefulness.

98. **(B)** Well designed office forms make clerical procedures easier to follow and result in simplifying these procedures. In turn, this results in increased production.

99. **(D)** This question is a matter of design. Factors in choices A, B, and C are important considerations. The number of copies to be reproduced by a mimeograph is not a consideration during the design stage.

100. **(C)** There is no point in using a form letter which will be used infrequently. Form letters are economical but they are impersonal. Anyone who has received a form letter in a serious matter knows that form letters are offensive.

101. **(C)** Form letters save time in preparing and typing replies on like matters, and free personnel to expedite less routine matters.

102. **(D)** The use of different sized type rather than different colors of ink will be economical and easier to produce. Since they will not be a permanent record,

functionalism rather than aesthetics should be emphasized.

103. **(B)** All the answers indicate one side of the large sheets to be cut equals 4¼″ because 4 sheets can be cut from either the 17″ × 22″ or the 17″ × 28″ sheets. Both 5½″ and 2¾″ can be cut from the 22″ side with no waste (4 sheets and 8 sheets respectively); 8 sheets of 3½″ can be cut from 28″, again with no waste. Only 3¾″ × 4¼″ cannot be cut from the larger sheets without having leftover paper.

104. **(C)** When designing a form from which information can be copied onto a ledger, the most important thing to remember is to make the copy job as easy to do as possible. The best way to do this is to put the material in the same order on the form as it is on the ledger.

105. **(A)** Form letters are usually inflexible, and are not subject to being easily changed. They are printed in bulk, and even a minor change will require a reprinting.

MORALE

1. "If a situation can be established whereby the individual can for the most part furnish his or her own motivation, where stimulation comes from the perception of a larger and more inclusive task, the rationale of which is clear to him or her and accepted by him or her then a higher level of performance and morale may be achieved." The implication of the above quotations for the administrator is that
   (A) orders usually should permit the subordinate to exercise discretion
   (B) employees perform better when they understand the reasons for procedures
   (C) more emphasis should be given to teaching theory to all levels of the department
   (D) motivation depends primarily upon rational considerations.

2. Of the following, the morale of employees is probably most closely dependent on the
   (A) situation existing at hand
   (B) abilities of the administrators
   (C) tightness of discipline in the department
   (D) day-to-day working conditions and personal relations.

3. Of the following, morale is usually most dependent on the
   (A) relationships between superiors and subordinates
   (B) relationships among subordinates
   (C) rates of pay
   (D) possibilities of promotion.

4. In dealing with his staff, an administrator's frank acknowledgment of his difficulties in solving agency problems has the effect of
   (A) solidifying criticism of the administrator
   (B) lowering staff morale
   (C) lowering the administrator's prestige
   (D) promoting good feeling.

5. Employee harmony and morale are best sustained when the exercise of individual initiative on the part of each employee is
   (A) encouraged by the opportunity to try out each new idea
   (B) developed in such a way that each member of a group will contribute toward a group objective
   (C) stimulated in such a way as to lead to a feeling of personal achievement rather than group achievement
   (D) discouraged as disruptive to the group's activity and morale.

6. The good administrator would assign personnel by which of the following methods in order to achieve the best functioning of the department and the best morale in the department
   (A) by an impartial method, that is, by "drawing lots" method with frequent changes at "drawing" the better jobs
   (B) by an evaluation of the qualifications of the workers as well as the necessary requirements of the position

(C) by ranking the positions according to pay and assigning supervisors on basis of seniority

(D) any of the above, as they are equally valuable.

7. A well-conceived pay plan within a department is one that
   - (A) does away with jealousies which arise when employees are paid at unequal rates
   - (B) distinguishes more responsible jobs from those of lesser responsibility
   - (C) makes pay between private and public employment equitable
   - (D) gives clear title to positions with different rates of pay.

8. Usually the general attitude of an administrator has
   - (A) little influence on the workers if they like their work
   - (B) little relation to morale if salaries paid are above the median rate for services performed
   - (C) a high degree of influence on the maintenance of morale
   - (D) limited effect on the workers if the physical environment in which they work is pleasant.

9. Which one of the following factors is generally considered to play the most important part in developing and maintaining a satisfactory state of morale among a group of employees?
   - (A) wage level
   - (B) working conditions
   - (C) immediate or first-line supervision
   - (D) intersocial relations within the group.

10. When an administrator takes time to so instruct subordinates that they understand the why and wherefore of their duties, he is
    - (A) making friends
    - (B) developing morale
    - (C) wasting time
    - (D) being dictatorial.

11. Of the following actions of an administrator, the one which is most likely to lead to high morale among subordinates is to
    - (A) insist that subordinates rigidly follow all the rules regardless of whether they are observed in other departments
    - (B) encourage subordinates to become friendly but discourage social engagements with them
    - (C) observe the same rules which the subordinates are expected to follow

(D) point out to his subordinates the advantages of having a cooperative spirit within the company.

12. One of the most vital factors in the development of the morale of the workers in the department is the
    - (A) relationship existing between the workers and the administrator
    - (B) relationship existing between the workers and their immediate superiors
    - (C) policy of allowing employees greater discretion in the way they perform their work
    - (D) quality of the work performed by specific employees.

13. Which one of the following traits of an administrator would be most likely to win and hold the respect of his unit?
    - (A) cheerful disposition
    - (B) seniority
    - (C) competence
    - (D) decisiveness.

14. The most important supervisory principle for the attainment of high morale is to
    - (A) be accessible to subordinates
    - (B) respect the feelings of subordinates
    - (C) give credit where credit is due
    - (D) be fair and impartial.

15. A competent supervisor is best judged by
    - (A) his or her command of words and the type of higher education he has
    - (B) his or her easy-going personality
    - (C) the speed with which subordinates do their assigned tasks
    - (D) the condition and morale of the subordinates.

16. In developing a sound employee relations policy in a department, administrators have found that more effective administration is obtained when
    - (A) employees are invited to consult and participate in the solution of personnel problems
    - (B) discussion is avoided by having the administrator make all decisions without consulting the employees
    - (C) decisions are made by administrators other than the immediate superiors
    - (D) there are formal rules and regulations to cover every situation.

17. The existence of high morale in an organization is best evidenced by the fact that

(A) its employees are willing to subordinate personal objectives to the organizations objectives

(B) employee working conditions are favorable and salary scales relatively high

(C) the number of disciplinary cases are few and infrequent

(D) the average length of service and tenure of employees are relatively long.

18. The greatest amount of improvement in the efficiency and morale of a unit will be brought about by the supervisor who
    (A) reminds his employees constantly that they must follow departmental regulations

(B) frequently praises an employee in the presence of the other employees in the unit

(C) invariably gives mild reproof and constructive criticism to subordinates when he discovers that they have made a mistake

(D) assigns duties to employees in conformance with their abilities and interests as far as practicable.

19. Of the following, the most usual concomitant of excessive absenteeism in any organization is
    (A) inadequate training
    (B) low morale
    (C) low pay
    (D) poor communications.

ANSWER KEY

1. B	5. B	9. C	13. C	17. A
2. D	6. B	10. B	14. D	18. D
3. A	7. A	11. C	15. D	19. B
4. D	8. C	12. B	16. A	

EXPLANATORY ANSWERS

1. **(B)** The quotation simply states that when a worker is able to comprehend how the work he or she is performing contributes to the overall accomplishment of agency objectives, the worker is likely to perform in a more efficient manner.

2. **(D)** Extensive studies have shown that everyday contacts on the job, such as those between fellow workers and between subordinates and superiors, are the most important factors affecting worker morale. The other possible answers would greatly affect morale only in special situations, such as when an administrator is abnormally harsh or overbearing and interferes in the daily activities of the unit.

3. **(A)** Studies have shown that in most work situations, the relationship between superiors and subordinates most closely affects the worker morale. A good supervisor can do a great deal towards alleviating or solving a possibly bad morale situation resulting from a conflict between two workers, lack of promotion opportunities, or from a low rate of pay. The lack of good relationships between supervisor and subordinates will, however, result in low morale, even if all the other factors are satisfactory to the staff.

4. **(D)** A good administrator knows that staff will generally support him or her if they believe the administrator is trying to do what is best for the agency. The fair and competent administrator who acknowledges that he or she does not have all the answers and does have difficulty with certain agency problems will probably receive the sympathy and cooperation of the staff without lowering his or her prestige or the staff's morale.

5. **(B)** Studies of individual and group behavior show that employee harmony and morale are best sustained when individual initiative is allowed to be shown within a group situation where the group is trying to solve a problem of common interest and importance. Thus, the most successful solution to a problem may very well come from a group discussion in which each member is expressing his

or her ideas. In this manner two things are accomplished—first, a problem is resolved and second, there is a display and growth of individual initiative and of group harmony.

6. **(B)** In order to achieve the highest morale and the best functioning of the agency, an administrator should fill each position with the staff member best qualified to fit that particular job. This involves evaluating both the qualifications of each staff member and the requirements of the particular job. The other answer choices fail to meet the dual purpose of achieving both good morale and effective functioning of an agency. Thus, filling all promotion jobs by seniority will solve a morale problem but may leave the supervisor with a promotee who cannot handle the new position. The same is even more likely to be true for the "drawing of lots" method.

7. **(A)** A pay plan provides for rates of pay for different jobs according to the different levels of responsibility within the same occupational group. A well-conceived pay plan within the civil service structure is based on the principle of equal pay for equal work. All positions involving the same work and requiring the same qualifications will, therefore, be established at the same salary range. A pay plan does not deal with jobs per se, that is the function of the classification plan which designates, for example, that all positions requiring the incumbents to do routine typing will be put into the same title—Typist. The pay plan states that all typists will be paid within a specific salary range. In establishing a pay plan in the public sector, studies are often made of comparable jobs in the private sector. Absolute pay equality with jobs in private industry is not always possible or desirable for public employment, because fringe benefits are generally better in public employment and must be considered when arriving at the public salary.

8. **(C)** The attitude of the administrator plays an important part in the maintenance of morale of subordinates. Workers may like the work and the work environment, have no problem with the salary, and may even remain with the

agency for these reasons, but if an administrator has a poor attitude, morale can only suffer.

9. **(C)** The immediate or first line supervisor's attitude is of prime importance in the development and maintenance of good morale. All of the other possible answers are important factors in building and maintaining good morale, but if a good relationship between workers and supervisor is lacking, poor morale will result. The other positive answers will *not* prevent poor morale.

10. **(B)** Explaining to workers *why* a job is done a certain way, instead of simply *how* the job is to be done, will lead to a spirit of group cooperation and good morale.

11. **(C)** The supervisor who observes the same rules he or she expects the subordinates to follow is most likely to gain their much needed support and respect. This also will result in a favorable level of morale.

12. **(B)** Good morale depends largely on the relationship between first line supervisors and their immediate staff. All other relationships and all other morale building policies and practices are secondary to this most vital one.

13. **(C)** Workers are most likely to respect the administrator who has proven to be competent in his or her job. Competency implies decisiveness when a decisive answer is needed or a decisive action must be taken, but the competent leader is more than decisive—he or she is also correct in his or her decisions. A cheerful or an older leader may be well-liked, but not necessarily respected.

14. **(D)** A good supervisor follows all the points given in the possible answers; however, the *most* important fact in attaining a high morale is to make fair and impartial judgments.

15. **(D)** Just as morale is built and sustained by the workers' feeling that their supervisor is competent and fair, the supervisor is best judged for competency by the spirit of cooperation and unity displayed in his or her unit.

16. **(A)** Experience has shown that a good employee relations program is best developed by including the staff in the development of the program. Thus, for example, a discussion regarding the possible use of flexible working hours should include the participation of the staff in the planning process. Staff representatives will most likely contribute practical solutions to many of the problems raised by such a plan. Such participation will build the morale of staff, who then realize that top management knows that the agency is a team working towards common goals and seeking fair, impartial and practical solutions to problems affecting everyone. This does *not* mean that top management must accept all of the staff's ideas, because there are matters which must remain unknown to the staff and which will affect final decisions. Also, top management must bear the consequences of all bad decisions! What this *does* mean, is that top management believes in the staff participation and is willing to listen to the staff's ideas on mutual concerns.

17. **(A)** The best indication of high morale in any organization is when the staff thinks of the good of the whole group before they think of personal objectives and are willing to forego many personal plans in order to help the group. The worker who cancels a planned party willingly, in order to help the team meet an emergency deadline, and the worker who postpones a vacation to get an important job done are examples of staff whose morale is high. Working conditions, high salaries, good discipline and low turnover may all be positive signs that an organization seems to be functioning effectively, but none show that the morale of the organization is high. It is when the workers in the organization refuse or are unwilling to voluntarily do *more* than is absolutely required to keep their jobs that poor morale is evident.

18. **(D)** Efficiency and morale are influenced positively when workers understand and like their jobs. The employee who is in the wrong job, either because he or she cannot do it well or dislikes the work, will be neither the most efficient worker nor one with good morale. None of the other possible answers will satisfy both the improvement in efficiency and in morale referred to in the question.

19. **(B)** Studies of excessive absenteeism generally show poor morale among the employees. The worker whose morale is low, because he or she does not feel that he or she is part of a team effort and has not the desire to help the group meet its goals, is the worker who develops headaches or slight colds and stays home at the slightest provocation. The worker with high morale is the one who knows that his or her contribution is important to the group and feels responsible for getting it done promptly and correctly and therefore attempts to get to work even at the possible expense of his or her health.

CONFERENCES, MEETINGS, AND INTERVIEWS

DIRECTIONS FOR ANSWERING QUESTIONS

Each question has four suggested answers, lettered A, B, C, and D. Decide which one is the best answer and on the sample answer sheet (all answer sheets are at the front of the book) find the question number and darken the area, with a soft pencil, which corresponds to the answer that you have selected.

1. If a representative committee of employees in a large department is to meet with an administrative officer for the purpose of improving staff relations and of handling grievances, it is best that these meetings be held
   (A) at regular intervals
   (B) whenever requested by an aggrieved employee
   (C) at the discretion of the administrative officer
   (D) whenever the need arises.

2. A bureau chief has scheduled a conference with the unit heads in his bureau to obtain their views on a major problem confronting the bureau. The *least* appropriate action for him to take in conducting this conference is to
   (A) present his own views on the solution of the problem before asking the unit heads for their opinions
   (B) call upon a participant in the conference for information which this participant should have as part of his job
   (C) weigh the opinions expressed at the conference in the light of the individual speaker's background and experience
   (D) summarize briefly, at the conclusion of the conference, the important points covered and the conclusions reached.

3. Of the following practices and techniques that may be employed by the conference leader, the

one that the conference leader should ordinarily avoid is
   (A) permitting certain participants to leave the conference to get back to their work when the discussion has reached the point where their special interests or qualifications are no longer involved
   (B) encouraging the participants to take full written notes for later comparison with the minutes of the meeting
   (C) helping a participant extricate himself from an awkward position in which the participant has placed himself by an ill-advised remark
   (D) translating the technical remarks of a speaker for the benefit of some participants who would otherwise fail to grasp the meaning of the remarks.

4. Your office staff consists of eight clerks, stenographers and typists, cramped in a long narrow room. The room is very difficult to ventilate properly, and, as in so many other offices, the disagreement over the method of ventilation is marked. Two cliques are developing and the friction is carrying over into the work of the office. Of the following, the best way to proceed is to
   (A) call your staff together, have the matter fully discussed giving each person an opportunity to be heard, and put the matter to vote; then enforce the method of ventilation which has the most votes

(B) call your staff together and have the matter fully disclosed. If a compromise arrangement is agreed upon, put it into effect. Otherwise, on the basis of all the facts at your disposal, make a decision as to how best to ventilate the room and enforce your decision

(C) speak to the employees individually, make a decision as to how to ventilate the room, and then enforce your decision

(D) study the layout of the office, make a decision as to how best to ventilate the room, and then enforce your decision.

5. Assume that you have been placed in charge of a unit where the quality of the work performed is poor. You plan to discuss the matter of improving the quality of the work at a staff meeting of the unit. Of the following courses of action which you might take at this meeting, the best one is to

(A) describe a few cases of exceptionally poor work performance; then have the employees performing this work explain why their work was done poorly

(B) inform the staff that you will be criticized by your own superior if the quality of the unit's work does not improve; then discuss, in general terms, the problem of improving the quality of the work

(C) discuss the problem of improving the quality of the unit's work; then call upon each employee by name for his suggestions for improving the work he performs

(D) present the problem to the staff; then indicate and discuss specific methods for improving the quality of the work.

6. The *least* accurate of the following statements regarding the conduct of a conference is that

(A) when there is great disparity in the rank of the participants at a conference, the conference leader should ordinarily refrain from requesting an opinion point blank from a participant of relatively low rank

(B) when the aim of a conference is to obtain the opinion of a group of approximately the same rank, the rank of the conference leader should ordinarily not be too much higher than that of the participants

(C) in general, the chances that a conference will be fruitful are greatly increased if the conference leader's direct superior is one of the participants

(D) a top administrator invited to present a brief talk sponsoring a series of conferences for line supervisors should generally arrange to leave the conference as soon as appropriate after he has made his speech.

7. "To the executive who directs the complex and diverse operations of a large organizational unit, the conference is an important and, at times, indispensable tool of management. The inexperienced executive may, however, employ the conference for a purpose for which it is ill fitted." Of the following, the *least* suitable use of the conference by the executive is to

(A) reconcile conflicting views or interests

(B) develop an understanding by all concerned of a policy already adopted

(C) coordinate an activity involving line supervisors

(D) perform technical research on a specific project.

8. Committee conferences among bureau heads of coordinate rank are least likely to be effective when their primary purpose is the

(A) coordination of specific functions

(B) formulation of broad policies

(C) execution of detailed plans

(D) elimination of duplicated activities.

9. You call a conference of bureau unit heads to discuss and adopt a certain plan of administrative action. In this conference you act as chairman because, in the main, the problem has been yours to solve, you have given it the original thought, and you are the one to present it to the group. In this conference you should not

(A) see that different points of view are advanced

(B) decide on details of the program

(C) attempt to integrate all ideas into a united policy

(D) realize that the quality of the decision rests on the ability to pool knowledge.

10. If you are in charge of a bureau, the purpose that it is generally not desirable to seek to accomplish by means of a private, personal conference with your superior is to

(A) obtain the transfer of an employee whose service is unsatisfactory

(B) determine the appropriate action for reducing "loafing" in your bureau

(C) secure approval for a new policy to be instituted in your bureau

(D) obtain additional employees to conduct the work of the bureau.

11. Administrators frequently have to get facts by interviewing people. Although the interview is a legitimate fact gathering technique, it has definite limitations which should not be overlooked. The one of the following which is an important limitation is that

(A) people who are interviewed frequently answer questions with guesses rather than admit their ignorance

(B) it is a poor way to discover the general attitude and thinking of supervisors interviewed

(C) people sometimes hesitate to give information during an interview which they will submit in written form

(D) it is a poor way to discover how well employees understand departmental policies.

12. In an office where applicants for employment are interviewed, it is most desirable that the office furniture be arranged so that the

(A) person being interviewed is seated where he can see the notes being recorded by the interviewer

(B) person being interviewed cannot be seen by other interviewers

(C) conversation between the interviewer and the person being interviewed cannot be overheard by others

(D) interviewer faces the person being interviewed but has his back to others who are waiting to be interviewed.

13. Assume that you are interviewing a new entrance level clerical employee for the purpose of determining where the worker would be best placed. In making your determination, the characteristics, to which you should give greatest weight is the employee's

(A) interest in the jobs you describe

(B) mechanical aptitude

(C) poise and self assurance

(D) fluency of verbal expression.

14. Of the following, the purpose for which you would least frequently prefer the privacy of a personal conference with an employee under your supervision is to

(A) discuss his satisfaction with working conditions

(B) reprimand him for an error he has made

(C) determine the reasons for his frequent absences

(D) praise him for the excellence of his work.

15. The public administrator has many administrative tools available to solve the problems with which he is faced. One of the most important of these is the conference. When compared to other administrative tools, the greatest value of the conference is to solve problems which

(A) are familiar and rather simple

(B) do not involve any research or analysis

(C) are new and difficult

(D) do not require a solution in the foreseeable future.

16. The one of the following which usually can *least* be considered to be an advantage of committees as they are generally used in government and business is that they

(A) provide opportunities for reconciling varying points of view

(B) promote coordination by the interchange of information among the members of the committee

(C) act promptly in situations requiring immediate action

(D) use group judgment to resolve questions requiring a wide range of experience.

17. For an office supervisor to confer periodically with his subordinates in order to anticipate job problems which are likely to arise is desirable mainly because

(A) there will be fewer problems for which hasty decisions will have to be made

(B) some problems which are anticipated may not arise

(C) his subordinates will learn to refer the problems arising in the unit to him

(D) constant anticipation of future problems tends to raise additional problems.

18. The staff conference, as a training method, can be used *least* effectively when

(A) the backgrounds of the participants are diversified

(B) there is wide difference of opinion concerning questions to be discussed

(C) the participants are experienced in the problems to be discussed

(D) the subjects discussed pose no problems.

19. An administrator made a practice of distributing agenda to all participants before a staff meeting was to be held. In general, this practice is
    (A) good; participants can give prior thought to the problems to be discussed
    (B) bad; participants are less spontaneous and candid in their discussions
    (C) good; protracted discussion of one topic and neglect of others is prevented
    (D) bad; the problem of keeping the discussions confidential is made more difficult.

20. Of the following, the most important reason for holding periodic staff conferences is to
    (A) brief the staff on the plans and prospects of the organization
    (B) hear the grievances and problems of the subordinate members of the staff
    (C) obtain suggestions from subordinate members of the staff
    (D) obtain uniformity in interpretation of policies and procedures.

21. At staff conferences, one member of the staff frequently has good ideas but expresses them poorly. For the supervisor to persuade this staff member to keep quiet at staff meetings but to explain his ideas in advance to the supervisor so that the latter may present them at the meeting in a more readily understandable manner would be
    (A) unwise, since it would curtail both the subordinate's satisfaction and any additional ideas he might develop at the conferences
    (B) unwise, since it would be annoying to the staff to have someone presenting ideas which were not his own
    (C) wise, since this subordinate's ideas would receive more ready acceptance if well presented, especially when presented by the supervisor
    (D) wise, since this would facilitate the smooth running of staff meetings.

22. Assume that you are a training conference leader and that you have just begun a series of conferences on supervisory techniques for new supervisors. Each conference is scheduled to last for three hours. A thorough discussion of all the mate-

rial planned for the first session, which you had estimated would last until 4 p.m., is completed by 3:30 p.m. For you to summarize the points that have been made and close the meeting would be
    (A) advisable; the participants will lose interest in the conference if it is permitted to continue merely to occupy the remaining time
    (B) inadvisable; the participants should be asked if there are any other topics that they would like to discuss
    (C) advisable; the participants in a training conference should not be kept from their regular work for long periods of time
    (D) inadvisable; material scheduled for discussion at future sessions should be used for the remainder of this session.

23. Some public agencies conduct exit interviews with employees who quit their jobs. The one of the following which is generally considered to be the chief value to a public agency of such an interview is in
    (A) ascertaining from the employee the reasons why he is leaving his job
    (B) obtaining reliable information on the employee's work history with the agency
    (C) persuading the employee to reconsider his decision to quit
    (D) giving the employee a final evaluation of his work performance.

24. As an administrator, you are conducting a training conference dealing with administrative principles and practices. One of the members of the conference, Mr. Smith, makes a factual statement which you know to be incorrect, and which may hinder the development of the discussion. None of the other members attempts to correct Mr. Smith or to question him on what he has said, although until this point, the members have participated actively in the discussions. In this situation, the most advisable course of action for you to take would be to
    (A) proceed with the discussion without commenting on Mr. Smith's statement
    (B) correct the statement that Mr. Smith has made
    (C) emphasize that the material discussed at the conference is to serve only as a guide for handling actual work situations
    (D) urge the members to decide for themselves whether or not to accept factual statements made at the conference.

25. Assume that you are giving a lecture for the purpose of explaining a new procedure. You find that the employees attending the lecture are asking many questions on the material as you present it. Consequently, you realize that you will be unable to cover all of the material you had intended to cover, and that a second lecture will be necessary. In this situation, the most advisable course of action for you to take would be to
   (A) answer the questions on the new procedure as they arise
   (B) answer the questions that can be answered quickly and ask the employees to reserve questions requiring lengthier answers for the second lecture
   (C) suggest that further questions be withheld until the second lecture so that you can cover as much of the remaining material as possible
   (D) refer the questions back to the employees asking them.

26. As the supervisor of a unit in an agency, you have just been instructed to put into effect a new procedure which you know will be disliked by your subordinates. Of the following, the *most* important reason for calling a meeting of your staff before putting the new procedure into effect is to
   (A) help you to determine which workers will be reluctant to cooperate in carrying out the new procedure
   (B) allow you to announce that the new procedure must be put into effect despite any objections which might be raised
   (C) enable you to explain that you don't approve of the new procedure and to give the reasons why it must nevertheless be put into effect
   (D) permit you to discuss the purpose of the new procedure and to present the reasons for its adoption.

27. The most important reason for a supervisor to encourage his staff to make suggestions for improving the work of the unit is that such suggestions may
   (A) indicate who is the most efficient employee in the unit
   (B) increase the productivity of the unit

(C) raise the morale of the employees who make the suggestions
(D) reduce the amount of supervision necessary to perform the work of the unit.

28. A stenographer assigned as secretary to a bureau chief offers a suggestion for improving the working conditions in the bureau. This suggestion is rejected by the bureau chief because of several major defects. The most appropriate of the following actions for this stenographer to take is to
   (A) continue to present this suggestion periodically until the bureau chief adopts it
   (B) persuade other bureau employees to present the same suggestion so that the bureau chief may be led to believe that there is a very strong sentiment for the adoption of this suggestion
   (C) acknowledge that there are objections to the adoption of the suggestion and continue making suggestions whenever such suggestions seem warranted
   (D) revise the wording of the suggestion so that it appears to be a different one and present it later to the bureau chief as an entirely new suggestion.

29. An experienced and competent stenographer offers her bureau chief a suggestion for eliminating some of the clerical work performed in the bureau. This suggestion had been made some time ago by another employee and had been rejected because it would necessitate the performing of this clerical work by another bureau which is ill-equipped to handle this work. Of the following, the most desirable action for the bureau chief to take is to
   (A) inform the stenographer flatly that the suggestion had been made before and had been rejected
   (B) explain fully why the suggestion cannot be adopted
   (C) postpone immediate action on her suggestion and inform her at a later date that the suggestion had been considered and rejected because of technical reasons
   (D) inform her that he will investigate the matter thoroughly.

ANSWER KEY

1. A	7. D	13. A	19. A	25. A
2. A	8. C	14. D	20. D	26. D
3. B	9. B	15. C	21. A	27. B
4. B	10. B	16. C	22. A	28. C
5. D	11. A	17. A	23. A	29. B
6. C	12. C	18. D	24. B	

EXPLANATORY ANSWERS

1. **(A)** The confidence of the workers must be gained by scheduling regular meetings. Otherwise, it may seem to them an empty gesture. If something is to be discussed the workers will know just when they can bring it up. Without a scheduled pattern, management could delay a meeting if a controversial matter is up for discussion, thus destroying worker confidence in the operation.

2. **(A)** A bureau chief who wants to obtain the views of unit heads on a subject should never give his or her own views first because it will hamper subordinates from expressing their own, especially opposing views. In addition, the administrator appears to be seeking staff approval for something that has already been decided.

3. **(B)** A good conference leader makes sure that attendees actively participate in a conference, and not take detailed notes for comparison with the minutes from the meeting.

4. **(B)** Supervisors who have experienced the situation described know that not everyone can be fully satisfied with the final decision. The best way to handle it is to try to get a compromise solution that everyone at the meeting can accept. If this is not possible, the manager must make the decision based on the facts, and must be prepared to handle the inevitable complaints. Voting is not a solution because the losers will still have a valid grievance. Deciding the issue without first holding a conference on the matter does not show strong leadership qualities needed in a good supervisor.

5. **(D)** Your initial approach is to be completely honest with the staff. They must be informed that the work has been poor, and that it must be improved. Be specific in your criticisms and then discuss the methods of improvement. This requires that you do your homework in advance, and be prepared with concrete ideas.

6. **(C)** It is generally not good procedure for the conference leader's superior to participate because it inevitably hampers the specific role the leader should play in guiding the group. As a general rule, the conference leader should be at least as high in rank as any other participant. Otherwise, he or she will tend to look to the high level official to answer questions and render judgments rather than lead the group to make its own decisions and answer its own questions.

7. **(D)** Conferences are occasions to exchange ideas. It is not a time to perform complex work or to discuss matters which are not common to all participants.

8. **(C)** The execution of detailed plans should be carried out by each bureau under its own bureau chief. The coordination of these plans and activities may require conferences among bureau heads.

9. **(B)** The purpose of the conference is to tell the bureau heads about the plan and have it adopted, with or without any modifications the group feels are needed. Under these circumstances there is no need to decide on the details of the plan or program, just to have it adopted. Later work meetings will undoubtedly have to be scheduled with individual bureau heads to determine the actual steps involved in the plan.

10. **(B)** As head of a bureau you should not need to have a private conference with your superior to handle such personnel problems as loafing on the job. That is why you are a supervisor. The other possible answers are matters you should discuss because they involve possible policy changes or are matters which the supervisor must approve before action can be taken.

11. **(A)** Using the interview method to obtain facts succeeds only if the person interviewed possesses these facts.

Even the best interviewer may not always be able to distinguish between a fact and a guess.

12. **(C)** Interviews with applicants for employment should be private so that other applicants cannot hear the questions being asked and thus gain an advantage. In addition, the applicant can talk freely about matters he or she would rather not have exposed.

13. **(A)** The question suggests that several vacancies are to be filled, and all other things being equal, the choice of assignment might well be made on the basis of the interests of the new employee. This is an initial assignment, however, and at a later date, because of other factors, a change might have to be made. Interest in performing a certain type of work does not guarantee that an individual has the ability to do it. Remember, this is a first act.

14. **(D)** The basic principle involved is that reprimands of any sort should be held privately whereas praise should generally be given in the presence of others.

15. **(C)** Compared to other administrative tools, the conference is most valuable in helping solve new and difficult problems where the knowledge of many experts can be shared in order to arrive at a workable solution.

16. **(C)** Conferences are generally time-consuming and not usually geared to making decisions when immediate action must be taken. The other possible answers indicate major advantages of conferences.

17. **(A)** To get the job done an office supervisor must be aware of everything going on in the unit. One way to do this is to confer periodically with subordinates to learn about likely future problems, so that solutions can be worked out in advance and avoid hasty decisions.

18. **(D)** If no problems are presented in the subject matter under discussion, the staff conference is generally not an effective training technique because there is, in effect, nothing to be learned through an exchange of ideas.

19. **(A)** Staff should know the subjects to be discussed at a staff meeting beforehand so that they come to it prepared to sensibly discuss them. Such a procedure may make workers less candid and spontaneous, but these are not necessarily needed in most staff meetings, which are usually confined to imparting or exchanging pertinent information. An agenda may or may not prevent protracted discussion. This is in any case a matter for the administrator to control. Regular meetings are not usually the place to discuss confidential matters.

20. **(D)** The primary purpose of period staff meetings is to help get the work of the unit done properly by making sure that all staff members understand and are following the agency's policies and procedures in an accepted uniform manner.

21. **(A)** No one likes to hear his or her ideas spouted by someone else, even if the contribution is acknowledged by the speaker. In this case, the worker would be both unhappy to hear his or her ideas presented and, more important, be too inhibited to offer new ideas during the meeting because the supervisor has made it clear that he or she is inarticulate. A more productive solution would be for the supervisor to help the worker learn to speak more coherently.

22. **(A)** The training session should be concluded when the matters to be learned have been taught, and there is nothing more to be said on these matters. Otherwise, the import of the training may be lost in idle conversation or discussions without purpose or used as "filler." The termination of the session at this point would not detract from the importance that this session has already achieved in the minds of the trainees.

23. **(A)** Exit interviews are an important means of learning why employees leave the organization. Such data improves employee relations, points out trouble spots in the agency, provides data for wage studies being conducted, etc.

24. **(B)** The only action you can take is to correct the statement, since no one else has. If not corrected, further discussions may be hindered.

25. **(A)** The wisest procedure is to continue answering pertinent questions on the material already presented, so that you know it has been thoroughly understood. Waiting until the next lecture to answer questions on material already presented will cause workers to forget their questions and possibly misunderstand something that has been taught. By answering questions at the time the material is discussed, you reinforce the correct procedure, and can prepare for the second lecture with the confidence that the staff has absorbed all the previous material.

26. **(D)** A worker who understands the reasons for something is more willing to join with other workers in the unit trying to get the job done as directed. The supervisor should refrain from indicating personal displeasure with the procedure because he or she must represent management's point of view. The basic principle to remember is a worker is more willing to follow a supervisor's directions and carry out a procedure which has been explained to the extent the worker's misgivings are overcome.

27. **(B)** A supervisor's primary function is to get the work done correctly, efficiently, and in a timely manner. He or she should encourage any and all suggestions from the staff which will further increase production. Good suggestions come from the most unlikely sources.

28. **(C)** The stenographer should accept the major deficiencies in his or her suggestions, and continue to make any

other suggestions he or she feels would help the agency. All of the other possible answers are inappropriate because they indicate the worker has failed to understand and accept the reasons for the rejection.

29. **(B)** Since there is nothing to indicate the situation has changed, the bureau chief should again reject the suggestion, and explain to the worker why it is not being accepted. Explaining the reason for the failure to accept any suggestion is a basic principle of handling staff suggestions. It prevents the worker from feeling that he or she has wasted their time, and will encourage the worker to find better ways to improve the work of the unit and agency in the future.

RECRUITMENT

DIRECTIONS FOR ANSWERING QUESTIONS

Each question has four suggested answers, lettered A, B, C, and D. Decide which one is the best answer and on the sample answer sheet (all answer sheets are at the front of the book) find the question number and darken the area, with a soft pencil, which corresponds to the answer that you have selected.

1. "The problem of determining the type of organization which should exist is inextricably interwoven with the problem of recruitment." In general, this statement is
   (A) correct; since organizations are manmade they can be changed
   (B) not correct; the organizational form which is most desirable is independent of the persons involved
   (C) correct; the problem of organization cannot be considered apart from employee qualifications
   (D) not correct; organizational problems can be separated into many parts and recruitment is important in only a few of these.

2. You are in charge of a central stenographic unit. The Appointing Officer of your Department has authorized you to nominate a provisional stenographer to fill a vacancy. You call the United States Employment Service and they send you a young lady. Her employment record consists of five years of service with one concern as a stenographer, from which position she was dismissed. She states that during her last year with the concern a new supervisor was assigned, and that he was a very disagreeable person. She further states that he was unfair in his treatment of his subordinates and on one occasion she protested. He chose to treat this action as insubordination and had her dismissed summarily. To refuse to consider this person for the position would be

   (A) cautious, as the reason she gave for her dismissal may not be the true reason
   (B) foolish since such an employee might be a valuable employee
   (C) intelligent because you will be responsible for the selection you make
   (D) wise as she has demonstrated an inability to get along with people.

3. A placement officer in a department follows the procedure of consulting the supervisor of the unit in which a vacancy exists concerning the kind of worker he wants before attempting to fill the vacancy. This procedure is, in general
   (A) undesirable; it makes the selection process dependent on the whim of the supervisor
   (B) desirable; it will make for a more effectively working organization
   (C) undesirable; if the kind of worker the supervisor wants is not available, he will be dissatisfied
   (D) desirable; the more people who are consulted about a matter of this kind, the more chance there is that no mistake will be made.

Answer Questions 4 through 9 on the basis of the following paragraph:

Plan 1 "Hire broadly qualified people, work out their assignments from time to time to suit the needs of the enterprise and aptitudes of individuals. Let their progress and recognition be based on

155

the length and overall quality of the service, regardless of the significance of individual assignments which they periodically assume."

Plan 2 "Hire experts and assign them well-defined duties. Their compensation, for the most part, should be dependent on the duties performed."

4. For Plan 1 to be successful, there must be assured to a much greater extent than for Plan 2, the existence of
   - (A) a well-developed training program
   - (B) a widely publicized recruitment program
   - (C) in general, better working conditions
   - (D) more skilled administrators.

5. Plan 1 would tend to develop employees who were
   - (A) able to perform a variety of functions
   - (B) conversant only with problems in the particular field in which they were employed
   - (C) in general, not satisfied with the work they perform
   - (D) intensely competitive.

6. Large governmental organizations in the United States tend, in general, to use
   - (A) Plan 1
   - (B) Plan 2
   - (C) Plan 1 for technical positions and Plan 2 for clerical positions
   - (D) Plan 2 for administrative positions and Plan 1 for clerical and technical positions.

7. "In organizations which operate on the basis of Plan 1, placement of a man in the proper job after selection is much more difficult than in those which operate on the basis of Plan 2." This statement is, in general
   - (A) correct; the selection is not on the basis of specific aptitudes and abilities
   - (B) not correct; specific aptitudes and abilities would tend to be determined in advance as would be the case with Plan 2
   - (C) correct; it is much more difficult to determine specific aptitudes and abilities than general qualifications
   - (D) not correct; placement would be based on the needs of the organization, consequently only a limited number of positions would be available.

8. "Administration in an organization operating on the basis of Plan 1 would tend to be less flexible than one operating on the basis of Plan 2." This statement is, in general
   - (A) correct; recruitment of experts permits rapid expansion
   - (B) not correct; the absence of well-defined positions permits wide and rapid recruitment without an extensive selection period
   - (C) correct; well defined positions allow for replacement on an assembly-line basis without an extensive breaking in period and thus permits greater flexibility
   - (D) not correct; Plan 1 presents greater freedom in movement of individuals from one position to another and in redefining positions according to capabilities of employees and the needs of the moment.

9. "To a greater extent than Plan 2, Plan 1 leads to conflict and overlapping in administrative operations." In general, this is the case because
   - (A) employees paid on the basis of duties performed tend to be more conscious of overlapping operations and tend to limit their activities
   - (B) experts refuse to accept responsibilities in fields other than their own
   - (C) the lack of carefully defined positions may conceal many points at which coordination and reconciliation are necessary
   - (D) there tends to be more pressure for "empire building" where prestige is measured solely in terms of assignment.

10. The information requested in the application blank which is to be filled out by persons applying for a position
    - (A) should not be accepted as correct unless accompanied by a notarized oath
    - (B) should be the same for all positions in order to permit cross-verification
    - (C) should depend upon the purposes to be served by the blank
    - (D) should not be of a personal nature.

11. The emphasis in public administration during recent years has been less on the
    - (A) need for the elimination of the spoils system and more on the development of policy and techniques of administration that contribute to employee selection and productivity

(B) development of policy and techniques of administration that contribute to employee selection and productivity and more on the need for the elimination of the spoils system

(C) human relation aspects of administration and more on the technical problems of classification and placement

(D) problems of administration of governmental units in the United States and more on those of international organizations.

12. "An attempt should be more to determine which elements in the recruitment procedure are static, which are variable and repetitive, and which are variable and due to chance." The one of the following which is the best reason for following this procedure is that if the elements which are static are isolated then it is possible to

(A) set up routines for dealing with them

(B) revise the procedure in order to make them variable

(C) determine which elements are variable

(D) provide some periodic follow up and adjustment.

Make use of the following paragraph in answering Questions 13 and 14.

"The most significant improvements in selection procedures can be expected from a program designed to obtain more precise statements of the requirements for a particular position and from the development of procedures that will make it possible to select not just those applicants who are generally best, but those whose abilities and personal characteristics provide the closest fit to the specific job requirements."

13. According to the above paragraph, better selection procedures will result from

(A) simplification of job descriptions

(B) better recruiting procedures

(C) obtaining of more detailed experience data from applicants

(D) detailed statements of training and skills required for positions.

14. According to the above paragraph, the most desirable applicant for a position is

(A) the one whose qualifications are most nearly the same as the job requirement

(B) the one whose abilities and personal characteristics are of the highest order

(C) generally not the same as the best qualified person

(D) the person who has the greatest interest in obtaining the position.

15. The one of the following which is most generally accepted as a prerequisite to the development of a sound career service is

(A) agreement to accept for all higher positions the senior eligible employee

(B) the recruitment of an adequate proportion of beginning employees who will eventually be capable of performing progressively more difficult duties

(C) strict adherence to the principle of competitive promotion from within for all positions above the entrance level

(D) the development of a program of periodically changing an employee's duties in order to prevent stagnation.

16. One argument which is presented against a strict career system in the civil service is, "The employees who are recruited today for low level jobs become the administrators of tomorrow. At the present time the employees we are attracting for the low level jobs are untrained and poorly educated. Thus it follows that the administrators of tomorrow will be untrained and poorly educated." The one of the following which is a correct criticism of the reasoning is that

(A) the argument is logically correct but the conclusion is false as the hypothesis that we are attracting untrained and poorly educated people for our low level jobs is false

(B) the conclusion does not follow logically from hypotheses

(C) the argument is logically correct, but the conclusion is false because it is a false hypothesis that tomorrow's administrators will come from employees who hold low level jobs

(D) the argument is logically correct, and the conclusion is correct.

17. Of the following, the fact which is the most likely cause for a lower separation rate on account of poor performance in public service than in private employment is that usually

(A) civil service employees have undergone a more exacting method of selection

(B) it is impossible to discharge a civil service

employee once he has passed his probationary period
(C) civil service employees wish to have security of employment
(D) the ablest persons are generally the ones who seek public employment.

18. The one of the following factors which is most influential in determining the proportion of qualified applicants who refuse public employment when offered is
(A) the interim between application and offer of a position
(B) the specific nature of the duties of the position
(C) the general nature of economic conditions at the time when the position is offered
(D) the salary paid.

19. Of the following factors which are influential in determining which employment a young man or woman will choose, government employ is generally considered superior in
(A) salaries
(B) opportunities to move into other similar organizations
(C) prestige and recognition
(D) leave and retirement benefits.

20. "It is dangerous to public health, welfare and security to pack the administrative branch of government with political appointees—even though political parties feel they cannot survive without such practice." This danger lies mostly in the fact that
(A) the turnover of the public personnel will be too high
(B) too many persons of the same political party will hold important positions
(C) the public servants who have started at the bottom will have no opportunity for advancement
(D) the persons placed into important positions may be lacking in adequate technical ability.

21. The one of the following results which would most nearly prove that scientific job placement tends to decrease the rate of job turnover is that the use of scientific job placement
(A) always follows a period with an increasing turnover rate
(B) is never followed by a period with increasing turnover rate

(C) is never followed by a period with a decreasing turnover rate
(D) frequently follows a period with a decreasing turnover rate.

22. The determination of the fitness of a person to fill a position solely on the basis of his experience is
(A) desirable; experience is the best test of aptitude for a position when it is rated properly
(B) understandable; the applicant may not be giving correct factual information in regard to his experience
(C) desirable; a uniform rating key can be applied to evaluate experience
(D) undesirable; it is difficult to evaluate from experience records how much the applicant has gained from his experience.

23. The one of the following which is frequently given as a major argument against a tightly knit promotion-from-within policy is that
(A) it takes too long for an employee in the lower grades to reach the top
(B) all persons both in and out of the government are equally entitled to civil service jobs
(C) persons are placed in executive jobs who are too well acquainted with the existing organization
(D) it leads to the presence of executive jobs of clerks who still operate as clerks.

24. Some organizations interview employees who resign or are discharged. This procedure is usually
(A) of great value in reducing labor turnover and creating good will toward the organization
(B) of little or no value as the views of incompetent or disgruntled employees are of questionable validity
(C) dangerous; it gives employees who are leaving an organization the opportunity to pay off old scores
(D) of great value in showing the way to more efficient methods of production and the establishment of higher work norms.

25. "The problem of the procurement and effective utilization of the material objects in the operation of an enterprise has much in common with that of procurement and utilization of personal service." Of the following, the most unreasonable statement regarding this quotation is that, in both cases, solution of the problem requires

(A) the same degree of supervision for effective administration

(B) classification of needs according to some consistent principle

(C) the creation of a special procurement service

(D) machinery and procedure to set up proper controls over use.

26. Of the following, the greatest stress in selecting employees for office supervisory positions should ordinarily be placed on
   (A) intelligence and educational background
   (B) knowledge of the work and capacity for leadership
   (C) sincere interest in the activities and objectives of the agency
   (D) skill in performing the type of work to be supervised.

27. It is generally considered desirable to attract more men into the teaching profession primarily because it is believed that
   (A) men are generally better at maintaining discipline and coaching teams
   (B) children usually respect men more than women, and commonly achieve greater maturity and self-control under the guidance of men teachers
   (C) men are needed for eventual promotion into positions of administrative leadership
   (D) children should have an opportunity to be associated with men as well as women in school.

28. "Legal proof that an applicant for a position in an education system has served sentence in a penal institution, no matter how early in his life, should constitute an automatic rejection of his application." This basis for rejection is
   (A) desirable primarily because children will not respect teachers who have broken the laws of adult society
   (B) undesirable primarily because applicants for teaching positions cannot reasonably be expected to have higher standards of conduct than citizens in any other occupation or profession
   (C) desirable primarily because educational systems should not employ such people for teaching

(D) undesirable primarily because it indicates little discrimination in terms of type and extent of crime or of subsequent conduct.

29. Verified evidence of continued deep emotional disturbances in the records of an applicant for a teaching position should point to a rejection of his application mainly because
   (A) educational systems should not employ people for teaching positions who have a history of emotional disturbance
   (B) every child has the right to be taught by healthy, well-adjusted teachers
   (C) it is generally agreed that people once afflicted with mental or emotional disturbances cannot become inspiring teachers
   (D) some emotional experiences tend to have lasting deleterious effects upon a person's mental health.

30. Selection of candidates for employment on the basis of aptitude test results is made on the assumption that the candidates making the highest test scores
   (A) possess the most knowledge about the job for which they were tested
   (B) will need a minimum amount of training on the job for which they were tested
   (C) will be the most satisfactory employees after they have received training
   (D) are those who will have the highest interest in succeeding on the job for which they were tested.

31. The rate of labor turnover in an organization may be arrived at by dividing the total number of separations from the organization in a given period by the average number of workers employed in the same period. In arriving at the rate it is assumed that those separated are replaced. If the rate of turnover is excessively low in comparison with other similar organizations, it usually indicates that
   (A) the organization is stagnant
   (B) promotions within the organization are made frequently
   (C) the organization's recruitment policies have been ineffective
   (D) suitable workers are in short supply.

ANSWER KEY

1. C	8. D	15. B	22. D	29. B
2. B	9. C	16. B	23. D	30. C
3. B	10. C	17. A	24. A	31. A
4. A	11. A	18. A	25. A	
5. A	12. A	19. D	26. B	
6. B	13. D	20. D	27. D	
7. A	14. A	21. B	28. D	

EXPLANATORY ANSWERS

1. **(C)** The quality of candidates for an examination and thus the quality of new employees, ultimately depends on the success of the recruiting programs. The type of organization in turn ultimately depends on the type of employees, their qualities and their ability to perform the work of the agency.

2. **(B)** Under the circumstances, you should consider the young lady for possible provisional appointment because she meets the basic qualification requirements, and has demonstrated a degree of stability of employment. The reason for her discharge is subject to verification, and she can be dismissed during this time if she proves unsatisfactory.

3. **(B)** Whenever vacancies exist, a good placement officer consults the supervisor to discuss the individual qualities and qualifications that would best suit the unit's needs. The officer then attempts to find as nearly the right person for that particular job as possible.

4. **(A)** Plan 1 calls for broadly qualified people to work on many different assignments, and therefore requires an exceptionally good training program. Experts are called for under Plan 2. Both plans require the existence of all the factors listed in the other possible answers.

5. **(A)** Calling for broadly qualified people who will move from assignment to assignment, Plan 1 will obviously result in workers who can perform many tasks.

6. **(B)** Large governmental organizations in the U.S.A. generally hire people who meet the specific qualification requirements for specific titles and jobs, and are expected to work "in-title" or in work closely related to that title.

7. **(A)** The assumption in the utilization of Plan 1 is that those who are hired are capable of being trained to fill a variety of positions. For proper placement of these individuals it would be prudent to take into consideration any special aptitudes and abilities. This has not yet been done during the hiring process.

8. **(D)** Plan 1 provides a greater flexibility of operation because it gives administration a greater ability to cope with unexpected needs, and change plans and staff assignments. None of the other possible answers are true statements.

9. **(C)** There may come into existence, jobs which require special skills which are not easily acquired. Adjustments will then have to be made.

10. **(C)** The amount and nature of information to be included in an application blank depends upon what is going to be done with the blank. Different application forms call for a variety of information, such as work history or educational requirements, because the positions to be filled may require information to ensure proper selection.

11. **(A)** Surveys of recently published material and actual practice in public administration show that prior emphasis on the elimination of the spoils system has been virtually eliminated. The emphasis now is to develop scientific techniques and policies in selecting employees, technical discussions of ways to increase productivity, and the human relations aspects of public administration.

12. **(A)** The more the static elements of the recruitment procedure can be routinized, the better the recruitment

officer can expedite them, and concentrate on weighing the more variable elements.

13. **(D)** The quotation says that the best improvements in the selection procedure can be expected when requirements are most specific and selection procedures are tailored to find the candidate whose abilities and personal characteristics best fit the specific job. It therefore follows that the better selection procedure will result if detailed statements of specific training and skills are required.

14. **(A)** Significant improvements in detailing requirements are desired to facilitate selection of the right person to fit the job. A person with abilities and personal characteristics of a high order is desirable, as is one eager to obtain the position, but these are no good if the person does not match the position to be filled.

15. **(B)** The senior qualified employee may not be the most suitable person for a job. All higher level jobs are not filled by competitive promotion from within the agency because many jobs require that they be filled on a noncompetitive basis or even on an exempt basis. In general, a sound career service means that beginning employees should be sufficiently competent that they will, given experience, be able to assume more difficult work.

16. **(B)** Based solely on the quotation, the conclusion given is not logical because training is given to beginning workers and throughout their working careers. They will therefore be trained by the time they are eligible to become administrators. In addition, many beginning workers seek further education after initial appointment.

17. **(A)** Studies show that the principal reason for the lower separation rate due to poor performance is that government service generally requires employment candidates meet specific minimum requirements, and pass specific tests related to the work for which they are applying before appointment.

18. **(A)** Since a considerable amount of time elapses between the time a person first applies and the time when he or she is offered appointment, it is generally true that many persons refuse to accept a position offered because they have accepted other positions in the interim. The other possible answers do make some candidates decide not to accept public service jobs, but not to the extent that the time lapse does.

19. **(D)** The aspect of government employment generally considered superior to the private sector is the fringe benefits attached to public service. These include sick leave, vacation time, pension benefits, health insurance, etc.

20. **(D)** Many political appointees unfortunately do not result in "the best available individual to fill the vacant position." Therefore, to resort heavily to political appointees results in reduced effectiveness.

21. **(B)** Scientific job placement is designed to place the most nearly qualified person in the job, whereas turnover usually results from persons poorly matched to positions. Therefore, the utilization of scientific job placement should result in less turnover.

22. **(D)** Not all experience is good experience. An individual may have performed ineptly at a job for a considerable period of time before being detected for one reason or another. Just because a person has occupied a position of mechanic for a period of time does not make that person a good mechanic.

23. **(D)** Those who argue against a tightly-knit promotion-from-within policy point out that the person who starts as a clerk and passes successively higher clerical exams until he or she reaches a top executive position does not acquire the depth and knowledge and experience needed to think as an administrator. They contend that administration requires broader abilities to perceive and handle problems, qualities not generally gained by promotion from one clerical job to the next.

24. **(A)** "Exit interviews" reveal the reasons employees leave an organization. If the fault lies with the organization, this is perhaps the time for organizational change.

25. **(A)** Supervision over the administration of materials procurement is vastly different in degree from the procurement of personnel. The incorrect answers offer reasonable points of resemblance between the problems in procurement and in personnel.

26. **(B)** The best supervisors are not necessarily the ones who are most interested, skillful or intelligent. They are the ones who have the best leadership potential, and possess fairly complete knowledge of the unit's work.

27. **(D)** Fewer males than females are being attracted to the teaching profession especially at the elementary and secondary levels. Therefore, it is believed that young children would profit from associating with male and female teachers at this stage of their education.

28. **(D)** Automatic rejection of an applicant for a position in the education system because of penal incarceration is not good public policy. Discrimination should be made, for example, between a person convicted of a relatively minor offense many years ago and the recently released rapist. Further, the individual's behavior subsequent to release from prison should be taken into account. Standards of acceptability of ex-offenders for a position in the educational system, especially those in direct contact with students, should be drawn, but automatic rejection is not defensible.

29. **(B)** It probably would be harmful for a youngster in his or her formulative years to be exposed to an emotionally disturbed teacher. There would be a tendency for these emotional disturbances to be transmitted to the students.

30. **(C)** Aptitude tests in a particular field merely indicate those persons are more likely to absorb training and do better on the job after training.

31. **(A)** Progressive organizations need a regular infusion of new blood to bring in new ideas. Lower level employees need to feel that promotion opportunities are available because senior employees will be retiring or leaving for other jobs. Incompetent or borderline incompetents should be terminated. Excessively low turnover shows that little or none of these things are happening.

PART THREE

Control and Auxiliary Functions

FISCAL AND BUDGETARY CONTROL

DIRECTIONS FOR ANSWERING QUESTIONS

Each question has four suggested answers, lettered A, B, C, and D. Decide which one is the best answer and on the sample answer sheet (all answer sheets are at the front of the book) find the question number and darken the area, with a soft pencil, which corresponds to the answer that you have selected.

1. By means of the "debt limit" the State of New York regulates many facets of the debt of the City. The one of the following factors which is *not* regulated in this manner is the
   (A) purpose for which the debt is incurred
   (B) amount of debt which may be incurred
   (C) source from which the money may be borrowed
   (D) forms of debts which may be incurred.

2. The one of the following which is NOT necessarily a characteristic of a good buying procedure is that it
   (A) provides for proper analysis of purchases made
   (B) is simple
   (C) makes provision for substitutions where possible and necessary
   (D) makes sealed bids mandatory.

3. "When engaged in budget construction or budget analysis, there is no point in trying to determine the total or average benefits to be obtained from total expenditures for a particular commodity or function." The validity of this argument is usually based upon the
   (A) viewpoint that it is not possible to construct a functional budget
   (B) theory (or phenomenon) of diminishing utility
   (C) hypothesis that as governmental budgets provide in theory for minimum requirements, there is no need to determine total benefits

   (D) assumption that such determinations are not possible.

4. One of the primary purposes of the performance budget is to improve the ability to examine budgetary requirement by groups who have not been engaged in the construction of the budget. This is accomplished by
   (A) making line by line appropriations
   (B) making lump sum appropriations by department
   (C) enumerating authorization for all expenditures
   (D) permitting examination on the level of accomplishment.

5. "A budget is a plan whereby a goal is set for future operations. It affords a medium for comparing actual expenditures with planned expenditures." The one of the following which is the most accurate statement on the basis of this quotation is that
   (A) the budget serves as an accurate measure of past as well as future expenditures
   (B) the budget presents an estimate of expenditures to be made in the future
   (C) budget estimates should be based upon past budget requirements
   (D) planned expenditures usually fall short of actual expenditures.

6. With the exception of taxes on real estate and revenues required by law to be paid into any other

fund or account, all revenues of the City are paid into a fund called the

- (A) general fund
- (B) sinking fund
- (C) tax deficiency fund
- (D) debt service fund.

7. Assume that two machines, each costing $7375 were purchased for your office. Each machine requires the services of an operator at a salary of $1000 per month. These machines are to replace six clerks, two of whom earn $775 per month each, and four of whom earn $850 per month each. The number of months it will take for the cost of the machines to be made up from the savings in salaries is
- (A) less than four months
- (B) four months
- (C) five months
- (D) more than five months.

8. Suppose that the amount of stationery used by your department in August decreased by 16% as compared with the amount used in July, and that the amount used in September increased by 25% as compared with the amount used in August. The amount of stationery used in September as compared with the amount used in July is
- (A) greater by 5 per cent
- (B) less by 5 per cent
- (C) greater by 9 per cent
- (D) the same.

9. The city worker who is familiar with the City's fiscal affairs should know that the City issues Tax Anticipation Notes chiefly in order to secure cash funds to
- (A) finance the City's capital improvement projects in accordance with its "pay-as-you-go" policy
- (B) pay all or part of the anticipated cost of revenue-producing capital improvements
- (C) finance the expense budget in anticipation of the collection of real estate taxes
- (D) pay for expenditures which were unforeseen or which could not be determined at budget-making time.

10. The Comptroller publishes periodically in the City Record a statement of vouchers received in his office. A worker with a knowledge of budgetary control should know that these vouchers are

- (A) written orders on a bank to pay on demand a specified sum of money to a named person or agency
- (B) drafts upon the Treasurer for the payment of money only out of specified revenues, when and if those revenues are received
- (C) written forms attesting the propriety of the payment of money
- (D) estimates or proposed expenditures by City departments for a given period or purpose.

11. "No *stipend* was specified in the agreement." The word "stipend" as used in this sentence means most nearly
- (A) statement of working conditions
- (B) receipt for payment
- (C) compensation for services
- (D) delivery date.

12. Under the terms and conditions of the Expense Budget, department heads are held strictly accountable if they exceed appropriations without specific itemized approval. A Principal Administrative Associate familiar with methods of budgetary control should know that his department can best avoid exceeding its departmental appropriations for supplies and equipment by
- (A) having all obligations for purchases tentatively charged against appropriations as soon as the supplies and equipment have been requisitioned by the department
- (B) having all expenditures charged against the appropriate expense accounts as soon as the supplies or equipment have been received
- (C) changing expenditures to the appropriate expense accounts immediately after the invoices or packing slips have been received and approved
- (D) maintaining a double entry book-keeping system with budgetary accounting control exercised on an expenditure basis.

13. The one of the following which is usually *least* affected by an increase in the personnel of an organization is the
- (A) problems of employee relationships
- (B) average amount of work performed by an employee
- (C) importance of coordinating the work of organization units
- (D) number of first-line supervisors required.

14. To set up safeguards, during normal times, in order to make it extremely difficult for an office supervisor to secure new equipment and to force him to go to great lengths to justify such purchase is
    (A) wise because there is a great tendency for office supervisors to continually stock their offices with new equipment before the old is worn out
    (B) sensible because such a procedure is economical and in the long run saves money
    (C) unfair because only the office supervisor with ''pull'' or ''push'' will be able to get what he thinks he needs
    (D) foolish because office supervisors will be discouraged in their pursuit of new methods.

15. You are engaged in estimating the unit cost of a certain operation for the forthcoming budget. During the forthcoming year you plan to introduce a change in procedure which will allow two clerks, paid $12,000 each, to be transferred to other work but will increase the cost of materials, M, by 50 per cent. The number of units completed, N, is constant from year to year. Of the following, the decrease in unit cost over the period of one year which may be expected as a result of this change, other factors remaining equal, is
    (A) the product of the reciprocal of N and the difference between $24,000 and .5M
    (B) the difference between $24,000 and .5M
    (C) the reciprocal of N, multiplied by .5M
    (D) none of the foregoing.

16. In presenting figures which will be used for the preparation of the Departmental Expense Budget, the Administrator should review the figures for the current fiscal year in order to estimate
    (A) costs for additional real property
    (B) next year's operating expenses
    (C) expenditures for major plant alteration
    (D) purchases of new unusual equipment.

17. ''If we go from a one-shift to a two-shift basis, the cost of operation will decrease 5 per cent.'' The one of the following which would prove this assertion most completely is that investigation shows that
    (A) in no case did a change of this kind fail to result in a decrease of 5% in the cost of operation

(B) in all cases a change of this kind failed to result in a decrease of 5% in the cost of operation
(C) a decrease of 5% in the cost of operation resulted from a change of the kind described in many cases
(D) in no case in which a change of this kind was not made was there a decrease of 5% in the cost of operation.

18. A practice sometimes followed among some administrators in times of financial difficulty, when budget reductions are expected, is to request two or three times the material actually needed in order that, if the budget requests are reduced, at least part of the necessary funds will be granted. This is undesirable mainly because it
    (A) may result in less material being obtained than is actually necessary
    (B) makes accurate and scientific budget making for the city impossible
    (C) does not assure getting the amount requested
    (D) is not based on any definite knowledge of the degree to which budgets will be reduced.

19. For the most effective administrative management, appropriations should be
    (A) itemized
    (B) lump sum
    (C) bi-annual
    (D) semi-annual.

20. Of the following types of expenditure control in the practice of fiscal management, the one which is least important is that which relates to
    (A) past policy affecting expenditures
    (B) future policy affecting expenditures
    (C) prevention of improper use of funds
    (D) prevention of overdraft.

21. ''Savings of 20 percent or more in clerical operating costs can often be achieved by improvement of the physical conditions under which office work is performed.'' In general, the most valid of the following statements regarding physical conditions is that
    (A) conference rooms should have more light than mail rooms
    (B) the tops of desks should be glossy rather than dull
    (C) noise is reflected more by hard-surfaced materials that by soft or porous materials

(D) yellow is a more desirable wall color for offices receiving abundance of sunlight than for offices receiving little sunlight.

22. The true financial condition of a city is best reflected when its accounting system is placed upon
    (A) a cash basis
    (B) an accrual basis
    (C) a fiscal basis
    (D) a warrant basis.

23. The one of the following which is least characteristic of governmental reorganization is the
    (A) saving of large sums of money
    (B) problem of morale and personnel
    (C) task of logic and management
    (D) engineering approach.

24. In large cities the total cost of government is of course greater than in small cities but
    (A) this is accompanied by a decrease in per capita cost
    (B) the per capita cost is also greater
    (C) the per capita cost is approximately the same
    (D) the per capita cost is considerably less in approximately 50% of the cases.

25. Certain administrative functions, such as those concerned with budgetary and personnel selection activities, have been delegated to central agencies separated from the operating departments. Of the following, the principal reason for such separation is that
    (A) a central agency is generally better able to secure funds for performing these functions
    (B) decentralization increases executive control
    (C) greater economy, efficiency and uniformity can be obtained by establishing a central staff of experts to perform these functions
    (D) the problems involved in performing these functions vary significantly from one operating department to another.

26. Of the following the one which is not a disadvantage of the practice of making budget estimates solely on the basis of the previous year's budget is that it
    (A) does not anticipate economies and innovations
    (B) can be put into effect only when unit costs are known

(C) makes the budget less effective as an instrument of scientific planning
(D) assumes that future events will duplicate past experience.

27. Of the following, the least significant factor in determining whether last year's budget requests should be modified in preparing next year's budget for your bureau is the
    (A) magnitude of the funds that will be available
    (B) expected change in work load
    (C) possibility of introducing improved methods
    (D) increase of last year's budget allowance over the preceding year.

28. Suppose that you are assigned the task of collating and modifying preliminary budgetary requests made by bureau heads in your department. Of the following, the one which is the least acceptable reason for changing the magnitude of any single bureau's request is that
    (A) the request, when considered in relation to the purpose intended, is not sufficiently high
    (B) the work of the bureau has been partially taken over by another bureau
    (C) the request, when considered in relation to the purpose intended, is not sufficiently low
    (D) the money expended by the bureau during the previous year was substantially lower than that requested during that period.

29. When the discrepancy between the totals of a trial balance is $36, the least probable cause of the error is
    (A) omission of an item
    (B) entering of an item on the wrong side of the ledger
    (C) a mistake in addition or subtraction
    (D) transposition of digits.

30. "While the number of hours that persons who have been engaged to perform technical work actually spent in the performance of this type of work was the same in 1981 as in 1980, the percentage of the hours of technical work performed by this group has decreased in comparison with the total number of hours of technical work performed in the department." From this it follows that persons who have been engaged to perform
    (A) technical work spent a greater percentage of their time on non-technical work in 1981 than in 1980

(B) technical work performed a smaller percentage of the total work of the department in 1981 than in 1980

(C) non-technical work spent a greater percentage of their time on technical work in 1981 than in 1980

→ (D) non-technical work performed more hours of technical work in 1981 than in 1980.

31. Suppose that a division of a city department had its staff of 500 employees increased by 12%, and its total work load increased by 20%. Then, the work load of each employee has increased, most nearly, by
    (A) 6%
  — (B) 7%
    (C) 8%
    (D) 9%.

32. Your department requires the stock room to carry a two months' reserve of certain items at all times. If the department uses 250 units per month of one of these and if it requires 45 days in which to obtain a new supply, the minimum reorder point is most nearly
    (A) 600
    (B) 700
    (C) 800
  — (D) 900.

33. Of the following, the most fundamental reason for the use of budgets in governmental administration is that budgets
    (A) minimize seasonal variations in work loads and expenditures of public agencies
    (B) facilitate decentralization of functions performed by public agencies
  — (C) provide advance control on the expenditure of funds
    (D) establish valid bases for comparing present government activities with corresponding activities in previous periods.

34. In some governmental jurisdictions, the chief executive prepares the budget for a fiscal period and presents it to the legislative branch of government for adoption. In other jurisdictions, the legislative branch prepares and adopts the budget. Preparation of the budget by the chief executive rather than by the legislative branch is
  → (A) desirable primarily because the chief executive is held largely accountable by the public

for the results of fiscal operations and should therefore be the one to prepare the budget

(B) undesirable primarily because such a separation of the legislative and executive branches leads to the enactment of a budget that does not consider the over-all needs of the government

(C) desirable primarily because the preparation of the budget by the chief executive limits legislative review and evaluation of operating programs

(D) undesirable primarily because responsibility for budget preparation should be placed in the branch that must eventually adopt the budget and appropriate the funds for it.

35. The one of the following which is generally the *first* step in the budget-making process of a municipality that has a central budget agency is
    (A) determination of available sources of revenue within the municipality
    (B) establishment of tax rates at levels sufficient to achieve a balanced budget in the following fiscal period
    (C) evaluation, by the central budget agency, of the adequacy of the municipality's previous budgets
  → (D) assembling, by the central budget agency, of the proposed expenditures of each agency in the municipality for the following fiscal period.

36. "Some municipalities have delegated the functions of budget preparation and personnel selection to central agencies, thus removing these functions from operating departments." Of the following the most important reason why municipalities have delegated these functions to central agencies is that
    (A) the performance of these functions presents problems that vary from one operating department to another
    (B) operating departments often lack sufficient funds to perform these functions adequately
  → (C) the performance of these functions by a central agency produces more uniform policies than if these functions are performed by the operating departments
    (D) central agencies are not controlled as closely as are operating departments and so have greater freedom in formulating new policies

and procedures to deal with difficult budget and personnel problems.

37. Of the following, the one which can *least* be considered to be a proper function of an accounting system is to
    (A) indicate the need to curtail expenditures
    (B) provide information for future fiscal programs
    (C) record the expenditure of funds from special appropriations
    → (D) suggest methods to expedite the collection of revenues.

38. As it is used in auditing, an internal check is a
    ⇐ (A) procedure which is designed to guard against fraud
    (B) periodic audit by a public accounting firm to verify the accuracy of the internal transactions of an organization
    (C) document transferring funds from one section to another within an organization
    (D) practice of checking documents twice before they are transmitted outside an organization.

Questions 39 to 44

Column I includes characteristics of different types of budgets. By selecting the proper option in Column II, indicate whether each item in Column I refers to (A) line budgets, (B) lump sum budgets, (C) performance budgets, or whether it refers to (D) none of these types of budgets.

COLUMN I	COLUMN II
39. Aims at results rather than details (c)	(A) line budgets
40. Gives complete flexibility in use of funds for operations (B)	(B) lump sum budgets
41. Gives the classification of personnel (A)	(C) performance budgets
42. Guarantees sufficient funds for all operating needs (D)	(D) none of the above.
43. Is closely tied into a system of management analysis (c)	
44. Is specific in terms of employee salary (A)	

ANSWER KEY

1. C	10. C	19. B	28. D	37. D
2. D	11. C	20. A	29. C	38. A
3. B	12. A	21. C	30. D	39. C
4. D	13. B	22. B	31. B	40. B
5. B	14. D	23. A	32. D	41. A
6. A	15. A	24. B	33. C	42. D
7. C	16. B	25. C	34. A	43. C
8. A	17. A	26. B	35. D	44. A
9. C	18. B	27. D	36. C	

EXPLANATORY ANSWERS

1. **(C)** The sources from which money may be borrowed are not regulated by means of the "debt limit" set by the State of New York. Factors mentioned in the other possible answers are regulated by the "debt limit."

2. **(D)** The practice of making sealed bids mandatory for all items to be purchased may very well result in the jurisdiction having to pay more for the item than would otherwise be true. The lowest sealed bid received may very well be higher than the price available by other means of purchasing.

3. **(B)** Average or total benefits are not very meaningful. Some expenditures may derive small returns, but they might be necessary. Furthermore, other expenditures may result in great returns at the beginning, but these results may very well diminish as more money is spent in the same direction. Each expenditure should be studied and justified on its own.

4. **(D)** Performance budgeting is the appropriation of funds based on an agency's major activities. For example, funds would be appropriated for operating dental clinics in the Health Department, or for establishing eligibility clinics in a Social Services Department. This allows other groups such as taxpayers who are not actively involved in the planning of the budget to better understand how appropriated monies are actually being spent.

5. **(B)** The quotation states, in effect, that a budget is a plan for spending money for certain specified functions and that you can compare what is actually spent for each purpose with the amount of money planned, or budgeted, for it.

6. **(A)** The correct answer is self-evident.

7. **(C)** 1) The monthly cost of the present system without the machines is $4,950.00 (2 clerks at $775 each per month = $1,550.00 and 4 clerks at $850 each per month = $3,400.00, for a total of $4,950.00.)
   2) The monthly cost of the new system with the machines is $2,000.00.
   3) Thus $2,950.00 is saved in personnel costs each month by using the machines.
   4) The machines cost $14,750.00. It would therefore take five months for the cost of the machines to be made up, since $\frac{14750}{2950} = 5$.

8. **(A)** Using any number, say 100, for the amount of stationery needed in July, you would then know that 84 pieces were used in August (16% less than 100) and 105 pieces in September (25% more than 84). The difference between the amount used in September and the amount used in July is therefore 5.

9. **(C)** These notes are used to create a cash flow and have money available to meet immediate expenses and will be paid off when the real estate taxes are collected during the year. They are short term obligations and one should perceive the fact that money must be available at the beginning of the budgetary period before anticipated taxes are collected.

10. **(C)** Vouchers are formal affirmations that money should be paid in accordance with all pertinent rules, laws and recommendations.

11. **(C)** This answer is self-explanatory.

12. **(A)** The best way to make sure that appropriations for such items as supplies and equipment are not exceeded is to tentatively charge them against the appropriation approved for such items as soon as a requisition is received. If they are charged against the appropriation *after* the items, invoices, or packing slips are received, days and even weeks may pass before knowing just how much money is really left in the appropriation to fill requisitions that come in during the intervening period.

13. **(B)** Staffing is based on the average amount of work one worker can be reasonably expected to accomplish and on the total amount of work that has to be done. An increase in staff is generally needed because the work load has increased to the point where added personnel are necessary to handle that increase. Staff is not increased to change the average amount of work being done by the individual worker.

14. **(D)** If an office supervisor finds that it is extremely difficult to request new equipment and has to justify in great detail its need, he or she will tend to make do with existing equipment and not even try to develop new methods, especially those requiring new equipment. The procedure outlined in the question may not be very economical, since new procedures and new machines or equipment may, in the long run, prove to be more economical than keeping existing outdated equipment and procedures.

15. **(A)** This problem merely requires you to know that a reciprocal is one part of two numbers whose product is 1. Thus the reciprocal of 3 is ⅓. In this question the reciprocal of N, the number of units produced, is $1/N$. This now tells you something about one unit produced. Thus you can see that the difference in cost per unit would be the amount of money that would be saved annually in salaries ($24,000) minus the difference in cost between what would have been true if clerks had been used and what will be true if the material cost is increased and the clerks not used and then that number multiplied by the reciprocal of the total number of units produced.

Answer B is incorrect because it does not give you the decrease in *unit* costs, which is what is asked for in the question. Answer C is incorrect because it gives you the new cost (using only the cost of the material) and does not relate to the savings resulting from the fact that clerk's salaries do not have to be charged.

16. **(B)** A departmental expense budget involves only regular day to day operating expenses, not the expenditures given in the other possible answers.

17. **(A)** The correct answer is the only one that would prove that when a change was made, a decrease of 5% in the cost of operation was found. Answer B is the opposite of what we are trying to prove. Answer C can be eliminated, because without knowing how many cases of the total number of cases involved resulted in the 5% de-

crease, the assertion in the quotation is not proved. Answer D only proves that no decrease was found where the change was *not* made, which also does not prove that what the quotation says is true.

18. **(B)** Scientific and accurate budgeting is based on monetary requests for what is actually needed to do the agency's work properly. Otherwise the basis on which the budget is prepared is faulty. Other answers are possibly true, but are not reasons why the procedure indicated in the question is a poor one.

19. **(B)** Lump sum budgets are helpful to an administrator since they give the agency a total appropriation for a particular function or for all the agency's functions and then he or she can use it in the manner which is most effective in getting the work done.

20. **(A)** Past expenditure policies have relatively little effect on current expenditures control, while the other possible answers are important factors to consider for good fiscal management. What is important is what is to be accomplished during the current budgetary period.

21. **(C)** The implication of this question is that physical improvements in areas where work is performed can often lead to considerable increases in productivity. We must therefore select a valid physical change that is likely to result in an increase in productivity. Mail rooms need more light than conference rooms, because more work is performed there. A glossy desk would reflect light and would distract visibility. Yellow walls in a room receiving a good deal of sunlight would become too bright to work effectively. Choice (C), therefore, contains the only valid statement. Concerning a work location where there is a great deal of noise, it would be wiser to use porous materials wherever possible for they would absorb more noise than hard surfaces.

22. **(B)** Anticipating income involves drawing up a budget on what is to be accomplished and using that budget as a control to assure plans are achieved.

23. **(A)** Reorganization of an agency or of the entire governmental structure generally does *not* result in a substantial saving of money, since it usually does *not* result in laying-off a number of employees or in the cessation of a number of functions, or in a substantial reduction in the equipment used. The other possible answers give factors that generally do result from a reorganization of public agencies.

24. **(B)** In large cities both the total cost and the per capita cost of government is greater. In small cities governmental workers generally have lower salaries and there are usually fewer supervisors. In large cities additional services such as transit policy, aid to disadvantaged groups and so forth, must be provided for and paid by the citizens.

25. **(C)** Certain professional/technical governmental activities which serve all the various agencies in that jurisdiction and must be uniform in following policy, are usually centralized to a large extent. For example, the preparation and administration of the procedure to select employees for positions which are common to all agencies (e.g., clerks) is most efficiently, economically, and legally handled by a central core of experts. Central purchasing of common items for the use in all agencies (e.g., paper) is cheaper, more efficient and insures conformity of quality of items purchased.

26. **(B)** Budget estimates based solely on the previous year's budget can be made if unit costs are known. When you know, for example, that 100 reams of paper will cost X amount of dollars and that 500 reams will probably be used per year, based on previous use, it is possible to make a budget estimate on the cost of paper. The other possible answers are disadvantages in making a budget estimate solely on the previous year's budget.

27. **(D)** A budget request should be examined on the basis of the current need for that amount of money as well as the continued need for the function, the possible changes in the work load which will necessitate changes in the amount of money needed, and on the total amount of monies available for the function. The increase or decrease of last year's budget allowance over the previous year has little significance in determining whether this year's budget allowance should be modified.

28. **(D)** The fact that the amount of money a bureau spent during the fiscal year was substantially lower than the amount the bureau had requested is not, by itself, an acceptable reason for modifying its current budget request. The reasons for this phenomenon might be that certain policy changes altered some of the bureau's work responsibilities. The important point to remember in analyzing budget requests is that a budget should be based on the current monetary needs in order to accomplish the agency's current mandated activities, i.e., the purposes for which the money was appropriated.

29. **(C)** It is more likely to be an improper entry than a mistake in addition or subtraction. This is true for most errors in trial balances.

30. **(D)** In this question you are told that the number of hours spent by technicians in actual technical work did not change from 1980 to 1981, but that the percentage of time spent on technical work by these technicians decreased in comparison with the number of hours of technical work performed by the whole department. From this data you can only conclude that persons who were hired to do non-technical work did more technical work in 1981 than in 1980. Answers A and C cannot be implied from the quotation without information about the actual numbers of technicians and non-technicians employed in 1980 and 1981. Answer B cannot be determined at all from the data given.

31. **(B)** A staff of 500 increased by 12% would equal 560 on staff. Presuming that the original work load was 10,000 units per year, each worker therefore produced 20 units per year (10,000 ÷ 500). A 20% increase in the work load means a new work load of 12,000 units per year which is done by 560 workers, thus giving each worker a work load of 21.4 units per year (12,000 ÷ 560). This represents an increased work load of 7%.

32. **(D)** In this problem you are told that there must be 500 items available at all times and that 250 items are used each month. In 45 days you will use 375 items (250 + 125). Since it takes 45 days to obtain a new supply, you must reorder a minimum of 875 items.

33. **(C)** Good governmental administration demands that there be control over the way taxpayers' money is spent. The most fundamental reason for establishing a budget is to provide such a control *before* the monies are actually spent. Otherwise there is, in effect, no control. The other answer choices are possible uses of budgets, but are not the fundamental reason for their existence.

34. **(A)** The chief executive of a jurisdiction is held responsible for the success or failure of all operations, including their cost effectiveness. To do a job properly, the executive must determine which operations take priority, estimate their costs, and prepare a workable budget. Answer B is false. Answer C is not necessarily true and is a desirable policy if it is true. Answer D is not considered to be true by budget authorities.

35. **(D)** In preparing a jurisdiction's budget, the central budgeting agency must first gather data from each agency regarding its fiscal needs for the coming fiscal period. Only then can it evaluate the needs of each agency against total funds available and recommend cuts and eliminations. Answers A and B are not usually functions of a central budgeting office. Evaluation of previous budgets is useful *after* the current budget requests have been received.

36. **(C)** A centralized personnel selection or budgeting agency is better able to make certain that uniform policies are utilized for these important functions. Without such control a personnel selection system, based on merit and fitness, will be subject to individual agency interpretation of what is appropriate. Answer D is untrue. Answer B is not a basic reason and Answer A is not necessarily an argument in favor of a centralized performance of these activities.

37. **(D)** An accounting system should not be concerned with how to collect revenues. Some of the major functions of an accounting system are given in the other possible answers.

38. **(A)** Operations designed to prevent fraud, an inventory control, a tape on a cash register to record sales are examples of internal audits.

39. **(C)** Performance budgets emphasize the return for monies expended. Desired accomplishments are specified in the budget.

40. **(B)** The lump sum budget emphasizes the total amount of money to be spent. It is up to the executives to determine how it is to be spent.

41. **(A)** The line budget emphasizes line by line which personnel can be employed by title and salary.

42. **(D)** No budget can insure that monies will be available for all contingencies.

43. **(C)** Following a determination of what is to be accomplished, the setting of work standards could lead to a fairly accurate estimate of the money to be spent in accomplishing it.

44. **(A)** Each line indicates specifically the amount of salary to be paid to a worker holding a specific title.

PUBLIC RELATIONS

DIRECTIONS FOR ANSWERING QUESTIONS

Each question has four suggested answers, lettered A, B, C, and D. Decide which one is the best answer and on the sample answer sheet (all answer sheets are at the front of the book) find the question number and darken the area, with a soft pencil, which corresponds to the answer that you have selected.

1. Suppose that you were assigned in charge of a new headquarters bureau that will have extensive correspondence with the public and very frequent mail contact with divisions. It is decided at the beginning that all communications from the central office are to go out over your signature. Of the following, the most likely result of this procedure is that
   (A) the administrative head of the bureau will spend too much time preparing correspondence
   (B) execution of bureau policy will be unduly delayed
   (C) subordinate officers will tend to avoid responsibility for decisions based on bureau policy
   (D) uniformity of bureau policy as expressed in such communications will tend to be established.

2. Suppose that you have been asked to answer a letter from a local board of trade requesting certain information. You find that you cannot grant this request. Of the following ways of beginning your answering letter, the best way is to begin by
   (A) quoting the laws or regulations which forbid the release of this information
   (B) stating that you are sorry that the request cannot be granted
   (C) explaining in detail the reasons for your decision
   (D) commending the organization for its service to the community.

3. The relationship between any department and the press is like a "two-way street" because the press is not only a medium through which the department releases information to the public, but the press also
   (A) is interested in the promotion of the Department's program
   (B) can teach the Department good public relations
   (C) makes the Department aware of public opinion
   (D) provides the basis for community cooperation with the Department.

4. Assume that you have been asked to prepare an answer to a request from a citizen of the City addressed to the commissioner. If this request cannot be granted, it is most desirable that the answering letter begin by
   (A) indicating how to go about getting the request granted by another department
   (B) listing the laws which make granting the request impossible
   (C) saying that the request cannot be granted
   (D) discussing the problem presented and showing why the commissioner cannot be expected to grant the request.

5. Assume that you have been requested by the Chief of Department to prepare for public distribution a statement dealing with a controversial matter. For you to present the Department's point of view in a

175

terse statement making no reference to any other matter is, in general

(A) undesirable; you should show all the statistical data you used; how you obtained the data; and how you arrived at the conclusions presented

(B) desirable; people will not read long statements

(C) undesirable; the statements should be developed from ideas and facts familiar to most readers

(D) desirable; the department's viewpoint should be made known in all controversial matters.

6. The primary purpose of a public relations program of an administrative organization should be to develop mutual understanding between

(A) the public and those who benefit by organized service

(B) the public and the organization

(C) the organization and its affiliate organizations

(D) the personnel of the organization and the management.

7. You arrive in your office at 11 a.m., having been on an inspection tour since 8 o'clock. A man has been waiting in your office for two hours. He is abusive because of his long wait, and accuses you of sleeping off a hangover at the taxpayers' expense. You should

(A) say that you have been working all morning, and let him sit in the outer office a little longer until he cools off

(B) tell him you are too busy to see him and make an appointment for later in the day

(C) ignore his comments, courteously find out what his business is and take care of him in a perfunctory manner

(D) explain briefly that your duties sometimes take you out of your office and that an appointment would have prevented inconvenience.

8. During a citizen's conference, you are told very unfavorable personal comments concerning several top officials of the Department by a citizen. Of the following, it would usually be best for you to

(A) try to change the subject as soon as possible

(B) attempt to convince him that he is in error

(C) advise the citizen that your opinion might be like his, but that you can't discuss it

(D) review the improvements introduced by the present administration.

9. "If you want the friendship and cooperation of a man, do not do something for him, but get him to do something for you. His ego has been flattered by your request and, if you follow his advice, he has a vested interest in your project." To what extent is this principle of individual relations applicable to a problem of group relations, such as the development of favorable community attitudes toward the fire prevention activities of the Fire Department

(A) entirely; maximum public participation should be encouraged

(B) to some extent; the participation of certain groups, in certain functions, is desirable

(C) to a very minor extent; the efforts of community groups should be confined to suggestions, advice and recommendations

(D) to no degree; this principle is incompatible with the concept of democratic law enforcement.

10. The public is most likely to judge personnel largely on the basis of their

(A) experience

(B) training and education

(C) civic mindedness

(D) manner and appearance while on duty.

11. When employees consistently engage in poor public relations practices, of the following the cause is most often

(A) disobedience of orders

(B) lack of emotional control

(C) bullheadedness

(D) poor supervision.

12. A citizen's support of a department program can best be enlisted by

(A) telling him how another community has benefited from the use of the program

(B) telling him how backward the community is in its practices and why such a situation exists

(C) telling him that it is his civic duty to do all that he can to support the program

(D) informing him how the program will benefit him and his family.

13. The term "public relations" has been defined as the aggregate of every effort made to create and

maintain good will and to prevent the growth of ill will. This concept assumes particular importance with regard to public agencies because

(A) public relations become satisfactory in inverse ratio to the number of personnel employed in the public agency

(B) legislators may react unfavorably to the public agency

(C) they are much more dependent upon public good will than are commercial organizations

(D) they are tax-supported, and depend on the active and intelligent support of an informed public.

14. Of the following, the proper attitude for an administrative officer to adopt toward complaints from the public is that he should

(A) not only accept complaints but should establish a regular procedure whereby they may be handled

(B) avoid encouraging correspondence with the public on the subject of complaints

(C) remember that it is his duty to get a job done, not to act as a public relations officer

(D) recognize that complaints are rarely the basis for significant administrative action.

15. In a governmental agency, the basic objective of being directly concerned with public relations should be to

(A) promote the most efficient administration of the agency

(B) reduce annual reports which will be acceptable to the public

(C) increase the size of the agency

(D) broaden the "scope and activities of" the agency.

16. Which of the following has the least effect on a city department's public relations

(A) fluctuations in employment

(B) amount of budget

(C) organization plan of department

(D) size of department.

17. The main advantage for good sound public relations is to

(A) build up a good feeling and understanding between the department and the public

(B) gain public support for wage increases and better working conditions

(C) increase public interest in building projects

(D) attain a friendly and sympathetic press.

18. In dealing with the public it is helpful to know that generally most people are more willing to do that for which they

(A) are not responsible

(B) understand the reason

(C) will be given a little assistance

(D) must learn a new skill.

19. The inclusion of representatives of the public on advisory councils for government bodies is desirable primarily because

(A) the government body is able to obtain opinions of persons who have a public point of view

(B) the representatives of special interests are prevented from discussing differences of opinion

(C) the public is shown its interests are being guarded

(D) the public representatives can settle disagreements among other members.

20. Of the following, it is most important for municipal employees to

(A) have an intimate knowledge of the history of the City

(B) be trained to realize that their jobs are more important to the community than the jobs of private citizens

(C) have a basic knowledge of the state and federal constitutions

(D) be imbued with the importance of courtesy in dealing with the public.

21. A comprehensive public relations program must include a periodic review of all procedures affecting citizens for the purpose of making departmental procedures

(A) as fool-proof as possible even if it means making them somewhat long and complicated, as the public should not be expected to do the right thing if it is possible to do it a wrong way

(B) conform to what in the general consensus of opinion is a good practice

(C) self-evident processes for the management of the city government

(D) as simple and understandable as possible.

22. In preparing a report for release to the general public, the bureau chief should generally present at the beginning of the report
    (A) a description of the methods used in preparing the report
    (B) anticipate criticism of the report and the answer to this criticism
    (C) his conclusions and recommendations
    (D) a bibliography of the sources used in preparing the report.

23. In your capacity as an administrator you have been requested to develop a plan for improving the public relations effectiveness of the correspondence of the bureau heads. Of the following, the least valid consideration in initial presentation of your plan to your superior is
    (A) ability to present simultaneously restatements of an idea
    (B) the proper occasion for presentation of the plan
    (C) skill in bringing the matter to a decision
    (D) recognition of hierarchical authority.

24. It is a generally accepted principle of public administration that healthy public relations should be encouraged. Of the following, a basic assumption not underlying this principle is that, if the public gains a favorable impression of the work of civil service employees, then
    (A) the possibility of limiting the scope of governmental functions is increased
    (B) the public will lend increased support to the merit system
    (C) the resulting increased public prestige value of the governmental service will raise the level of recruitment
    (D) it will lead ultimately to more efficient government.

25. The supervisor of a large bureau, who was required in the course of business to answer a large number of letters from the public, completely formalized his responses, that is, the form and vocabulary of every letter he prepared were the same as far as possible. This method of solving the problem of how to handle correspondence is, in general,
    (A) good; if this method were applied to an entire department, the answering of letters could be left to clerks and the administrators would be free for more constructive work
    (B) bad; the time required to develop a satisfactory standard form and vocabulary is usually not available in an active organization
    (C) good; the use of standard forms causes similar requests to be answered in a similar way
    (D) bad; the use of standard forms and vocabulary to the extent indicated results in letters in "officialese" hindering unambiguous explanation and clear understanding.

26. Of the following steps in the planning of a public relations program, the one which should be undertaken *first* is to
    (A) contact editors of local newspapers
    (B) develop procedures for dealing with the public
    (C) establish civilian complaint procedures
    (D) study the public with which the department deals.

27. In preparing a report which will be released to the public, an administrator should *first* be sure that the report
    (A) has no irrelevant material
    (B) includes only statements which conform to the Department's policy
    (C) is free of all hackneyed and stereotyped phrases
    (D) presents ideas in a most logical order.

28. A very important announcement is to be made at a press conference, but you discover that the story has leaked to one of the city's newspapers. Of the following, the most advisable course of action for you to take *first* is to
    (A) deny the story until the press conference is held
    (B) give the story to the other papers at once and cancel the press conference
    (C) release the story to the papers at once, but still plan on holding the press conference
    (D) withhold any comment until the press conference.

29. Suppose that you have received certain information from a city official which is to form the basis of a press release. The information contains a statement which you believe is inaccurate. Of the following, the most advisable course of action for you to take *first* is to
    (A) cancel the press release
    (B) check the statement with the official

(C) eliminate the statement from the release
(D) rewrite the statement correctly.

30. When you are preparing a press release the most important consideration should be given to its
(A) format
(B) length
(C) style
— (D) timeliness.

31. A newspaper telephones to check a report about an official of your department which you feel may result in unfavorable publicity. Of the following, the most advisable course of action for you to take *first* is to
(A) give an absolute minimum of information and end the conversation as quickly as possible
(B) tell the reporter that you have no information concerning the matter
—(C) tell the reporter that you will look into the matter and call him back
(D) tell the reporter to hold the wire while you try to get some information on the matter.

32. At a press conference it turns out that many more reporters and photographers appear than there is room available. You cannot obtain another room on such short notice. Of the following, the most advisable course of action for you to take is to
(A) admit as many as you can and shut out the others
(B) divide the press into two groups and take them one group at a time
—(C) make a pool arrangement with the press
(D) postpone the press conference until another location can be found with sufficient space.

33. When, as a result of a shift in public sentiment, the elective officers of the city are changed, is it desirable for career administrators to shift ground without performing any illegal or dishonest act in order to conform to the policies of the new elective officers?
(A) No; the opinions and beliefs of the career officials are the result of long experience in administration and are more reliable than those of politicians
—(B) Yes; only in this way can citizens, political officials and career administrators alike have confidence in the performance of their respective functions
(C) No; a top career official who is so spineless as to change his views or procedures as a result of public opinion is of little value to the public service
(D) Yes; legal or illegal, it is necessary that a city employee carry out the orders of his superior officers.

34. An administrator of a large office has been bothered by an individual of some civic importance who makes a habit of frequently visiting him to discuss matters of no great significance. Of the following methods of discontinuing such interruptions it would be best for the administrator to
—(A) advise the caller that the pressure of duties makes it difficult for him to talk with the caller so often
(B) instruct a clerk to employ a variety of pretexts indicating that the administrator is not in the department whenever the individual calls
(C) instruct the clerk to tell the caller to discuss any matter with a subordinate
(D) see the caller but advise him to put into writing any matter he may wish to discuss.

ANSWER KEY

1. D	8. A	15. A	22. C	29. B
2. B	9. B	16. C	23. A	30. D
3. C	10. D	17. A	24. A	31. C
4. C	11. D	18. B	25. D	32. C
5. C	12. D	19. A	26. D	33. B
6. B	13. D	20. D	27. B	34. A
7. D	14. A	21. D	28. C	

EXPLANATORY ANSWERS

1. **(D)** A procedure as outlined in this question is designed to insure uniformity of policy appearing in communications which will be reviewed and signed by one individual. Any other procedure where two or more individuals were authorized to sign communications might result in diverse policy statements.

2. **(B)** The best policy in answering letters of request is to immediately refer to the subject matter of their letter. In this case you should begin by regretting that the request cannot be granted. In this way the requesting party knows at once which of the letters he or she wrote is being referred to, and what the answer is. There is no real good way of softening a rejection.

3. **(C)** Yes, the press will very often print just how the public feels about a controversial matter.

4. **(C)** Letters answering requests from citizens should begin by either denying or approving the request, or at least saying the matter is under consideration so that the correspondent knows immediately the status of the request. The other possible answers are either bad public relations policy (Answers A and D), or more suitably put in later parts of the reply.

5. **(C)** An agency's official point of view must be fully understood by the public so that even if they disagree, they can follow the logic and not develop antagonism towards the agency. To be most comprehensible, the viewpoint should develop from ideas and facts already known to the reader, contain as few statistics and technical data as possible, and be long enough to be fully understood while not repetitious.

6. **(B)** A public agency cannot function effectively without the support of its public, and public relations is directed at gaining this support.

7. **(D)** The best approach to take is not to apologize, but merely state that you were out of the office on official business. You then courteously remind the visitor that if an appointment had been set up, you would have kept it. The principle point to remember is that you are serving the public, but that means all the public, which is why you were not there when he arrived.

8. **(A)** Under the circumstances and as a public servant representing your agency in an official capacity, it would be most inappropriate for you to engage in discussion with a citizen about the faults of your superior. Change the subject as soon as possible.

9. **(B)** The practice of asking advice in group relations helps both to get certain projects done and obtain good community relations, but in many governmental projects public participation both hinders successful conclusion of a project, and may very well result in negative reactions from the public. Thus, although community participation in fire prevention is good public relations, and may help prevent fires, there is a point when firefighting and fire prevention must be left to the experts because of the level of expertise involved.

10. **(D)** All persons who have ever had contact with public agencies know that an agency is usually judged by the appearance and manner of the individuals who deal directly with the public. A slovenly, ill-spoken receptionist can ruin the public image more quickly than an incompetent clerk who is not in direct contact with the public.

11. **(D)** It is the direct supervisor's responsibility to be certain that the appearance and attitude of his or her workers towards the public creates a favorable public image. The supervisor must be faulted for any poor image resulting

from his or her unit's failure to practice good public relations.

12. **(D)** Public support of an agency project is best obtained by personalizing the benefits to be gained. For example, emphasis should be on how a cleaner street helps your family stay healthy; preventive health for the poor helps your pocketbook because otherwise you would have to pay for their hospital care; etc.

13. **(D)** Public agencies must obtain the informed support of the public. Otherwise, they either cease to exist, by being legislated out of existence or through cuts in funds, or become virtually useless because the public will not support them. The public will simply ignore their requests for action and active support. Note that commercial organizations also depend on the public good will in order to stay in business.

14. **(A)** To get the agency's work done properly and most economically, an administrator can use complaints from the public to know what problems are hindering successful completion of the agency's tasks. Therefore, a good administrator provides for an efficient procedure to handle complaints.

15. **(A)** All agency activities, including public relations, must have as their basic objective, to get the agency's work done efficiently and properly. The other possible answers are not basic objectives of a public relations policy.

16. **(C)** Of the choices given the organization plan would have least effect on public relations. Proper action should be taken that public relations is being discussed and not effectiveness. Public relations refers to the image set in the minds of the public.

17. **(A)** Good public relations is not confined to one area of concern, e.g., to get higher wages or press support for a building project, but with the development of an on-going rapport with both the general public and the individual groups within the larger public which are closely involved with and can support the agency's activities.

18. **(B)** Just as workers do work correctly if they fully understand its purpose and know why the preferred way is the best way, so people in general support a project when they understand the reason why it is necessary.

19. **(A)** A government body has the responsibility of fulfilling the needs and wants of the public. These needs can be transmitted to the public at these councils and the opportunity to do so will be appreciated.

20. **(D)** It is essential that all public servants be courteous in their dealings with the public because the public is their employer. The success of agency programs and even the continued existence of a worker's job may depend, in a large measure, on the favorable opinion of the public.

21. **(D)** Departmental procedures, especially those which are read by the public, must be as simple and understandable as possible. The public may have neither the training, experience, nor the time and interest to digest and follow complex wording or badly written procedures.

22. **(C)** A large portion of the general public has no interest in the methods used or the sources of material presented, and are probably not interested in replies to anticipated criticism. The public generally just wants to know the report's conclusions and recommendations, and this material should be supplied at the beginning of the report. If they want further details, they will read further into the report.

23. **(A)** The question requires the selection of the least valid choice given. The statement in choice (A) is, at best, gobbledygook.

24. **(A)** If the public gains a favorable impression of the work of civil servants, it will decrease, not increase, the possibility of limiting the scope of governmental functions. The other possible answers contain reasonable assumptions about the effect of good public relations with the public.

25. **(D)** Although form letters serve useful purposes (Answers A and C) and standardization of vocabulary is appropriate in many circumstances, the use of standard forms and vocabulary in every letter will result in a misunderstanding for the public who does not know the meaning of the "officialese" terms and language. What to an experienced public servant is perfectly clear may be incomprehensible and frustrating to the average reader.

26. **(D)** There are really many publics—the general public and those specific parts of it with which the agency deals. Thus, the Health Department may deal with the public-at-large, with the medical profession, with sick persons, with medical vendors, with other governmental agencies, etc. Each of these groups has different educational backgrounds, different degrees of knowledge of Health Department concerns, different aims and purposes. The first step in planning a public relations program is to learn about the different publics which concerns the agency, and determine what would be the best public relations approach to take towards each of them.

27. **(B)** All reports released to the public-at-large must contain only statements which are in accord with the agency's policy. This is the basis of all public relations work.

28. **(C)** Under these circumstances the only thing to do is release it at once to all the papers, but hold a conference anyway in order to answer pertinent questions, explain what happened as best you can, and try to repair any damage that has probably occurred in your relations with the press because of the leak. All the other possible

answers will only further damage your standing with the press.

29. **(B)** A public relations officer is not ultimately responsible for false data which he or she has received from a city official, but is responsible for checking the facts when he or she sees something that may be wrong. A public relations officer is a staff person, and is hired to help officials get the work done. He or she cannot change the release, but can make sure what the line officials really want to be released.

30. **(D)** If a press release is not timely it is of no use at all, even if the format, style and length are in accord with good public relations practice.

31. **(C)** As a public relations officer, your first responsibility is to see that unfavorable publicity is kept to a minimum. In the situation presented, the matter is potentially unfavorable to the agency, and may have to be discussed in detail with the agency head and other top officials before you get back to the reporter.

32. **(C)** Have a representative group of reporters appear at the news conference, the number which the room can accommodate, with the provision and acceptance of the reporters to be present that all information be disbursed in a timely fashion to the reporters which the room will not be able to accommodate.

33. **(B)** Anyone who has been in public service for a length of time has seen elected officials change and new policies adopted which are the opposite of the previous ones. People in the jurisdiction elected these officials to carry out the new policies, and officials are responsible for decisions reached and for ensuring these policies are carried out by the staff. Therefore civil service workers are obligated to change with administrations.

34. **(A)** This is the time for polite but decisive action. The truth must be told in a nice way. The administrator just does not have the time to devote to the individual, and any act of subterfuge is likely to have bad results.

STATISTICS AND CHARTS

DIRECTIONS FOR ANSWERING QUESTIONS

Each question has four suggested answers, lettered A, B, C, and D. Decide which one is the best answer and on the sample answer sheet (all answer sheets are at the front of the book) find the question number and darken the area, with a soft pencil, which corresponds to the answer that you have selected.

1. When fitting a curve to an observed set of points and calling it the "trend" we are making an assumption that
   (A) it is possible to find a curve of best fit
   (B) the elements of a set of points can be compared
   (C) the phenomenon under observation is variable
   (D) there is some degree of regularity in the phenomenon being observed.

2. The type of graph in which a zero base line at the bottom does not appear is a
   (A) cumulative frequency curve
   (B) frequency polygon
   (C) semi-logarithmic chart
   (D) histogram.

3. When interpreting per capita debt statistics of the city, the one of the following which has *least* significance is
   (A) financial history of the city
   (B) adjustment of population figures for seasonal variations
   (C) adequacy of the sampling
   (D) source of population figures used.

4. The one of the following which is most characteristic of indexes and index numbers is that they
   (A) are used to measure indirectly the incidence of a characteristic that is not directly measurable

   (B) are composed of a set of measures each of which is directly measurable
   (C) are composed of a set of measures none of which is directly measurable
   (D) are used to measure directly the incidence of a characteristic that is directly measurable.

5. As a rule, diagrams or charts involving area and volume comparisons should be avoided primarily because
   (A) it is difficult to differentiate between the sizes of areas or cubes with accuracy
   (B) they require unusual skill and too much time to prepare
   (C) geometric figures are not subject to exact determination
   (D) only frequency data can be accurately expressed in area or volume diagrams.

6. When the median, mean and mode of a frequency distribution coincide, we can correctly conclude that the
   (A) distribution is normal
   (B) standard error is zero
   (C) standard deviation is less than one
   (D) range of the distribution is narrow.

7. Prediction, as one of the major objectives of statistical research in municipal planning, is based primarily on the assumption that
   (A) some kinds of social, economic and physical data are intrinsically qualitative and subjective

183

(B) social interference or control cannot limit the outcome of a scientific social prediction
(C) many social and economic features of the city are amenable to quantitative description and analysis
(D) all types of social phenomenon can be measured as accurately as phenomena in the physical sciences.

8. The arithmetic mean, the mode and the median are in different studies used to
(A) summarize the information contained in a set of values by a single value which is typical of the whole set
(B) reduce the amount of labor involved in numerical calculations
(C) determine to what extent the observed sample differs from the expected
(D) reduce the range of variation among the factors under consideration.

9. Interpolation refers to the
(A) assumption of the mean of a distribution
(B) computation of intermediate values of a series
(C) interpretation of data
(D) extension of a curve beyond the available data.

10. "When planning a study to investigate the relationships existing among various forces, the variables should be defined in such a way as to render the correlations obtained as readily interpretable as possible." This recommendation is, in general
(A) poor; variables are not defined but are given as a condition of the study
(B) good; it will reduce the number of cases in which statistical results are meaningless or misleading
(C) poor; there is a danger of forcing a result when variables are defined too carefully
(D) good; definitions always formalize a process.

11. Of the following, the first step in the statistical analysis of a great mass of data secured from a survey is to
(A) compute the arithmetic mean as a preliminary step to further analysis
(B) plot the data to determine the characteristics of the data
(C) arrange the data into classes on the basis of likeness or difference
(D) scan the data to eliminate that which is apparently atypical of the trends of the survey.

12. Secondary sources of data are of use mainly because they
(A) are less likely to contain errors of arrangement of data than primary sources
(B) are more likely to include an adequate sampling
(C) are often more convenient to use
(D) usually explain the data and sources more fully than primary sources.

13. The one of the following statistical measures which evaluates the degree of individual diversity comprised in a group is the
(A) median
(B) coefficient of correlation
(C) standard of deviation
(D) coefficient of attenuation.

14. The most effective way of graphically demonstrating growth or development over periods of time is by means of a
(A) cumulative frequency chart
(B) normal curve chart
(C) simple column chart
(D) strata chart.

15. The most effective way of graphically presenting percentage distributions and comparing these percentages is by means of a
(A) correlation chart
(B) simple curve chart
(C) simple column chart
(D) strata chart.

16. The most effective way of graphically representing data subject to abrupt changes in magnitude with respect to time periods of irregular duration is by means of a
(A) pie chart
(B) normal curve chart
(C) staircase curve chart
(D) strata chart.

17. "A comparison shows that cities in each of the population groups as a whole fail to meet the standard of one acre for 100 persons. However, the 25% best cities in each class more than meet this standard, except in the case of the class of cities more than 1,000,000 or more in population." From this statement one may conclude that
(A) no cities of more than 1,000,000 in population meet the standard specified in the quotation

(B) exactly 75% of the cities covered in this quotation failed to meet the standard

(C) 25% of the best cities in most classes exceeded the specified standard

(D) some of the cities of more than 1,000,000 population may have exceeded the specified standard.

18. Statistical reliability of a test is determined by
    (A) comparison with criterion measures
    — (B) comparison of two scores on same test
    (C) critical analysis
    (D) consensus of opinion.

19. The method of showing how reliable a prediction has been made by a regression equation is to calculate the
    (A) standard error of measurement
    (B) coefficient of partial correlation
    —(C) standard error of estimate
    (D) index of reliability.

20. Deductive thinking means most nearly
    (A) sensing a felt difficulty
    (B) applying a generalization to a particular fact
    —(C) drawing a conclusion from a mass of data
    (D) considering the source and nature of a problem.

21. In the analysis of time series the attempt is made to segregate the observed changes due to the four most important types of movement which occur in time. The one of the following which is NOT one of these is
    (A) secular trends
    (B) cyclical movements
    — (C) associated trends
    (D) periodic movements.

Answer questions 22 and 23 on the basis of the following paragraph:

"If, during a study, some hundreds of values of a variable (such as annual number of latenesses for each employee in a department) have been noted merely in the arbitrary order in which they happen to occur, the mind cannot properly grasp the significance of the record; the observations must be ranked or classified in some way before the characteristics of the series can be comprehended, and those comparisons, on which arguments as to causation depend, can be made with other series. A dichotomous classification is too crude; if the values are merely classified according to whether they exceed or fall short of some fixed value, a large part of the information given by the original record is lost. Numerical measurements lend themselves with peculiar readiness to a manifold classification.''

22. According to the above statement, if the values of a variable which are gathered during a study are classified in few subdivisions, the most likely result will be
    (A) an inability to grasp the significance of the record
    (B) an inability to relate the series with other series
    —(C) a loss of much of the information in the original data
    (D) a loss of the readiness with which numerical measurements lend themselves to a manifold classification.

23. The above statement advocates, with respect to numerical data, the use of
    (A) arbitrary order
    (B) comparisons with other series
    (C) a two value classification
    — (D) a many value classification.

24. An example of discreet data is
    — (A) television sets per family
    (B) public housing population by age
    (C) speed of traffic movement at given intersections at various times of the day
    (D) life span of persons afflicted with certain types of heart disease.

25. One thousand applications have been submitted for a teaching license. It is planned to make an analysis of certain data on a representative sampling of these applications. Of the following, the best way to determine the proper size of the sample to be selected is to
    —(A) ascertain the results of an analysis of fifty applications, then to ascertain the significance of adding a second sample of fifty, and so on until no significant changes in results occur as samples of fifty are added
    (B) determine the reliability coefficient resulting from the correlation of scores or data obtained on a sample with those of the entire number of applications and select the sample for which the coefficient differs from one by a preassigned quantity.
    (C) include a number of cases sufficient to yield a standard error of the mean that is lower than the critical figure of 1.00

(D) select a sample of such size as would yield a normal distribution, or an approximation to it, of significant quantitative measures included in the data.

26. The most effective way of graphically comparing several series of data with respect to a single variable is by means of a
    (A) pie chart
  — (B) simple curve chart
    (C) staircase curve chart
    (D) strata chart.

27. A major difference between "statistics" and "statistical control" is that
    (A) statistical control is a single aspect of mathematical theory with goals
  —(B) statistical control involves comparison
    (C) statistics involves comparison with normal standards
    (D) statistics is the practical application of statistical control.

28. The one of the following which is the chief limitation of the organization chart as it is generally used in business and government is that the chart
    (A) engenders within incumbents feelings of rights to positions they occupy
  —(B) reveals only formal authority relationships, omitting the informal ones
    (C) shows varying degrees of authority even though authority is not subject to such differentiation
    (D) presents organizational structure as it is rather than what it is supposed to be.

29. On a flow process chart, the symbol commonly used for "inspection" is

    (A) ◯   (C) ▽

    (B) ◯   —(D) ▢

30. The symbol 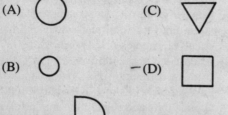 used in flow process charts stands for
    ⁻(A) delay
    (B) delete

(C) delivery
(D) detour.

31. On a flow process chart, a symbol commonly used for "transportation" is

    (A) ◯   (C) ▽

   — (B) ◯   (D) ▢

32. "Approximate figures serve as well as exact figures to indicate trends and make comparisons." Of the following, the most accurate statement on the basis of this quotation is that
    (A) it takes less time to obtain approximate figures than exact figures
    (B) exact figures are rarely used as they require too much computation
  ‑(C) for certain purposes, approximate figures are as revealing as exact figures
    (D) approximate figures can usually be used in place of exact figures.

33. A group of examiners has undertaken to study the role of personnel experience in influencing the quality of work done by personnel assistants. The adequacy of procedures employed and the results obtained by a group of personnel assistants have been rated by the examiner in charge and two of his colleagues to yield a score for each personnel assistant. The personnel assistants have been separated for the purpose of the study into a group of those who have had previous personnel experience and a group of those who have not. From the comparison of the mean scores of these two groups, to infer that the difference between the two averages must be due to differences in personnel experience would be
    ⁻(A) improper; the two groups may differ in factors other than experience
    (B) proper; if the difference in the means is significant
    (C) improper; the variances of the scores for each of the two groups should be equivalent
    (D) proper; if the differences in the variances are also taken into account.

Answer Questions 34 through 36 on the basis of the following table.

FREQUENCY DISTRIBUTION OF THE PERFORMANCE RATINGS OF 200 EMPLOYEES OF A NEW YORK CITY DEPARTMENT

Rating	No. Employees
50	1
55	2
60	4
65	10
70	15
75	30
80	50
85	60
90	25
95	2
100	1
	200

34. The value of the mean of the above distribution is most nearly
    (A) 80
    (B) 82
    (C) 84
    (D) 86.

35. The median of the above distribution is most nearly
    (A) 70
    (B) 75
    (C) 80
    (D) 85.

36. The mode for the above distribution is most nearly
    (A) 70
    (B) 75
    (C) 80
    (D) 85.

37. The least accurate of the following statements about graphic presentation is
    (A) it is desirable to show as many coordinate lines as possible in a finished diagram
    (B) the horizontal scale should read from left to right and the vertical scale from top to bottom
    (C) when two or more curves are represented for comparison on the same chart, their zero lines should coincide
    (D) a percentage curve should not be used when the purpose is to show the actual amounts of increase or decrease.

38. "This chart presents graphically a comparison of what is done and what is to be done. It is so ruled that each division of space represents both an amount of time and the quantity of work to be done during the particular unit of time. Horizontal lines drawn through these spaces show the relationship between the quantity of work actually done and that which is scheduled." The chart referred to is known generally as a
    (A) progress or Gantt chart
    (B) job correlation chart
    (C) process or flow of work chart
    (D) Simo work simplification chart.

Column I includes major characteristics of certain charts. By selecting the proper option in Column II, indicate whether each item in Column I is primarily associated with (A) flow charts, (B) process charts, (C) work distribution charts, or whether it is associated with (D) none of these charts.

COLUMN I

39. Details distribution of documents utilized in a single procedure

40. Gives the most details of procedure

41. Shows the amount of work done and to be done

42. Shows time spent by personnel on major assignments

43. Shows interrelationships of organizational units in carrying out one procedure

44. Used to compare time spent with importance of work produced in a unit

45. Used to control points where work accumulates

46. Used to determine the best sequence of flow of material

47. Used to equalize work assignments

COLUMN II

(A) flow charts
(B) process charts
(C) work distribution charts
(D) none of the above charts.

48. A task list should be made prior to the preparation of a
    (A) flow chart
    (B) flow process chart
    (C) work count
    (D) work distribution chart.

ANSWER KEY

1. D	11. C	21. C	31. B	41. D
2. C	12. C	22. C	32. C	42. C
3. C	13. C	23. D	33. A	43. A
4. A	14. C	24. A	34. A	44. C
5. A	15. D	25. A	35. C	45. D
6. A	16. C	26. B	36. D	46. A
7. C	17. C, D	27. B	37. A	47. C
8. A	18. B	28. B	38. A.	48. D
9. B	19. C	29. D	39. A	
10. B	20. C	30. A	40 .B	

EXPLANATORY ANSWERS

1. **(D)** In order for a series of points to be considered as a "trend," there must be a regularity in the phenomenon being observed. Thus, with a series of figures showing that every six months over a four year period the cost of living has gone up, we can say there is a trend towards increased cost of living.

2. **(C)** A factual question where the correct answer is self-explanatory.

3. **(C)** Per-capita debt statistics do not involve the use of sampling techniques.

4. **(A)** The correct answer is in effect a definition of the terms "index" or "index numbers." An index number is a number used to show change or magnitude as compared with that magnitude at a specific point of time. Thus if you use 100 as the index number, changes are shown as comparisons with that figure of 100.

5. **(A)** A pictorial graph might depict variables to the eye, but with limited accuracy. Where accuracy is required, other types of graphs might be more suitable.

6. **(A)** When the mean, median and mode coincide in a frequency distribution, the distribution is normal, i.e., there are as many measures below the central measure as there are above the central measure.

7. **(C)** Predicting the future is a part of municipal planning because there are social and economic factors that can be studied and compared in quantitative terms. Thus we can obtain reading scores for a representative group of students before and after a new reading program is instituted,

and can predict from the results the effect of the new program on the entire school population.

8. **(A)** The correct answer is a definition of measures of central tendency. The arithmetic mean, median and mode are all measures of central tendency.

9. **(B)** A factual question where the correct answer is self-explanatory.

10. **(B)** The quotation presents a good way to plan a study to investigate relationships among existing forces so that correlations are easily interpreted and results are meaningful. If you were studying, for example, the relationship between wealth and the amount of rent paid monthly, wealth must be clearly defined. Does it mean annual salary earned? total amount of money made each year? total money belonging to the family? Does it include property owned?

11. **(C)** The first step to take when confronted with a mass of data, is to arrange it in classes based on similarity. Thus, if you have 100 scores of people who took a test, the first thing to do is put all of the same scores together so that you are in effect dealing with fewer numbers and can make a more meaningful analysis from them. You cannot tell anything from 100 separate scores but you can from a distribution that shows 50 of the hundred received 75%, 15 received 80%, 10 received 90%, and 5 received 100%.

12. **(C)** If a statistician started from scratch to make a study on the housing situation in XYZ City, he or she would have to collect basic raw data for many months, before

even beginning to do the analysis desired. Secondary sources, if they are reliable, are the only way to obtain accurate figures, short of doing the job itself. Accurate raw data, like that obtainable from the U.S. Census in the above case, would be most helpful in carrying out the desired study within a reasonable length of time.

13. **(C)** A factual question. The correct answer defines a Standard of Deviation.

14. **(C)** A simple bar chart will best give you a graphic picture of growth over periods of time.

15. **(D)** A factual question where the correct answer is self-explanatory.

16. **(C)** A factual question where the correct answer is self-explanatory.

17. **(C and D)** The information given tells you:
1. Per class, the 25% best cities more than meet the standard of acre per 100 persons, *except*
2. in cities of more than 1,000,000, 25% of the best cities do not meet the standard of 100 acres per person.

From this statement, you can reasonably conclude that Answer C is correct. In most classes of cities, 25% of the best cities exceed the standard. Furthermore, Answer D is also correct. Some of the cities that have more than 1,000,000 persons may exceed the standard.

18. **(B)** The degree of reliability of a test is measured by performing the same test twice under the same conditions (e.g., the same person takes the same test) and comparing the results.

19. **(C)** A factual question where the correct answer is self-explanatory.

20. **(C)** The correct answer is a definition of deductive reasoning.

21. **(C)** A factual question where the correct answer is self-explanatory.

22. **(C)** In general information gathered in a study will be more meaningful and useful if it is expressed in a variety of ways. Thus the same information very often can support a multitude of arguments, for or against, depending on how it is presented.

23. **(D)** The chief point of the paragraph is that a many-value classification is preferable with respect to numerical data.

24. **(A)** Discrete data refers to a variable whose properties take only one value along a continuum of values—in this case, TV sets. You can have one TV set or two TV sets, but not 1¼ or 2½ TV sets. In contrast, the other possible answers are examples of continuous variables. Thus, for example, you can have ages one year; one year, one month; one year, two months, etc.

25. **(A)** To solve this problem, no complex stratifications about students is needed. You are looking for a representative sample of candidates and the best way to find some would be to use a random sample, i.e., of such size that each member of the candidate population has an equal probability of being selected. The best way to do this is to pick 50 candidates at random, do the analysis you want to do, then pick another random sample of 50 candidates, analyze them, and if the second analysis shows no significantly different results, the sample is appropriate. If there are significant differences, pick another 50 candidates at random and analyze them. If there are no significant differences, that size sample is sufficient, and so on until you have a sample of sufficient size and to which the addition of other candidates does not change the results, thus indicating that the size sample would be truly representative of the 1000 applicants.

26. **(B)** The simple curve chart would be the most useful because the reader of the chart would be able to compare the data with the variable. When the curve of the variable increases what is the status of the data and vice versa?

27. **(B)** Some organizations are statistically controlled, in that records of production are constantly compared to pre-conceived plans. Thus statistics are used primarily as a control to assure that desired results are met.

28. **(B)** Organization charts depict formal lines of authority in an organization. On the other hand, much work in an organization is performed on the basis of informal relationships in which workers accept the fact that particular work has to be performed and they are the ones to perform it. On these occasions, lines of authority are very often ignored. Informal relationships very often make an organization "go".

29. **(D)** A factual question where the correct answer is self-explanatory.

30. **(A)** A factual question where the correct answer is self-explanatory.

31. **(B)** A factual question where the correct answer is self-explanatory.

32. **(C)** The quotation says approximate figures can be used instead of exact figures in order to show trends and to make comparisons. The correct answer says just about the same thing. The answers given in the other three choices cannot be justified from the quotation.

33. **(A)** From the comparison of the mean scores of two groups of personnel assistants, one group having had previous personnel experience and one group not having had such experience, the difference in the quality of work done *cannot* be inferred to be due solely to the

difference in personnel experience, since other differences between the two groups (e.g., age, education, supervisor's ability, etc.) may be contributory factors.

34. **(A)** The mean is the sum of all the measures in a series divided by the number of such measures, i.e.—

$$\frac{\text{sum of ratings} \times \text{number of employers}}{\text{number of employees}} \quad \text{or}$$

$$\frac{15990}{200} = 79.5 \text{ or } 80$$

35. **(C)** The median of a distribution is the number above and below which half the numbers in the distribution fall. In this frequency distribution that number is 80.

rating	f	cum f
100	1	1
95	2	3
90	5	8
85	60	88
80	50	138
75	30	168
70	15	183
65	10	193
60	4	197
55	2	199
50	1	200

$\frac{200}{2} = 100$ The one hundredth number is at rating 80.

36. **(D)** The mode of a distribution is the number which appears most frequently. In this frequency distribution that number is 85.

37. **(A)** The incorrect answers are accurate statements about graphic presentations. It is *not* desirable to show a great number of coordinate numbers in a diagram because it is confusing to follow.

38. **(A)** A Gantt chart supports the principle that, "Time means money." It is an effective measure of the work performed as against the time it takes to perform it and the expenditure of monies towards its performance.

39. **(A)** Answer (A) depicts all operations of a procedure.

40. **(B)** A process chart is generally more complete than the flow chart.

41. **(D)** None of the listed charts do this. (This choice refers to the Gantt chart)

42. **(C)** This shows what is being done and how much time is being spent doing it.

43. **(A)** Answer (A) depicts just how the procedure is accomplished.

44. **(C)** Answer (C) shows what is being done and how much time is being spent doing it.

45. **(D)** Although flow charts and flow process charts depict how a procedure is accomplished in an organization, they really do not depict physical movement and therefore they do not indicate the locations of bottlenecks and therefore cannot be used to control them. Office layout charts are at times used to depict the physical movement involved in an operation.

46. **(A)** The flow chart lays out the process step by step, thus sequential difficulties can be rectified.

47. **(C)** The work distribution chart will indicate the amount of work each individual is doing by task. Inequalities can thus be rectified if they exist.

48. **(D)** The tasks performed must be identified before a work distribution chart is prepared. The list of tasks must be complete so that every bit of activity in the organization can be accounted for.

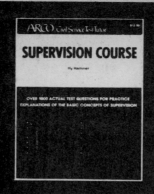

SELECTED CIVIL SERVIC[

TITLE	NUMBER	PRICE
ACCOUNTANT-AUDITOR	05544-8	10.00
Administrative Assistant (order PRINCIPAL ADMINISTRATIVE ASSOCIATE–ADMINISTRATIVE ASSISTANT)		
Administrative Manager (order STAFF POSITIONS–METHODS ANALYST–SENIOR ADMINISTRATIVE ASSISTANT–ADMINISTRATIVE MANAGER)		
ASSISTANT ACCOUNTANT	05613-4	8.00
Associate Staff Analyst (order STAFF ANALYST–ASSOCIATE STAFF ANALYST)		
Auditor (order ACCOUNTANT–AUDITOR)		
Battalion Chief (order FIREFIGHTER PROMOTION EXAMINATIONS)		
Captain Fire Department (order FIREFIGHTER PROMOTION EXAMINATIONS)		
Captain Police Department (order POLICE PROMOTION EXAMINATIONS)		
CIVIL SERVICE CLERICAL PROMOTION TESTS	06186-3	8.00
CIVIL SERVICE HANDBOOK	05166-3	5.00
Civilian Police Aide (order POLICE ADMINISTRATIVE AIDE–CIVILIAN POLICE AIDE)		
Clerical Promotion Tests (order CIVIL SERVICE CLERICAL PROMOTION TESTS)		
COMPLETE GUIDE TO U.S. CIVIL SERVICE JOBS	05245-7	5.00
Court Clerk (order COURT OFFICER–SENIOR COURT OFFICER–COURT CLERK)		
COURT OFFICER–SENIOR COURT OFFICER–COURT CLERK	05615-0	9.00

TITLE	NUMBER	PRICE
Deputy Sheriff (order HOME STUDY COURSE FOR SCORING HIGH ON LAW ENFORCEMENT TESTS)		
Detective–Investigator (order HOME STUDY COURSE FOR SCORING HIGH ON LAW ENFORCEMENT TESTS)		
FIREFIGHTER PROMOTION EXAMINATIONS	05611-8	10.00
FOOD SERVICE SUPERVISOR	04819-0	8.00
HOME STUDY COURSE FOR SCORING HIGH ON LAW ENFORCEMENT TESTS	05410-7	9.00
Lieutentant Fire Department (order FIREFIGHTER PROMOTION EXAMINATIONS)		
Lieutenant Police Department (order POLICE PROMOTION EXAMINATIONS)		
MANAGEMENT ANALYST–ASSISTANT–ASSOCIATE	03864-0	8.00
Management Analyst Assistant (order MANAGEMENT ANALYST–ASSISTANT–ASSOCIATE		
Management Analyst Associate (order MANAGEMENT ANALYST–ASSISTANT–ASSOCIATE)		
MASTERING WRITING SKILLS FOR CIVIL SERVICE ADVANCEMENT	05774-2	8.00
Methods Analyst (order STAFF POSITIONS–METHODS ANALYST–SENIOR ADMINISTRATIVE ASSISTANT–ADMINISTRATIVE MANAGER)		
NURSE–REGISTERED NURSE–PRACTICAL NURSE–PUBLIC HEALTH NURSE (also order NURSE'S AIDE HANDBOOK)	05248-1	8.00
OFFICE ASSOCIATE	04855-7	8.00
OFFICE HANDBOOK FOR CIVIL SERVICE EMPLOYEES	05605-3	8.00

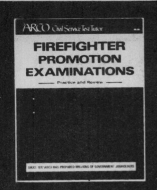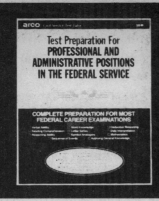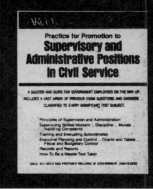

'EST TUTORS

TITLE	NUMBER	PRICE
Parole Officer (order *PROBATION OFFICER–PAROLE OFFICER*)		
POLICE ADMINISTRATIVE AIDE–CIVILIAN POLICE AIDE	05411-5	8.00
POLICE PROMOTION EXAMINATIONS	05604-5	12.00
Police Sergeant (order *HOME STUDY COURSE FOR SCORING HIGH ON LAW ENFORCEMENT TESTS* and *SERGEANT, P.D.*)		
Practical Nurse (order *NURSE–REGISTERED NURSE– PRACTICAL NURSE–PUBLIC HEALTH NURSE* and *NURSE'S AIDE HANDBOOK*)		
PRACTICE FOR PROMOTION TO SUPERVISORY AND ADMINISTRATIVE POSITIONS IN CIVIL SERVICE	05763-7	8.00
PRINCIPAL ADMINISTRATIVE ASSOCIATE–ADMINISTRATIVE ASSISTANT	05617-7	10.00
PRINCIPAL CLERK–PRINCIPAL STENOGRAPHER	05536-7	8.00
Principal Stenographer (order *PRINCIPAL CLERK–PRINCIPAL STENOGRAPHER*)		
PROBATION OFFICER–PAROLE OFFICER	05619-3	8.00
Professional Administrative Career Examination (order *TEST PREPARATION FOR PROFESSIONAL AND ADMINISTRATIVE POSITIONS IN THE FEDERAL SERVICE*)		
Public Health Nurse (order *NURSE–REGISTERED NURSE– PRACTICAL NURSE–PUBLIC HEALTH NURSE* and *NURSE'S AIDE HANDBOOK*)		
Registered Nurse (order *NURSE–REGISTERED NURSE– PRACTICAL NURSE–PUBLIC HEALTH NURSE* and *NURSE'S AIDE HANDBOOK*)		

TITLE	NUMBER	PRICE
Security Officer–Inspector (order *HOME STUDY COURSE FOR SCORING HIGH ON LAW ENFORCEMENT TESTS*)		
Senior Administrative Assistant (order *STAFF POSITIONS–METHODS ANALYST–SENIOR ADMINISTRATIVE ASSISTANT–ADMINISTRATIVE MANAGER*)		
SENIOR CLERICAL SERIES	05523-5	8.00
Senior Court Officer (order *COURT OFFICER–SENIOR COURT OFFICER–COURT CLERK*)		
Senior grades of Clerk (order *SENIOR CLERICAL SERIES*)		
SERGEANT, P.D. (also see *HOME STUDY COURSE FOR SCORING HIGH ON LAW ENFORCEMENT TESTS*)	05278-3	12.00
SOCIAL SUPERVISOR	04190-0	10.00
STAFF ANALYST–ASSOCIATE STAFF ANALYST	05522-7	10.00
STAFF POSITIONS–METHODS ANALYST–SENIOR ADMINISTRATIVE ASSISTANT–ADMINISTRATIVE MANAGER	03490-4	6.00
Statistics Clerk (order *SENIOR CLERICAL SERIES*)		
STENOGRAPHER–TYPIST GS-2 TO GS-7	05412-3	8.00
SUPERVISING CLERK– STENOGRAPHER–OFFICE ASSOCIATE	04309-1	8.00
SUPERVISION COURSE	05618-5	10.00
Supervisor (Child Welfare) (order *SOCIAL SUPERVISOR*)		
TEST PREPARATION FOR PROFESSIONAL AND ADMINISTRATIVE POSITIONS IN THE FEDERAL SERVICE	05921-4	10.00
VOCABULARY, SPELLING, AND GRAMMAR	05806-4	6.95

ORDER THE BOOKS DESCRIBED ON THE PREVIOUS PAGES FROM YOUR BOOKSELLER OR DIRECTLY FROM:

ARCO PUBLISHING, INC.
215 Park Avenue South
New York, N.Y. 10003

To order directly from Arco, please add $1.00 for first book and 35¢ for each additional book for packing and mailing cost. No C.O.D.'s accepted.

Residents of New York, New Jersey and California must add appropriate sales tax.

MAIL THIS COUPON TODAY!

ARCO PUBLISHING, INC., 215 Park Avenue South, New York, N.Y. 10003
Please rush the following Arco books:

NO. OF COPIES	TITLE #	TITLE	PRICE	EXTENSION
			SUB-TOTAL	
			LOCAL TAX	
			PACKING & MAILING	
			TOTAL	

I enclose check ☐,   M.O. ☐, for $_____   or charge my ☐ VISA   ☐ MASTERCARD

Account #_____ Exp. Date_____

Signature_____

NAME _____

ADDRESS _____

CITY _____ STATE _____ ZIP _____

Every Arco book is guaranteed. Return for full refund within ten days if not completely satisfied.

NOT RESPONSIBLE FOR CASH SENT THROUGH THE MAILS